Anonymus

Refrigerators and Food Preservation in foreign Countries

Anonymus

Refrigerators and Food Preservation in foreign Countries

ISBN/EAN: 9783742802224

Manufactured in Europe, USA, Canada, Australia, Japa

Cover: Foto ©Gila Hanssen / pixelio.de

Manufactured and distributed by brebook publishing software (www.brebook.com)

Anonymus

Refrigerators and Food Preservation in foreign Countries

SPECIAL.—CONSULAR REPORTS

REFRIGERATORS AND FOOD PRESERVATION

IN

FOREIGN COUNTRIES.

REPORTS FROM THE CONSULS OF THE UNITED STATES, ON THE USE
OF REFRIGERATORS AND NATURAL AND MANUFACTURED ICE,
FOR THE PRESERVATION OF FOOD IN THEIR SEVERAL
DISTRICTS, IN ANSWER TO A CIRCULAR FROM
THE DEPARTMENT OF STATE.

ISSUED FROM THE BUREAU OF STATISTICS, DEPARTMENT OF
STATE. ALL REQUESTS FOR THESE REPORTS SHOULD
BE ADDRESSED TO THE SECRETARY OF STATE.

WASHINGTON:
GOVERNMENT PRINTING OFFICE.
1890.

REFRIGERATOR CIRCULAR.

DEPARTMENT OF STATE,
Washington, November 25, 1889.

To the CONSUL OF THE UNITED STATES
At ——— ———:

SIR: With a view to extending their trade to foreign markets, the manufacturers of refrigerators in the United States desire information in regard to the use of such articles in foreign countries, viz:

(1) Are refrigerators used in your consular district, and to what extent?
(2) Are there any peculiar features required in the construction of refrigerators for your district?
(3) Where are the refrigerators in use in your district manufactured?
(4) Sizes, formations, and prices of refrigerators in use in your district?
(5) How is ice secured in your district, and the price per 100 pounds thereof?

It is believed that many countries would adopt the American system of preserving foods and liquids, if made acquainted therewith; hence you are requested to investigate this phase of the subject as much as possible.

Where refrigerators are not in use you are requested to report upon the conditions which prevail relative to the preservation of foods and liquids, and whether the American refrigerators could not be so modified as to meet local requirements in your district.

Report, also, upon the best manner of introducing refrigerators into your district.

I am, sir, your obedient servant,

ALVEY A. ADEE,
Second Assistant Secretary.

CONTINENT OF AFRICA.

EGYPT.

REPORT BY VICE-CONSUL-GENERAL GRANT, OF CAIRO.

So-called refrigerators are in general use in the larger towns of Egypt, but are of an inferior quality, often being mere ice-boxes.

No peculiar features are required. Those in use are principally of local manufacture. They are very plain and simple, and could well be replaced by American articles, were it not for the great expense of transportation.

There are two types of refrigerators made here, one like a chest, being a simple ice-box lined with zinc, which sometimes has a zinc shelf over the ice and sometimes not. It generally contains a zinc compartment for the purpose of keeping cold water. The other has a door. Neither of them are made with double doors or linings filled with sawdust or other material, and there is therefore waste of the ice.

The prices of the two kinds mentioned vary, according to size, from 60 francs, or $12, to 90 francs, or $18, and perhaps 100 francs, or $20.

In Egypt ice is manufactured, there being two manufactories in Cairo, one in Alexandria and one in Suez. There is said to be one also in Mansourah. At different times attempts have been made to import natural ice from America and from Sweden, but they failed on account of the lower price of manufactured ice. The ice manufactured in Cairo is frozen at 50° centigrade by means of compressed air, without the aid of acids or chemicals. It is sold at 40 cents for a block weighing 44 pounds, and at proportionate rates for the half block.

There being no plans or illustrations of American refrigerators at this office it would be difficult to investigate satisfactorily the question of their successful introduction into Egypt, but there appears to be nothing to hinder the ready sale of this article here except the price, which must necessarily be high on account of the great cost of transportation. Nevertheless the founding of an establishment in Egypt by some enterprising company, for the purpose of manufacturing refrigerators on the American principle, might be feasible, as labor is cheap here. But such a company would have to seek other markets for its products besides Egypt.

Water is generally kept cool in cheap, porous earthen jars or bottles, called "goulies," manufactured in Upper Egypt, the best of them coming from Keneh. The coolness is produced by the transpiration of the water through the jar and by the consequent evaporation.

Milk is preserved by boiling; butter is kept in water.

Usually every house or apartment is provided with a small safe or cupboard, perforated with holes to allow of a current of air, attached to the window-sill of the kitchen or dining-room.

LOUIS B. GRANT,
Vice-Consul-General.

UNITED STATES CONSULATE-GENERAL,
    Cairo, April 21, 1890.

MADEIRA.

REPORT BY CONSUL JONES, OF FUNCHAL.

During the winter season snow and hail fall on the mountains, and this is gathered and put into caves and brought down, as required, in the early morning.

It is very expensive—worth $1.50 for what a man can carry in a basket.

Mr. Reid, the proprietor of four hotels in this city, has requested Mr. Summers-Clerk, a celebrated architect of London, to look into an American refrigerator now in use in that city, and give his opinion on same.

I should like to have some illustrations showing the refrigerator, price-list, etc.

T. C. JONES,
Consul.

UNITED STATES CONSULATE,
    Funchal, January 20, 1890.

MOROCCO.

REPORT BY VICE-CONSUL STALKER, OF TANGIER.

Refrigerators are used in this consular district to a very limited extent, and there are no peculiar features required in their construction.

These were manufactured in the United States.

Sizes, formations, and prices are unknown.

Ice is imported from Gibraltar, at about $5 per 100 pounds.

ROBERT STALKER,
Vice-Consul.

UNITED STATES CONSULATE,
    Tangier, January 31, 1890.

REUNION.

REPORT BY COMMERCIAL AGENT RAYEUR.

Refrigerators are not in a great demand in our country, because the people are not very fond of ice.

In June and July we have ice and snow on the top of two of our mountains; but few people mind it; nevertheless, in one of our hotels ice is used to cool beverages in summer, but on so small a scale that refrigerators have no chance to be sold here.

EDOUARD RAYEUR,
Commercial Agent.

ST. DENIS (ISLAND OF REUNION),
January 22, 1890.

SENEGAL.

REPORT BY CONSUL STRICKLAND, OF GORÉE DAKAR.

Refrigerators are used to some extent in this consular district. No peculiar features are required in their construction.

There are no refrigerators that I am aware of in this consular district except American, and as yet not many of these.

Eddy's small box-shaped refrigerator for families, price $15, is the one now mostly depended on.

Ice, until lately, has been manufactured as wanted by steam machines, but early last summer the bark *Mejunticork* brought a shipment here from Boston, which was stored at Dakar in an ice-house of wood, constructed for the purpose, and retailed at about 4½ cents per pound. It did not, however, prove a paying speculation on account of the rapid melting of the ice after it was uncovered for sale, but this difficulty is now sought to be obviated by dividing the ice-house into compartments and uncovering one at a time.

A small shipment of ice was also imported last season at St. Louis from Portland, with similar results.

There will be some demand for small-sized refrigerators for families in the future, but parties are at hand to furnish them.

PETER STRICKLAND,
Consul.

UNITED STATES CONSULATE,
Gorée-Dakar, February 4, 1890.

ZANZIBAR.

REPORT BY CONSUL PRATT.

Refrigerators are used in this consular district to a very limited extent. There are no peculiar features required in their construction. The refrigerators in use in this district are manufactured here. No uniformity in size is observed.

Ice is chemically manufactured at a price of $3 per 100 pounds.

By the foregoing it will be observed that there can be little demand for refrigerators in this district, the high price of the manufactured ice precluding the practicability of its use as a preservative. The small local demand for ice is solely for use in cooling beverages.

SETH A. PRATT,
Consul.

UNITED STATES CONSULATE,
   Zanzibar, February 10, 1890.

SOUTH AFRICA.

REPORT BY CONSUL HOLLIS, OF CAPE TOWN.

Under the present condition of the ice market here but little can be said that would encourage the manufacturers of refrigerators to incur any expense in endeavoring to introduce their wares into this market.

The refrigerators used here are mostly of American manufacture and of the medium size.

The ice in use is the artificial or chemically made, and the quotation made me to-day for a daily supply of 10 pounds was 3 cents per pound.

I have no doubt that, given ice at a reasonable price, a much larger number of refrigerators would be imported; but with ice at the price named, and an almost total failure to meet the demand on the hottest days when most needed, it is not surprising to learn that the largest houses do not average more than four or five sales a year.

I have informed a New York manufacturer of ice-machines of the condition of the business of ice manufacture here, and think it probable that he will make an improvement in this line by entering this market with the most modern machine.

In this climate ice could be used with comfort all the year round and would be under more favorable conditions.

The condition of this trade, as briefly outlined above, is applicable to the whole country.

GEO. F. HOLLIS,
Consul.

UNITED STATES CONSULATE,
   Cape Town, February 15, 1890.

CONTINENT OF AMERICA.

BRITISH NORTH AMERICA.

AMHERSTBURG.

REPORT BY CONSUL TURNER.

In answer to the interrogatories contained in Department circular under date of November 25, 1889, I have the honor to report: Refrigerators are used in this consular district by all who can afford to purchase them. There are no peculiar features required in the construction. The refrigerators in use in this district are principally of American manufacture. Sizes, formation, and prices are, 3 by 5, 4 by 6, and 5 by 7 feet; average in price from $15 to $40. Ice is secured from the Detroit River and Lake Erie; price from 15 to 20 cents per 100 pounds. It is believed that the people of this consular district would adopt the American system of preserving foods and liquids, if made acquainted with them, by establishing agencies for that purpose where refrigerators are not in use. The conditions which prevail relative to the preservation of foods and liquids, are ice-boxes. American refrigerators could be so modified as to meet local requirements.

Josiah Turner,
Consul.

United States Consulate,
    Amherstburg, January 27, 1890.

BRITISH COLUMBIA.

REPORT BY VICE-CONSUL MARVIN, OF VICTORIA.

Refrigerators are used in this consular district to a limited extent.

There are no peculiar features required. Those in use in this district are manufactured at Montreal.

The sizes are 4 by 6 feet, and the prices from $10 to $50.

Ice is secured in ice-houses, and the price thereof is 2 cents per pound.

In this consular district the heat of summer is never extreme, and therefore the demand for refrigerators is small, and those that are in use in this district are chiefly of Canadian manufacture. It would be useless to think of introducing refrigerators into this district, as the climate during the two or three hottest months of the year is never so intense as to require them, and the duty is too high to import them.

EDGAR MARVIN,
Vice-Consul.

UNITED STATES CONSULATE,
Victoria, December 30, 1889.

CHATHAM.

REPORT BY COMMERCIAL AGENT EDDY.

Refrigerators in use in this consular district are the same as used in Michigan. They are generally manufactured in this consular district, although some are imported from the United States.

Ice in this district is secured in same manner as in Michigan, and the price per ton is $2, and 10 cents per 100 pounds.

I would also report that the American system prevails to a great extent in preserving foods and liquids in this district.

JEROME EDDY,
Commercial Agent.

UNITED STATES COMMERCIAL AGENCY,
Chatham, Canada, January 22, 1890.

COATICOOK.

REPORT BY CONSUL ROBERTS.

Refrigerators are used in this consular district, but not to a large extent. A few of the leading families of the vicinity have them, and some of the grocers and meat dealers make use of them at their places of business.

No peculiar features are required. Those in use are manufactured in Canada. The sizes and formations are, I find, similar to those of the refrigerators in use in the New England States. A common size here is 18 by 36 inches. The prices of refrigerators in this vicinity are from $10 to $18.

In this consular district ice is secured by the use of tools similar in character to those used for the same purpose in the New England States. The price of ice to the consumer is 20 cents per 100 pounds.

On account of the usually short duration of the warm or summer season of each year in this portion of the Dominion, and on account, also, of the consequent small demand for the use of ice in the preservation of foods and liquids, this consular district, in my judgment, does not present a very inviting field for the introduction of American refrigerators. The best manner of introducing them, however, would be, I believe, for the manufacturer to procure a hardware dealer in Coaticook, and also one in Rock Island (in the township of Stanstead), to act as agents for their sale.

FRANK W. ROBERTS,
Consul.

UNITED STATES CONSULATE,
Coaticook, January 13, 1890.

FORT ERIE.

REPORT BY CONSUL WHELAN.

In the consular district of Fort Erie refrigerators are pretty generally used, and about to the same extent, comparatively, and under like conditions, as in the States bordering on the Great Lakes. The features and styles embodied in the refrigerators manufactured and used in those States would entirely answer the requirements of this consular district. Those used here are manufactured in Brantford and other parts of the province of Ontario

The following tables give the sizes, description, and prices of the refrigerators used here.

Description.	Length.	Depth.	Height.	Price.
	Inches.	*Inches.*	*Inches.*	
Wood lined, bronze trimmings, oak-grained, casters	28	18	42	$11.00
Zinc lined, new patent latch, casters, thick wall	32	18	42	14.00
Zinc lined, hard wood, thick walls, bronze trimmings, casters	26	17	40	15.00
Do	28	18	42	17.00
Do	30	19	44	19.00
Do	33	21	46	21.00
Zinc lined, bronze trimmings, locks and hinges, casters	34	20	46	24.50
Do	41	22	48	28.50
Do	47	23	50	33.50
Ice-chest, hard wood	30	22	30	10.00
Do	34	23	31	11.00
Do	40	25	32	13.00
Counter refrigerators: Ice-chamber, water-cooler, and tap; lower part, under ice-chamber has glass front ends, and forms a show-case for exhibition of butter or other provisions needing ice	24	24	27	13.00

In all these refrigerators, except the chest, the ice-chamber is on top.

The dealers get 25 per cent. off these prices, and the Canadian duty on refrigerators is 35 per cent.

Query: Can United States manufacturers compete?

Ice is secured here in the ordinary ice-house, just as in the United States, and is sold by the ton for from $2.50 to $3.00. It is retailed at the rate of 25 to 30 cents per 100 pounds.

JAMES WHELAN,
Consul.

UNITED STATES CONSULATE,
Fort Erie, February 10, 1890.

GASPÉ BASIN.

REPORT BY CONSUL DICKSON.

Refrigerators are almost an unheard-of piece of furniture in this district; even the stores and hotels do not use them.

Snow takes the place of ice in this district; the stores, hotels, and about all of the inhabitants have snow-houses on their premises.

The fresh fish that is shipped from here to the United States is packed in snow, which is deemed superior to ice, as it keeps the fish cool but does not freeze them.

There is no ice put up in this district to speak of; just a small amount, for the use of steamers that run here during the summer months.

In regard to the last clause of this circular, to report upon the best manner of introducing refrigerators into this district, I am unable to offer any encouragement in this line at present, for there are no cities or large towns in this district; the villages number from 200 to 500 inhabitants each. There is no such thing as an ice-cart delivering ice from house to house in this district.

ALMAR F. DICKSON,
Consul.

UNITED STATES CONSULATE,
Gaspé Basin, January, 1890.

LONDON.

REPORT BY COMMERCIAL AGENT LEONARD.

Upon diligent inquiry I learn that refrigerators are used only in cities and larger towns; there is rarely any demand for them in the country, owing, it is alleged, to the fact that most or quite all the farmers are supplied with good cellars and out spring-houses, with cool water running through the latter. There are no striking or peculiar features in construction different from those manufactured in the United States except in the matter of finish. Dealers say our refrigerators are more tastefully finished. Nearly, if not all, as far as I am able to learn, now being sold here are of home production. Formerly the Baldwin ice-chest, of Vermont, was sold in this market. A few also from some Buffalo manufacturer were sold here. None of either are now kept in stock, the whole trade being supplied by home manufacture. In size they correspond with those manufactured in the United States for domestic purposes. Some contain ice only on the top, others contain ice both top and body of chest ranging in price from $10 to $20, according to size and finish.

Ice is secured here in great abundance. It is taken from the north branch of the Thames River and from spring ponds in the immediate vicinity of the city. The latter is much purer and better and sells at 12½ cents per 100 pounds.

I have made particular inquiry as to the possibility of introducing refrigerators where not now in use. I am told that it would be difficult for the reason already given. The farmers depend upon their cool cellars and out spring-houses. I will continue my investigations, and if I find anything of special note will report it promptly. I am inclined to think, from the favorable expressions made of American manufactures of ice-chests in their finish, that with proper effort there might be some increase of trade and preference given to our productions. I can not promise much with the home manufacturers looking up the trade, pressing sales, large and small, whenever they can.

H. Z. LEONARD,
Commercial Agent.

UNITED STATES COMMERCIAL AGENCY,
  London, January 16, 1890.

KINGSTON.

REPORT BY CONSUL TWITCHELL.

Refrigerators are in general use in this consular district among the wealthy class of citizens. No peculiar features are required in their construction. Some of the refrigerators used are manufactured here; the largest proportion are imported from the United States; they are similar to those in New York State; price from $8 to $35.

Ice is cut from the harbor during the winter, and is delivered to customers at about 25 cents per 100 pounds.

WM. TWITCHELL,
Consul.

UNITED STATES CONSULATE,
  Kingston, January 17, 1890.

MANITOBA.

REPORT BY CONSUL TAYLOR, OF WINNIPEG.

On account of the northern climate, refrigerators are used to limited extent only in this district in proportion to population. In the country, cellars where water is congealed during winter to a considerable depth and closed during summer are a very convenient substitute.

Ordinary patterns and grades of refrigerators as used in United States are occasionally manufactured here, but are mostly brought from Toronto, Brantford, and London in Eastern Canada. Those generally in use are of the following dimensions: 41 by 33 by 21 inches, price $18; 41 by 40 by 21 inches, $20; 48 by 46 by 21 inches, $25.

The duty by the Canadian tariff on refrigerators, classified as "furniture," is 35 per cent. ad valorem.

Ice is readily secured in all parts of Manitoba and elsewhere in this consular district, price $1 per ton; delivered and distributed in summer by ice companies to families at $5 per season of five months at 10 pounds daily, and larger quantities at less rates.

JAMES W. TAYLOR,
Consul.

UNITED STATES CONSULATE,
Winnipeg, June 14, 1890.

MONTREAL.

REPORT BY CONSUL-GENERAL KNAPP.

Refrigerators are used in this consular district, their use, however, being mostly confined to the cities and villages. As to just what extent they are used it is impossible to state. The climate here during the greater part of the year is so cold that refrigerators are not in such demand as they are in a warmer climate. Still they are used here to a considerable extent and their use is increasing.

I am unable to find that there are any peculiar features required in their construction.

The refrigerators used here are mostly manufactured in Montreal, Ottawa, and Brantford, Canada.

The principal manufacturers in Montreal are George W. Reed and Joseph E. Barill. Some refrigerators are also imported from the United States, those so imported being manufactured principally by the Jewett Manufacturing Company, Buffalo, N. Y., and by the Baldwin Manufacturing Company, Burlington, Vt.

The refrigerator most in use here is the North Star refrigerator, manufactured in this city.

To secure an equable cool temperature throughout this refrigerator the ice compartment is placed in the top, thus allowing the cold air to descend from the ice.

To effect a thorough circulation as well as ventilation, a current of air is created and passed through by means of ventilators on the sides. (and which are used to regulate this at pleasure) into the air-chamber, from whence it enters into and circulates throughout the compartments, making its exit on the opposite side to which it enters through similar air-chambers and ventilators.

The shelves are made of galvanized-iron wire, which does not rust, and the rack is covered with zinc. This last not only protects the bottom of the ice-box but also serves to keep the ice free from its meltings, and economizes.

This refrigerator is manufactured in different sizes, with prices varying according to size.

Width.	Depth.	Height.	Price.
Inches.	Inches.	Inches.	
35	22	45	$23.00
38	23	47	26.00
41	24	49	30.00
44	25	51	35.00
48	26	53	40.00

The North Star refrigerator is, as stated above, the one principally used in this district; other refrigerators used to some extent do not vary materially from the one above described in sizes and prices, and while in formation they may differ somewhat, they are of ordinary construction, with no peculiar features characterizing their formation.

Ice is secured in this consular district principally from the rivers St. Lawrence and Richelieu. The ice secured by ice companies is furnished to customers at 29 cents per 100 pounds.

CHAS. L. KNAPP,
Consul-General.

UNITED STATES CONSULATE-GENERAL,
Montreal, February 6, 1890.

NOVA SCOTIA.

REPORT BY CONSUL-GENERAL FRYE, OF HALIFAX.

Refrigerators are in use in Nova Scotia to a moderate extent. There are no peculiar features required in their construction for this province. Most of the refrigerators sold in Nova Scotia are manufactured in some part of Canada—some in this province and some in Ontario. A few are or have been imported from the United States, and they are said to be better finished than the Canadian make; but owing to the Canadian duty, which is 30 per cent. ad valorem, they can not be sold at a profit in competition with those manufactured in Canada.

The sizes most in use for domestic purposes are: Width, 2 feet 6 inches; height, 44 inches. They are similar in arrangement and appearance to the American refrigerators, different styles being used, and are sold for about the same price that the American article sells for in the United States.

Ice is easily secured in winter in this country wherever there are streams or fresh-water lakes, which are abundant. The ordinary price of ice, per ton, is about $1.50. This season, owing to the greater demand abroad, the price is about $2.50. By the 100 pounds it is sold for 25 cents. Families using moderate quantities during the warmer seasons of the year, obtain it for from $3 to $6 per season, according to the quantity used.

Ice is stored to considerable extent in winter both for shipment and for domestic use. Some families who do not use the refrigerators have small houses or large closets, in which a supply is kept for daily use in summer. I doubt if these store-rooms or closets are constructed on modern or improved plans. In one of the meat-markets in Halifax, however, a large apartment is now being constructed by a professional builder of refrigerators from Boston, who has constructed several of them in other parts of the Dominion. It will cost about $1,500, and will be a decided improvement upon anything of its kind in this city, if not in this province.

It is not probable that under the present Canadian tariff American refrigerators can be successfully sold here, unless the manufacturers can furnish them cheaper than at their present prices. To find a market the refrigerators must be of better appearance, finish, and quality, and as cheap, or nearly as cheap, as the Canadian article. Purchasers unacquainted with refrigerators can not always judge what kinds possess the best preserving qualities, and are apt to buy the cheaper article, provided it looks well and appears to be convenient in its arrangements. The only way, therefore, to find a market here for the American refrigerator would seem to be to place the very best article in the market at the lowest price, and to advertise it liberally. In the hands of enterprising and competent agents they might, and I believe would, find some sale here. Like many other luxuries the refrigerator becomes a necessity, as people become accustomed to its use and learn its value.

WAKEFIELD G. FRYE,
Consul-General.

UNITED STATES CONSULATE-GENERAL,
Halifax, April 3, 1890.

OTTAWA.

REPORT BY CONSUL-GENERAL LAY.

Refrigerators are largely used in this consular district for domestic purposes and by butchers, brewers, pork-packers, green grocers, hotels, restaurants, etc.

Those in use are mostly box-shaped, with sides of wood, having spaces filled with non-conducting material and dead air spaces. The ice-box is on top or on the side, and the air is drawn through ventilators, passing over the ice and descending to the storage chamber. One style in rather general use here is the "Hauralean" patent, which is similar to the American "Lorillard" patent. They are manufactured for domestic purposes in the principal cities, Toronto and Ottawa. Cold-storage houses are put up and used in Morrisburg, Iroquois, Prescott, Brockville, and Kingston, usually for the storage of butter and eggs, meats, etc., where ice is cheap and from whence large shipments are made.

The sizes, formations, and prices of the refrigerators in use are as follows: 36 by 32 by 18 inches, ash, $20; 42 by 32 by 18 inches, ash, $25; 48 by 34 by 21 inches, ash, $30; 48 by 40 by 27 inches, ash, $40; 72 by 54 by 30 inches, ash, $60.

The above is the ordinary domestic refrigerator, box-shaped. Special sizes are made for hotels, restaurants, etc.

Ice is usually sawn into blocks 3 feet long. It is then packed in large ice-houses; price, put in, from 35 to 50 cents per ton, according to distance of haul. Price of ice at retail, in summer, about 40 cents per 100 pounds.

Comparing the American system with the Canadian, it is claimed here that Canada has an equally good one. But it can hardly be said that perfection has been attained in the consumption of ice, in the even distribution of air, in the carrying off of noxious gases generated by articles of food, or in the perfect dryness of the air. There have been about fifteen Canadian patents issued for refrigerators within the past ten years.

Refrigerators are used very universally except in the country districts. Nearly every household goods dealer is an agent for some refrigerator, and no one style possesses sufficient merit to become universally adopted.

The best manner of introducing refrigerators into this district would be to have reliable traveling agents to visit important cities and towns and select household dealers, like the companies do here, and give them a liberal commission for a time to sell them; also, to show the refrigerators at the agricultural fairs which are held, annually, in the fall; also, by a judicious system of advertising.

RICHARD G. LAY,
Consul-General.

UNITED STATES CONSULATE GENERAL,
Ottawa, February 6, 1890.

PORT HOPE.

REPORT BY COMMERCIAL AGENT SHAFFER.

Refrigerators are almost universally used in hotels, butchers' stalls, and private houses. No peculiar features required in construction, except those mentioned below.

The refrigerators in use in this district are manufactured in Toronto and in Michigan. Hotels and private houses use the Leonard refrigerator, for the most part, manufactured in Michigan.

The sizes are 8 by 10 and 12 feet in height, according to the business for which they are required.

Butchers use 12 by 14 by 14 feet high; they are double lined with felt paper between the boards.

Fruiterers and fish dealers use a smaller size with an outer and an inner "skin" 2 inches apart, and this space is filled with charcoal; a part of the top portion is reserved for ice, and on the sides there are spaces for the cold air from the ice-chamber to enter the refrigerator; and in the rear there is a warm air-chamber for carrying off the warm air.

The cost is from $250 to $600.

Average sizes, 27 by 18 by 42 inches, $16; 30 by 20 by 45 inches, $22; 36 by 21 by 48 inches, $30; 40 by 24 by 50 inches, $40; 43 by 26 by 60 inches, $50; 48 by 25 by 45 inches (drawing-room style), $75.

The ice is secured from the rivers and lakes by cutting it with a cross-cut saw into blocks 2½ feet long and 1½ feet wide. It costs the consumer 50 cents per 100 pounds.

Generally, I think the people are familiar, in this district, with the various kinds of American refrigerators, and if they do not adopt them it will not be from ignorance of their superiority.

LUTHER M. SHAFFER,
Commercial Agent.

UNITED STATES COMMERCIAL AGENCY,
Port Hope, January 30, 1889.

PORT ROWAN.

REPORT BY COMMERCIAL AGENT SCHOOLEY.

Refrigerators are in use in this consular district only to a limited extent. There are no peculiar features required in the construction. They are manufactured principally in Toronto, Hamilton, and Brantford.

Sizes and prices are as follows: From 24 to 40 inches in length, 18 to 20 inches in depth, 27 to 45 inches in height; generally of square design; from $11 to $30 for ordinary house use.

Ice in this district is cut from ponds. The price is $1 per load, delivered in ice-house, each load containing about 1½ tons. It is generally retailed to customers for the season, ranging from $2 to $15 and $25, according to the quantity used.

I may here add that many private houses have their own ice-houses and they are greatly utilized. In many cases ice-chests, simply made of wood and lined with zinc, are largely used. As there are only villages and towns, there being no cities in my district, refrigerators are not used to such an extent as in the cities. A good deal of dependence is also placed in the cellars, they being built with a due regard to the preservation of foods and liquids.

As to introducing refrigerators into this district, the greatest drawback is regarding prices; there being also a duty of 35 per cent. which makes it almost prohibitive.

R. H. SCHOOLEY,
Commercial Agent.

UNITED STATES COMMERCIAL AGENCY,
Port Rowan, January 21, 1890.

PORT STANLEY AND ST. THOMAS.

REPORT BY CONSUL QUIGGLE.

Refrigerators are used in this consular district to about the same extent as in similarly situated parts of the United States. There are no peculiar features required in their construction other than those ordinarily found in American-made refrigerators. They are manufactured at Toronto, London, Brantford, and Harriston, in the Province of Ontario; sizes and formations are about the same as standard American refrigerators. Prices range from about $10 to $25, retail. It is seldom that any are sold at a higher figure than the latter.

The mode of securing ice is so obvious in this northern latitude as to require no explanation. The price of ice in the summer season is usually from 12 to 15 cents per 100 pounds.

The best manner of introducing refrigerators into this district would be by furnishing dealers with descriptive catalogues and placing the prices so low, and making the discounts so liberal, that they could afford to pay the Canadian duty of 35 per cent. ad valorem and sell them as cheap as those of domestic manufacture.

JAMES C. QUIGGLE,
Consul.

UNITED STATES CONSULATE,
Port Stanley and St. Thomas, January 17, 1890.

ST. HYACINTHE.

REPORT BY COMMERCIAL AGENT MOORE.

Only the smaller sizes of refrigerators are used here by private families. In stores large ice-boxes, constructed like those you would find in every meat or provision store in the United States, are not in general use; if there are any, they are constructed after their own plans and are merely large boxes.

In the market here, where meats are sold on every Saturday, there are no ice-boxes or cold storage. The butchers take their meat which is unsold and put it in the large cold-storage rooms (of an American firm of egg packers here), made after plans by Mixer & Co., American refrigerator makers. They are charged one-half cent per pound for this privilege and keep their meat there until the next market day.

There are no peculiar features required in the construction of refrigerators for this district. Those in use are manufactured in the province of Ontario.

The prices, etc., given here are taken from the price-list of the manufacturers of refrigerators on sale here, Messrs. Gould & Knowles, Brantford, Ontario. The measurement is the outside measurement.

Description.	Length.	Depth.	Height.	Price.	Shipping weight.
	Inches.	Inches.	Inches.		Pounds.
Cheap grade	28	18	42	$10.00	164
Medium grade	26	17	40	14.00	140
Do	28	18	42	16.00	160
Do	30	19	44	18.00	175
Do	33	21	46	20.00	200
Best grade	34	20	46	23.00	215
Do	41	22	48	17.00	255
Do	47	23	50	32.00	318
Ice-chests	30	22	30	9.00	146
Do	34	23	31	10.00	150
Do	40	25	32	12.00	180
Counter refrigerator, glass side for show-case	24	24	27	12.00	142

Ice is cut from the river on which the town is situated; nearly every person has his own ice-house, which he fills himself.

It is never sold by the pound, but ice men charge $8 for the season of five months, delivering 20 pounds daily.

The best manner to introduce refrigerators would be to place them in the hands of some merchant here, or else send a commercial traveler, and by judicious advertising.

THOMAS EWING MOORE,
Commercial Agent.

UNITED STATES COMMERCIAL AGENCY,
St. Hyacinthe, February 3, 1890.

ST. JOHNS, QUEBEC.

REPORT BY CONSUL FISK.

Refrigerators are generally used in this district. No peculiar features required. A refrigerator that is good for New England would be good for this district.

Those in use here are manufactured at Brantford and London, Ontario, Montreal, Quebec, and to some extent at Burlington, Vt.

The formations are quite like the refrigerators in common use in New England. The ice compartment is generally in the top. Single and double doors are used, with zinc or wood for lining. In some, to effect a thorough circulation and ventilation (as claimed), a current of air is created and passed through by means of ventilators on the sides into the air-chamber, from whence it enters and circulates throughout the compartments.

Prices.

	Length.	Depth.	Height.	Price.
	Inches.	Inches.	Inches.	
No. 1	34	20	46	$23.00
No. 2	41	22	48	27.00
No. 3	47	23	50	32.00
No. 10	60	28	68	45.00

Ice is secured from the streams. The price is about 20 cents per 100 pounds.

H. C. FISK,
Consul.

UNITED STATES CONSULATE,
St. John's, Quebec, February 10, 1890.

ST. STEPHEN.

REPORT BY CONSUL GOODNOW.

Very few refrigerators are used in this district, and those in private families, they are of all kinds, sizes, and of local manufacture; there is no demand at present for them.

Ice is cut on this (St. Croix) river 2 miles above the town, hauled here by teams, and stored at an expense of 50 cents per ton; in summer time it is sold for 50 cents per 100 pounds.

EDWARD C. GOODNOW,
Consul.

UNITED STATES CONSULATE,
St. Stephen, January 30, 1890.

SHERBROOKE.

REPORT BY CONSUL WHITE.

Refrigerators are used in this consular district very generally, more perhaps than would be natural to suppose in a latitude as far north as this is, and where there is but very little warm weather compared with other sections of the country.

There are no peculiar features required in their construction. It is safe to say that fully 75 per cent. of them are manufactured in the United States.

As an invariable rule, the size and formation consist of the ordinary size and style in general use by private families, hotel proprietors, dairy and market men throughout the eastern and northern part of the United States, which are so well known that I deem it inexpedient and unnecessary to enter into a detailed account and description of the construction of these ordinary house and market refrigerators.

In some countries where there is an extremely warm climate the year round, it has been proved and demonstrated that ice can be manufactured by an artificial process much cheaper than to transport it from colder countries, but in a country like this, where, during the winter months, the temperature is so cold that the mercury ranges at times as low as 45° below zero, there seems to be no occasion to resort to artificial means to secure ice in this immediate locality. It is cut and taken from the rivers, ponds, and lakes in this locality at a cost of about 40 or 50 cents per ton and preserved in ordinary ice-houses.

Ice-dealers furnish ordinary private families for $5 a season and charge hotel and market men and other parties using a large quantity at the rate of $2.50 or $3.00 a ton.

D. M. WHITE,
Consul.

UNITED STATES CONSULATE,
  Sherbrooke, March 13, 1890.

THREE RIVERS.

REPORT BY CONSUL SMITH.

Refrigerators are in general use in this consular district.

So far as I can learn there are no peculiar features in their construction. They are manufactured in this city.

They are of all sizes; prices range from $18 to $50.

While those in use here are generally inferior to those manufactured in the United States, the climate, even in mid-summer, is so cool and the people are so poor, that I can offer no encouragement to American makers to attempt the introduction of their wares.

NICHOLAS SMITH,
Consul.

UNITED STATES CONSULATE,
  Three Rivers, December 2, 1889.

MEXICO.

GUAYMAS.

REPORT BY CONSUL WILLARD.

Refrigerators are used to a very limited extent in this consular district. The few that are used are of American manufacture, but the whole number imported for the past five years will not exceed thirty.

There is no system of preserving food in this part of Mexico beyond that practiced from the early days of the settlement of this coast, viz: drying in the open air the flesh of animals, the atmosphere being such that in three days' exposure to the sun it is perfectly dried. The same is then made into bales or packages and will keep from one to two years.

The ice which we have in this part of Mexico is made artificially; there are but two ice-machines in this consular district; one at Guaymas of the capacity of 5 tons daily. The consumption in the summer months, from June to November, is 3 tons per day. The ice-machine at Hermosillo (capital of Sonora) has the same capacity, and the consumption is about the same as at Guaymas. No ice is imported from the United States as a regular business. Price in Guaymas per pound 2½ cents; in large quantities, 1½ cents.

The preservation of liquids has not been attempted.

Regarding the best manner of introducing refrigerators into this district, I am unable to give a clear idea; the people still pursue the old-time custom of their forefathers, and although this consular district borders on the United States, with daily railway communication, no change, excepting to a limited extent, has been made in the manner of living, and no new system of preserving food and liquids attempted. There are no canning establishments for the preservation of either beef or fish in this consular district.

A. WILLARD,
Consul.

UNITED STATES CONSULATE,
Guaymas, March 1, 1890.

LA PAZ.

REPORT BY CONSUL VIOSCA.

While this country is so utterly unprovided with the facilities for procuring ice enough during summer to satiate the craving appetite of one-third of its consumers, and that at the enormous price of from 12 to 25 cents per pound at which it is sold, when any of it from across the Gulf has reached the market, it becomes thus impossible to make a report of any utility to the manufacturers on the refrigerator subject.

JAS. VIOSCA,
Consul.

UNITED STATES CONSULATE,
   La Paz, February 1, 1890.

PASO DEL NORTE.

REPORT BY CONSUL SAMPSON.

Very few refrigerators are used in this consular district.

Ice is secured from the Artificial Ice Company of El Paso, Tex. Price, 75 cents per 100 pounds.

A. J. SAMPSON,
Consul.

UNITED STATES CONSULATE,
   Paso del Norte, February 20, 1890.

TUXPAN.

There being neither ice nor machines for its manufacture in this district, refrigerators could not be sold in this market.

JOHN DRAYTON,
Consul.

UNITED STATES CONSULATE,
   Tuxpan, January 18, 1890.

CENTRAL AMERICA.

COSTA RICA.

REPORT BY CONSUL MACKEY, OF SAN JOSÉ.

Refrigerators are used in Co-ta Rica to but a limited extent, their use being confined to the capital, San José, and the two ports Punta Arenas and Limon.

The latter places are small, neither exceeding more than 2,500 inhabitants. San José has a population of 25,000, but the standard of comfort is not sufficiently high to bring refrigerators into general use. They are used principally in the drinking saloons and retail grocery stores of the towns mentioned.

There are no peculiar features required in their construction for this district.

Those in use are manufactured in New York or San José.

Only the smaller sizes are used, and those of the simplest form. Those manufactured here hold, as a rule, 5 pounds of ice; those imported are made to hold from 25 to 30 pounds. The cost of the former is $10, United States currency; of the latter, about double that sum.

There are ice factories in San José and Punta Arenas, and consumers are supplied daily with the ice required at a cost of 1½ cents (United States currency) per pound.

My reply to the Department's circular is brief, for the reason that the trade here in refrigerators is insignificant, and likely to continue unimportant, on account of climatic and social conditions.

BECKFORD MACKEY,
Consul.

UNITED STATES CONSULATE,
San José, February 10, 1890.

NICARAGUA.

BLUEFIELDS.

REPORT BY CONSULAR AGENT SIMMONS.

"No" and "none" are the only replies I can make to interrogatories 1, 2, 3, 4, and 5 of the refrigerator circular.

During the past two years the writer has industriously sought, for his personal needs, an apparatus for the preservation of foods and liquids, one that should cheaply maintain a sufficiently low temperature, and not necessarily for production of ice, for which the demand is not enough to warrant the expense of machinery. To the very many letters of inquiry sent to all parts of the United States circulars only were received in reply, representing machines for making ice; expensive, involving employment of steam-engines, and skilled labor to conduct them.

One ton of ice per week would at present fully supply all demands, and its price must not exceed 5 cents (*soles*) per pound to insure the sale of so much. What is wanted are refrigerating apparatus for the preservation of meats, etc., and cheap enough to meet private needs, machines that will maintain a uniform temperature of 38° to 40° Fahr. One such on a large scale would meet all town requirements and serve to promote the sale of meats, poultry, etc., of American importations. Facilities for the introduction of everything needed are furnished by steam lines from the ports of New Orleans, Savannah, Philadelphia, and New York.

JNO. H. SIMMONS,
Consular Agent.

U. S. CONSULAR AGENCY,
Bluefields, January 25, 1890.

MANAGUA.

REPORT BY CONSUL WILLS.

Refrigerators are used to such a limited extent in my consular district that I can not say they are used at all.

The ice company brought in a few refrigerators, with the materials for their factory, duty free; finding no demand for them, they were put upon the market below cost. The price paid was $21; they were offered at $15, but not sold.

Another gentleman has lately imported fifteen, costing from $3 to $15 each. He finds no sale for them.

They are manufactured by Macy & Co., New York.

Ice is manufactured only in Managua, and shipped to the different towns. The wholesale price at the factory is $2.50 per 100 pounds, but it is retailed by special agents at 5 cents a pound. Parties using ice buy a pound at a time, generally before each meal.

Perishable goods are purchased only in sufficient quantities for the day. The markets are open every day, including Sundays.

CHAS. H. WILLS,
Consul.

UNITED STATES CONSULATE,
Managua, April 15, 1890.

SOUTH AMERICA.

ARGENTINE REPUBLIC.

REPORT BY CONSUL BAKER, OF BUENOS AYRES.

I am in receipt of the circular of the Department of State asking certain information in regard to the use of refrigerators in the Argentine Republic, with a view to extending the trade of American manufacturers of such articles in this country.

In reply I have to state that the people of this Republic fully appreciate the value and convenience of the American refrigerators, and for a number of years, ever since the manufacture of artificial ice was commenced in this country, these articles have not only been imported here, but they have found a very ready and increasing sale. Now, not only are they used by hotels, cafés, eating-houses, *confiterias*, and drinking saloons generally, but in all the dwelling-houses of the wealthier classes.

I know of no particular features which are required in their construction to meet the tastes of this community, but you will see in use all the various shapes and sizes, from the mere ice-box to those which have the pretentions of a sideboard. As, however, ice is an expensive article of luxury, I suppose those whose construction requires the smallest quantity and least consumption of ice would be preferred.

There may be some few refrigerators imported from other countries, but the great bulk of those on sale here are from the United States.

In regard to sizes, formations, and prices, there is nothing that I can say further than that these depend on the requirements, the tastes, and the means of those who purchase them, just as is the case in the United States.

The great drawback to the universal use of refrigerators in the Argentine Republic is the fact that there is no natural ice here, and no importations from northern latitudes. All the ice used is manufactured; and while the quantity is every year growing larger and the quality is equally being improved, yet the expense is so great, other things being considered, that it is only those with somewhat plethoric purses who can indulge in its general use. Two years ago the price was 90 cents per 25 pounds, but, owing to increased facilities in its manufacture, you can now buy a very good quality for from 2 to 3 cents per pound for large quantities. At retail, from the groceries, it sells for 5 to 8 cents per pound, according to the demand. These prices are in Argentine paper money, which, reduced to gold, would make the price of ice about 1 cent per pound for large quantities, and $2\frac{1}{2}$ to 4 cents per pound at retail, estimated in United States coin.

A few years ago the attempt was made to import ice from the United States to Buenos Ayres, but it proved to be a failure owing to the fact that sea-going vessels at that time were obliged to anchor about 8 miles from the shore and have their cargoes transferred to lighters; so that with such exposure under a fervent sunshine ice cargoes melted about as rapidly as they were delivered. But since then a great change has been effected in the handling of cargoes here. Now Buenos Ayres has a good and convenient harbor, where vessels discharge alongside of commodious wharves or docks without delay and without trouble; and it seems to me, if parties should first make arrangements for ice deposits on these docks, that it would be a paying business to import ice to Buenos Ayres from the United States. I think there is no doubt that it could be delivered from the United States much cheaper than it can be manufactured here. Thus, with its more general use owing to greater cheapness, there would be an increased demand for American refrigerators.

E. L. BAKER,
Consul.

UNITED STATES CONSULATE,
Buenos Ayres, February 12, 1890.

BOLIVIA.

REPORT BY CONSUL-GENERAL ANDERSON, OF LA PAZ.

My personal knowledge of the demand for refrigerators is confined to the department of La Paz, in which I have my official residence, not having visited either of the other seven departments of Bolivia, viz: Cochabamba, Potosi, Chuquisaca, Oruro, Tarija, Beni, and Santa Cruz. With the exception of the province of Fungas, lying in the northeast of this department and beyond the great Cordillera range, and a portion of the province of Cercada, lying south of this city some 8 leagues, and in the low valleys of the La Paz River, there is no demand whatever for refrigerators in the department of La Paz, owing to the favorable climatic conditions resulting from its varying altitudes of from 10,000 to 13,000 feet.

Here, as well as throughout the great departments of Potosi, embracing nine provinces, and Oruro, embracing three provinces, foods and liquids are kept in perfect preservation for from five to eight days in summer and from eight to twelve days in winter, by simply exposing them to the fresh air. The three departments to which I refer fall within the chief mountain districts of Bolivia, and embrace the great body of the population of the Republic.

The departments of Beni and Santa Cruz, lying still beyond the province of Fungas, have a climate similar to that of Fungas, but are so remotely situated and sparsely settled that neither offers an inviting field for the line of American goods referred to, although climatic conditions are favorable to their introduction. The departments of Cochabamba and Tarija embrace within their extensive limits a large number of low, warm, and exceedingly rich valleys, the products of which soon perish, as I am informed, for want of some adequate system for their preservation. The remaining department of Chuquisaca has a temperate climate as a rule.

The rural portion of this department is sparsely settled, the great bulk of the population living in Sucre, not only the capital of the department but of the Republic. It is apparent, therefore, from what I have here stated, that there is no general demand for refrigerators in this country; that the demand therefor, so far as the climate is concerned, is confined to the warm districts I have enumerated. The introduction of refrigerators into these districts is, in my judgment, an experiment worth trying.

A vast amount of the products of these sections of the country perish for lack of the American system of preserving foods and liquids. If, however, the manufacturers of refrigerators in the United States undertake this experiment they must do it in the light of the fact that the Indians are the producing class in this country, and that the introduction of modern appliances to take the place of their primitive methods of labor is regarded by them, as a rule, as an innovation not to be encouraged.

As to the manner of securing ice and its price per hundred pounds, I have to report that the supply of ice here at all seasons of the year is unlimited. The famous Illimani, which reaches an altitude of more than 23,000 feet, and other great peaks of the Andes system are not only perpetually covered with snow, but abound in solid beds and columns of ice as well.

The Indians climb to these mountain heights and, cutting the ice into blocks, lash them across the backs of llamas, and, with these celebrated burden-bearers of the Upper Andes, each carrying not exceeding 100 pounds, the limit of their ability as pack-animals, they descend, as sure of foot as the llamas themselves, to the ice markets of the country, where they sell it at from 20 to 40 cents per 100 pounds.

T. H. ANDERSON,
Consul-General.

UNITED STATES CONSULATE-GENERAL,
La Paz, March 15, 1890.

BRAZIL.

RIO DE JANEIRO.

REPORT BY CONSUL-GENERAL DOCKERY.

Replying to the Department's circular of date November 25, 1889, asking information in regard to the use of refrigerators in this consular district, I beg to report that after careful investigation I find that they are now used in this city to a limited extent. The demand, however, is slowly increasing each year, and 200 to 300 will probably be sold this season. Those in use are principally imported from the United States, are small, cheaply constructed, and sell here for $10 to $50. No higher-priced article can now be sold here, but as the demand increases more costly ones can be introduced. Ice is manufactured here and retailed at $2\frac{1}{2}$ to $3\frac{1}{2}$ cents per pound. As a local company secured and now holds valuable concessions and exclusive privileges for cold-air preservation which are not now in use, the chances for the successful introduction of any other method are not good at present.

Up to now, the supply of articles of food has been for the day only, but, with facilities to keep it, a change of custom may reasonably be looked for. Ice having been put on the market at a figure placing it within the reach of the people, from being a luxury it will come into general use, and with that will come the increased demand for refrigerators.

My conclusions are that a market can be opened here for the successful introduction of American refrigerators. To do so will require a careful study on the part of our manufacturers to produce such goods as will suit the trade. A large stock of the manufactured article should be brought here and considerable money spent in advertising and pushing the sale. I believe the result will come slowly, but very satisfactorily.

I shall refer more fully in a general dispatch to the necessity of our manufacturers becoming more thoroughly acquainted with and adapting their products to the wants of this market if they would enter into competition with the English and Germans. A splendid opportunity is now presented.

O. H. DOCKERY,
Consul-General.

UNITED STATES CONSULATE-GENERAL,
Rio de Janerio, February 15, 1890.

BAHIA.

REPORT BY CONSUL BURKE.

As to information concerning refrigerators, as called for in the circular dated November 25, 1889, I have the honor to say but very little can be given, as the use of this article in this place is confined to the hotels and a few restaurants. Not a half dozen were imported during the past year. They are almost an unknown quantity in private houses. One may be found here and there, but they are so little used that hardware merchants do not keep them in stock. In one of the large hardware stores I found one, which the merchant had imported on order from England. This and another one made up his entire importation of refrigerators for the year 1889. It was a small one, perhaps $2\frac{1}{2}$ feet square; retail price, 40 milreis ($21.84); constructed much the same as American refrigerators of the same size. It was lined with zinc inside, with a place for depositing the ice, and shelves that were movable, making the space between them larger or smaller according to size of the articles placed within.

I saw one of a German make, size about 4 feet in height, 4 in length, and 2½ in breadth. At the top of this was the ice-chest, extending through its length and breadth dimensions and about 6 inches in depth. Underneath this ice-chest were the slides and the shelves, the shelves being movable. Below the ice-chest are two partitions, or, rather, two compartments, with a partition running up and down through the center of the refrigerator. In this partition is a faucet to draw the water from the ice-box. The interior of the refrigerator is lined with zinc. The cost of this refrigerator, when exchange was high, was 120 milreis ($65.52), laid down here in Bahia. The freight on it was 28 milreis ($15.29), and the duty 38 milreis ($20.77), together with other expenses, making, as mentioned above, 120 milreis all told. England and Germany furnished the very few that are here.

The prevailing opinion among Brazilians is that it is unhealthy and injurious to use ice in this climate. Even many foreigners hold the same opinion and rarely use ice. Those families that use ice buy it late in the afternoon as the ice-cart goes through the city, place the ice bought in a small box of saw-dust when the ice is used at dinner, which takes place from 6.30 to 8 p. m.

From one to three kilos is the quantity purchased by those families that use it. By families it is not used at all to preserve foods.

As meats can be bought at any time of the day and fruit also, no more of anything is purchased than is required for the day; therefore in such cases the refrigerator is dispensed with. Canned goods are also very largely used.

Ice is very expensive, selling at 200 reis, about 10 cents, per kilo, or say 5 cents per pound.

Yet I do not think it is the price of the ice that prevents people from using it more extensively, but because its use, as I said, is regarded as being unhealthy and injurious. But perhaps the chief reason why families do not use refrigerators is because they never have used them and can not appreciate how good a thing it is to have them. As far as I can learn no special effort has ever been made to introduce them and merchants sent for them only on order simply, because there has not been nor is there to-day any demand for them.

The first thing to do if any business is expected is to create a demand for them. This can be done only, it seems to me, by showing families how good, useful, and necessary a thing a refrigerator is.

If this could be done and ice drop one-half in price, there would be a sale for refrigerators.

And I do not know of any better method of introducing this article than by a sort of canvassing tour amongst the business men and men of leisure. To canvass from house to house would hardly do. Either that method or the establishing of an agency here with refrigerators on hand all the time, making a strong effort to work up the trade to create a demand.

I think our American refrigerators, just as they are manufactured, are adapted for this climate. The only thing is to show the people the advantage of such an article in preserving goods and liquids, and that ice, though expensive, is not injurious if taken with moderation, and that a refrigerator may be both "a thing of beauty and a joy forever," especially in a hot climate.

Should any manufacturers desire to correspond with any firm here on the subject of taking the agency, offering terms, inquiring for terms, etc., I would recommend the firm of Corta Santos & Co. But the correspondence should be in Portuguese.

DAVID N. BURKE,
Consul.

UNITED STATES CONSULATE,
Bahia, March 15, 1890.

PERNAMBUCO.

REPORT BY CONSUL BORSTEL.

No refrigerators are used in this consular district, except a few hotels that are provided in that way.

The few in use at the hotels are manufactured in the United States at Burlington, Vt.

The Baldwin refrigerators, size 2 by 1.8 and 3 feet high, price $20. The Macey Diamond refrigerator, size 2.6 by 1.8 and 3 feet high, price $22.50. An ice-chest for cooling beer or wine, showing no marked name, price $16.50.

All ice here is artificially made by machinery; price per 100 pounds, $2.50.

Meats and fish can not be preserved more than one day in this hot climate, hence the little use made of refrigerators.

I have not the least doubt that the American refrigerators could be introduced here by an energetic man who would canvass from house to house for the sale of same, but he must speak Portuguese, and not become soon disheartened if he does not meet with success at first; it is almost impossible to get the people here interested in anything even if it is to their benefit.

It would be impossible for one to make any suggestions in regard to modifying the American refrigerators to meet local requirement, because, not being in the business, I have never given the subject any attention.

H. CHRISTIAN BORSTEL.

UNITED STATES CONSULATE,
Pernambuco, January 30, 1890.

BRITISH GUIANA.

REPORT BY CONSUL WALTHALL, OF DEMERARA.

Refrigerators are in general use in this colony, though to what extent I am unable to ascertain with accuracy.

No peculiar features are believed to be required in their construction. So far as ascertained they are exclusively of American manufacture, and I am informed that the "Eureka" refrigerator and the "Diamond" ice-box are the kinds of which most have been sold. The sizes and prices vary.

The ice trade is at present in the hands of a firm (Messrs. Birch & Co.) who have a contract with the Government, by which they are required to furnish it, whether in larger or smaller quantities, at a uniform price of 1 cent per pound. On the other hand, the Government accords them the exclusive privilege of supplying the Government offices, hospitals, and other public institutions. They are bound to keep on hand at all seasons a sufficient supply for these purposes, and in case of failure are liable to a fine for every day of the deficiency. As regards the supply for private individuals and families, the business is open to competition, but although supposed to be in contemplation, no such competition has as yet been set on foot.

W. T. WALTHALL,
Consul.

UNITED STATES CONSULATE,
Demerara, February 20, 1890.

CHILI.

IQUIQUE.

REPORT BY CONSUL MERRIAM.

Refrigerators are used in this consular district to a very limited extent, their use being confined to the hotels and a very small number of well-to-do families.

No peculiar features are observed in the refrigerators here used, nearly all of which are imported from England and Germany.

The sizes vary from 2 to 3 feet in height, of about the same length and width, and are sold for from $20 to $40 American gold, or its equivalent in Chilian currency.

The ice consumed in this city is all manufactured by a German, who has no opposition or competition in the business, and who sells it in rectangular cakes at the rate of $10 (Chilian currency) per quintal of 100 pounds, or say $5 American gold, although, in fact, the quintal of ice never weighs more than 80 pounds.

91A——3

Were there competition in the manufacture of ice and a consequent reduction of, say, 50 per cent. in the price, its consumption would, doubtless, be much increased, and there would be a corresponding increase in the use of refrigerators.

This is not a promising field for the introduction of refrigerators under the present conditions of ice manufacture.

J. W. MERRIAM,
Consul.

UNITED STATES CONSULATE,
Iquique, February 28, 1890.

TALCAHUANO.

REPORT BY CONSUL VAN INGEN.

All the ice used in this part of the country is brought down from the Andes, which are close by, in carts to the nearest railway station and thence transshipped to destination; but the quantity is very insignificant and is only for household use. There are no refrigerators used here.

All the preserved food and liquids used here are imported.

JOHN F. VAN INGEN,
Consul.

UNITED STATES CONSULATE,
Talcahuano, March 27, 1890.

DUTCH GUIANA.

REPORT BY CONSUL BROWNE, OF PARAMARIBO.

The articles that come nearest to refrigerators, in use in this colony, are ice-chests, which are imported here from Boston, and by Mr. A. N. Bixby.

There is no particular feature that I know of required in the construction of refrigerators for this district.

The ice-chests in use in this district are manufactured in the United States and in Holland.

The size of the ice-chests in use here is as follows: Length, 2½ feet; width, 20 inches; height, 2 feet; thickness of box, 3 inches.

Ice is imported in this colony from Boston by Mr. A. N. Bixby, shipping merchant, and is put up in an ice-house built according to the principle of those in use in the United States.

The price per 100 pounds of ice is $3. Price of the ice-chests, $10.

I would state, for the information of the manufacturers of refrigerators in the United States, that in this district we have only one city, and that is Paramaribo, which place has a population of 27,000, and of that number, to the best of my opinion, there are not more than from 400 to 500 people who use ice.

Nine-tenths of the population are poor and can not afford to purchase a refrigerator.

In regard to the preservation of food, the people here only buy enough to last from day to day, so that there is no danger of it spoiling in that length of time.

I think the best means for the manufacturers in the United States to introduce their refrigerators in this colony (that is, if they should think well of doing so, after reading this report) would be to send an agent down here with samples of the different kinds of refrigerators, and probably he might be able to dispose of some.

THOMAS BROWNE,
Consul.

UNITED STATES CONSULATE,
Paramaribo, January 22, 1890.

ECUADOR.

REPORT BY CONSUL-GENERAL SORSBY, OF GUAYAQUIL.

The total number of refrigerators in use in this district is about fifty, all of which are in use by private families. There are two large ones in use—one by the Lager Beer Association and the other by a saloon.

There are no special features required.

Those in use are of American patent and make. The sizes are 4 by 2½ by 2½ feet. Price here, $35 gold, two and three compartments, Jewett's Queen.

The Lager Beer Association manufactures the ice with an American machine, the La Vergen. The price of the ice is, wholesale, $2 gold per 100 pounds and 7 cents gold retail.

Food and liquids are not preserved, everything of that nature, when used at all, being imported. R. B. Jones & Co. would be the best parties to whom circulars, etc., should be sent.

WILLIAM B. SORSBY,
Consul-General.

UNITED STATES CONSULATE-GENERAL,
Guayaquil, January 20, 1890.

COLOMBIA.

BARRANQUILLA.

REPORT BY VICE-CONSUL WHELPLEY.

The Colombian housekeeper has a prejudice against keeping fresh meat uncooked; it must be cooked the day of killing; fish or fowl the same—a natural and necessary usage in a climate where the mercury stands at 84° to 86°, and the air teems with insect life to such an extent that two hours' exposure is often sufficient for the deposit of larvæ.

Given such atmospheric conditions, and the natural effect on animal food, when ice was an unattainable luxury, as it was a few years ago, and we must consider such a prejudice on the part of the housekeeper as reasonable.

Cooked food of any description left over from the meals of the family is considered the rightful perquisite of the servant, who may have several persons dependent upon her and with whom she shares the gleanings from the master's table. Consequently no cooked food is kept over from one meal to another; no perishable viands are preserved from one day to the next. This custom, hereditary from the days of Spanish rule, and the patriarchal simplicity of the early settlers with their large retinues of household slaves and poor dependents, is another reason why refrigerators are not considered a necessity.

The kitchens are generally in detached buildings or isolated inclosures, apart from the residences. The swarms of ants and other predatory insects, attracted by the odor of food, renders it necessary, and is another reason why its immediate consumption is preferable to its temporary preservation.

From my own household experience I believe that in a country so infested with insect pests the feet of any closet, safe, or refrigerator should be set in metal cups, the cups to be filled with water when necessary, or salt and kerosene, to prevent the entrance of vermin.

There are but two refrigerators, I believe, in actual use, and these were made in New York. But as the supply of artificial ice has heretofore been very uncertain, owing to defects in machinery or mismanagement, these can hardly be said to be in use.

The largest portable refrigerator, 5 feet by 5 feet by 5 feet (from Boston), was intended for a depository in an ice-cream establishment—a failure.

Steam-boats have their ice-boxes built in store-room or pantry.

The large earthen water jars, "Tinajas," keep the water sufficiently cool for drinking, generally 10° or 12° below the temperature of the air, and in the minds of many ice is a luxury of doubtful merit in a sanitary point of view. The limited consumption, from 500 to 700 pounds daily, may be increased hereafter, as there is a new apparatus being put up at the present time, promising a better quality and at cheaper rates. Ice is now from 5 to 7½ cents a pound. So far the drinking saloons, club-rooms, hotels, and steam-boats are the consumers, and as yet it is but rarely used in families. Economy in household expenses also has due weight among a people more accustomed to plain but substantial fare rather than luxurious living.

The duty on a refrigerator would be 20 cents a kilogram, with 25 per cent. additional. As to the best manner of introduction, perhaps circulars sent to the consulate for distribution would be the best preliminary step, if accompanied by illustrations and price-lists in Spanish. The progress of new ideas, in conflict with hereditary domestic customs, must necessarily be slow, but the ultimate victory will be on the side of the greatest economy.

S. M. WHELPLEY,
Vice-Consul.

UNITED STATES CONSULATE,
Barranquilla, January 24, 1890.

COLON.

REPORT BY CONSUL VIFQUAIN.

Refrigerators are not in use in this consular district.

For this district they should be so constructed as to be saving of the ice.

I have found three refrigerators. One at the Pacific Mail Office, the Allegretti patent; it is used to keep cigars, hence not a success as refrigerator. I have found two at a store for sale, where they are liable to remain. They belong to the Jewett Manufactory, and they are both different. One is called the Queen; it sells for $40 Colombian currency, or $25 gold. The other is the Labrador; it sells for $35 Colombian currency, or $22 gold. There is no demand for them because they require too much ice. These refrigerators are manufactured in New York.

Ice is imported from the United States; principally from the Kennebec River. The ice traffic is in the hands of a monopoly; this monopoly is, by its contract with the Government, obliged to sell ice at 5 cents per pound.

This is in answer to the questions, and I submit the following for the information of the manufacturers of refrigerators.

If there is any country in the world where refrigerators are needed, this must be the country. But such a refrigerator is needed as will have a due regard for the saving of the ice, as this article is very dear.

The means resorted to here to preserve foods and liquids are ice-boxes of the "Ideal" model, manufactured in New York, from No. 2 upwards; they sell for from $10 to $20, Colombian currency, or from $6.50 to $13, American gold. They are a very unhandy affair, but answer the purpose better than refrigerators, simply because the latter use too much ice. A medium-sized refrigerator, saving of the ice, would be of great service to the people here, and would prove of good sale, provided the qualities of the same had been fairly tested. The best method for the manufacturers of good refrigerators to introduce them here is to send an active agent, with the knowledge of the Spanish language, on the spot; if this be considered too expensive, let them select a good house here.

VICTOR VIFQUAIN,
Consul.

UNITED STATES CONSULATE,
Colon, January 8, 1890.

PANAMA.

REPORT BY CONSUL-GENERAL ADAMSON.

Refrigerators are used in this consular district to a very limited extent. Dealers decline stating the number sold in a year, but I believe one dozen would more than supply the annual demand of this market.

There are no peculiar features required in the construction of those for this district. Those in use in this district are manufactured in the United States, probably New York.

The only ones I have seen are marked "Mace's diamond refrigerator." They are of four sizes, averaging about 3 feet in height, 30 inches wide, and 18 inches deep, containing in the upper half a zinc ice-box of about 24 by 15 by 15 inches, underneath which is the place for the food to be preserved; average price, $14 gold.

All the ice used here is brought from the State of Maine. The business is a monopoly. The Government stipulates with the monopolists that ice must be sold at not more than 5 cents, Colombian coin, per pound.

It is not customary in any of the countries of Spanish America to take the pains to preserve food such as is taken by our American housekeepers.

The people seem to provide only for their immediate wants, and ice is so expensive that there would not be much economy in saving food by the use of ice and refrigerators.

I do not know of any way by which the demand for refrigerators in this district can be increased to any great extent as long as the sale of ce continues to be a monopoly.

THOMAS ADAMSON,
Consul-General.

UNITED STATES CONSULATE GENERAL,
Panama, January 27, 1890.

VENEZUELA.

REPORT BY CONSUL BIRD, OF LA GUAYRA.

Refrigerators are used to a very limited extent in Venezuela.

There are no peculiar features required in their construction, except that they should be made of walnut, to withstand the ravages of the wood maggot, so destructive to ordinary American woods.

Those in use here are imported from the United States.

The usual sizes and forms made in the United States are found to be suitable here. The prices are more than 100 per cent. greater than in the United States, owing to the fact that, duties being assessed on the gross weight, refrigerators pay heavy duty. For instance, one weighing 300 pounds, made of walnut, would pay $33.29 duty and $4.16 transit tax. If made of ordinary wood it would pay $19.98 duty and $2.50 transit tax. By ordinary wood is meant maple, pine, oak, etc.

Ice is manufactured in Caracas, and is sold at $4 per 100 pounds. None is imported. It is believed that if a proper ice depot were established in La Guayra and importations of natural ice introduced from the United States a profitable trade might be eventually built up. By the tariff it is admitted free of duty. While ice is so dear here, the use of refrigerators will be necessarily very limited.

WINFIELD S. BIRD,
Consul.

UNITED STATES CONSULATE,
    LaGuayra, January 11, 1890.

BRITISH WEST INDIES.

BERMUDA.

REPORT BY CONSUL BECKWITH, OF HAMILTON.

Refrigerators are used here extensively in hotels, saloons, and private houses.

There are no peculiar features required in their construction.

All used here are manufactured in the United States.

Those used here are of the same formations, sizes, and prices as those used in the States.

Ice is imported here from Maine in American vessels. Price per 100 pounds, 75 cents.

HENRY W. BECKWITH,
Consul.

UNITED STATES CONSULATE,
Hamilton, January 1, 1890.

JAMAICA.

REPORT BY CONSUL ALLEN, OF KINGSTON.

Refrigerators are in general use in this consular district and throughout the island of Jamaica.

They are of ordinary construction, such as are in general use in the United States.

Those in use in this district are manufactured in the United States. Sizes 4 by 2 by 3 feet and upwards, as in the United States.

The price of ice is 75 cents for 100 pounds. All ice consumed in this district is manufactured by one company from machines of American pattern, and the management of the factory is under the direction of an American expert.

The steamers plying between the United States and outports of this island bring small quantities of ice occasionally, but the quantity being thus brought is limited and in no way affects the price of the article, thus this entire consular district is virtually dependent on Kingston for its supply.

W. G. ALLEN,
Consul.

UNITED STATES CONSULATE,
Kingston, February 3, 1890.

LEEWARD ISLANDS.

REPORT BY CONSUL JACKSON, OF ANTIGUA.

Little trade can be expected in this quarter owing to the hand-to-mouth method of living, the high price of ice, and the general poverty that prevails among the bulk of the population. Although Maine ice is in good supply, and we a population of 35,000, generally very thirsty, the consumption of ice rarely exceeds 300 pounds a day.

The retail price is $2 per hundred, but if it were furnished at half the price I doubt if the consumption would show much improvement.

A few refrigerators of American make were imported by the party having the ice contract here, and have been sold cheap to encourage the use of ice. They give good satisfaction.

In the Dominica consular agency district ice is kept in supply and retailed at 3 cents per pound; but the circumstances surrounding that place are much more aggravated than obtain in Antigua, consequently a very limited demand must exist for refrigerators.

The consular agency districts of Anguilla, Montserrat, Nevis, and Portsmouth are without ice, and a few pounds only would be consumed however cheap it could be supplied.

CHESTER E. JACKSON,
Consul.

UNITED STATES CONSULATE,
Antigua, February 28, 1890.

NASSAU.

REPORT BY CONSUL M'LAIN.

There are very few refrigerators in use in this colony, there being no supply of ice outside of this city and the high price of the article forbidding its general use in Nassau. I do not suppose there are fifty refrigerators, including all kinds, good, bad, and indifferent, in use in the entire Bahamas. They are never kept in stock by the merchants, and dealers inform me that the demand for them is so small as not to be worth mentioning. Now and then some person needs one and the merchant orders it for him.

Any ordinary refrigerator will meet all the requirements of the people of this colony.

The few in use are of American manufacture.

They are small ones, such as retail at from $8 to $12 in the United States, and are of all conceivable forms and patterns. A few, known as the "Eddy" and the "Arctic," have been imported within a year or two.

The supply of ice comes from Maine, imported in schooners. No attempt has ever been made to manufacture ice here, those interested having figured out that it would not pay to do so. The use of ice is confined to comparatively few families, and probably the quantity sold per annum will not exceed 400 to 500 tons. The price varies, ranging from 2 cents to 4 cents per pound. A large ice-house is owned by the Government, which is rented to parties who give bonds to keep a supply of ice always on hand, to be sold at not to exceed 4 cents per pound. The hotel here has its own ice-house and imports 200 tons per annum.

Families who desire to preserve meats or poultry for a few days send it to the "ice-house," where it is kept for a small consideration. Beef, mutton, etc., are used the same day as killed as a rule; poultry killed when needed; fish sold alive every day in the market.

I do not see any way of introducing refrigerators into this colony at present more extensively than they are coming in at this time. It is only now and then that one is needed, and it is at once ordered by some merchant from New York.

Ice is too dear, the people are too poor, the need of refrigerators is not felt enough to warrant any expectations that a trade worth having can be developed in this article in the Bahamas. The only consolation is that whenever any are purchased they are bought in the United States.

THOS. J. MCLAIN, JR,
Consul.

UNITED STATES CONSULATE,
Nassau, N. P., January 8, 1890.

TOBAGO.

REPORT BY CONSULAR AGENT KEENS.

Refrigerators are not at all used on this island.

Ice is seldom imported, occasionally a few hundred pounds are procured from Trinidad or Barbadoes for special occasions, when its cost is very high, but it is not generally used by the inhabitants.

I have no doubt that if this article could be procured at a low rate and in small quantities to meet the consumption of the island greater advantage would be taken of it, and refrigerators or machines for making ice on a small scale might be the means of establishing its use.

I think that it would be well if I were furnished with catalogues and price-lists of several makes so as to see what could be done in establishing such a system.

EDWARD KEENS,
Consular Agent.

UNITED STATES CONSULAR AGENCY,
Tobago, February 14, 1890.

TRINIDAD.

REPORT OF CONSUL SAWYER.

Refrigerators are in use in this district and to a large extent.

There are no peculiar features required in their construction other than the usual manufactured in the United States—chest and upright ones.

Those in use are manufactured in the United States, chiefly in Boston.

The sizes are various; small, medium, and large, chest and upright principally. Prices vary from $6 to $24 each.

Ice is imported into this island from the United States, principally from Boston. The price is generally $1 per 100 pounds excepting in times of scarcity.

MOSES H. SAWYER,
Consul.

UNITED STATES CONSULATE,
Trinidad, January 29, 1890.

FRENCH WEST INDIES.

GUADELOUPE.

REPORT BY CONSUL BARTLETT.

Refrigerators are not used in this consular district. I know of but one in Guadeloupe, and that I have myself at my little country place, and it is of the old style I purchased about fifteen years ago.

There being none used, this replies to interrogatories 2, 3, and 4.

There are two ice establishments, situated at Pointe-à-Pitre; one a French company, manufacturing artificial ice sold at their establishment, which manufactures only the quantity required daily; the other, part owned here and a portion in the United States, is called the "American Ice Company," which imports ice from Maine, which is secured in an ice-house built on the same principle as those in the State of Maine.

There is also an ice retailing establishment at Basse-Terre, to which the Government grants a subsidy of 2,000 francs per annum. There is a similar one at the Moule, which receives an annual subsidy of 1,200 francs from the town; another one, established at St. François, receives 600 francs subsidy per annum. There was one at Capesterre receiving an annual subsidy of 1,500 francs, but this subsidy having been withdrawn in January this year the establishment was subsequently closed.

The ice establishments at Pointe-à-Pitre do not receive any subsidy.

Ice purchased in town for the country is generally wrapped up in coarse woolen blankets.

The retail price of natural ice at Pointe-à-Pitre, for the present, is 25 centimes per kilogram, and at wholesale 150 francs per ton of 1,000 kilograms.

Artificial ice is retailed for 20 centimes (4.8 cents) a kilogram (2.205 pounds), and at wholesale 120 francs per ton of 1,000 kilograms.

Both natural and artificial ice are sold at retail in Basse-Terre for 30 centimes (5.8 cents) a kilogram.

At the Moule, St. François, and Capesterre it is retailed at 40 centimes a kilogram.

There is no ice sent round in carts, as customary with us. The families purchase their food in the morning sufficient for the daily supply. Bread is obtained fresh every day from the bakeries.

The butchers slaughter just sufficient for their daily sales, and should any quantity of beef happen to be left on hand, it is sent to the ice-house to be put in the ice-chest.

It seems to me that refrigerators ought to be used; and if the manufacturers of refrigerators were to address catalogues of their different kinds of refrigerators to the ice companies here, I have no doubt but that some of the families in Guadeloupe might be prevailed upon to make use of them.

CHARLES BARTLETT,
Consul.

UNITED STATES CONSULATE,
Guadeloupe, *February* 18, 1890.

MARTINIQUE.

REPORT BY CONSUL GARESCHÉ.

Refrigerators are used in this island to a very limited extent, principally by hotels and a few large boarding-houses.

Save one imported last year from Burlington, Vt., I know of none that are not of the primitive manufacture of this island.

From the above observations it can be inferred that not only are the refrigerators here used manufactured in this island, but that it would be impossible to give even an adequate idea of the sizes, formations, and prices thereof in this district.

Ice is almost entirely the product of machinery here, save, perhaps, an occasional cargo sent to Fort de France from the United States mainly for the use of the steamers of the Compagnie Generale Transatlantique.

Without distinction between the natural and artificial product, ice retails here the year round at 3 cents per pound, very little, if any, deduction being made for purchases in large quantities.

In conclusion I would say that refrigerators of moderate size might be profitably introduced here. At all events, since the modern article is almost entirely unknown, the venture might be worth the risk.

In my estimation, the best manner of introducing refrigerators would be to send a sample to each of the leading clubs here—there are two—and one to the leading hotel in Fort-de-France, and also to the only hotel in this city of St. Pierre. In this way their benefits could be appreciated, and the enterprising manufacturer who is willing to risk this much would profit by the education of this people.

Perhaps this would be ultimately cheaper than sending a commercial traveler here.

If any manufacturer desires to send one first-class specimen, of moderate price, I will gladly take charge of it and place it in such public location as may best serve to advertise the article.

WM. A. GARESCHÉ,
Consul.

UNITED STATES CONSULATE,
Martinique, *March* 12, 1890.

HAYTI.

REPORT BY MINISTER DOUGLAS, OF PORT AU PRINCE.

The refrigerators are not at all in general use here; they are, in fact, very rarely found either in families or in places of popular resort. The people here have never been accustomed to them, and do not feel the need or in general know the value or use of them.

Ice is brought here in vessels from the United States, usually from Maine. The price of it is $5 per 100 pounds. The articles exported from this country to the United States are of such a nature as to appear not to require samples of them to be transmitted to the collectors of customs of the ports of their destination, as contemplated in the circular of November 27, 1889.

FREDERICK DOUGLAS,
Minister.

UNITED STATES LEGATION,
Port au Prince, January 16, 1890.

SAN DOMINGO.

PUERTO PLATA.

In answer to refrigerator circular of November 25, 1889, I have to report that no refrigerators are used in this district, nor is ice obtainable for any purpose.

THOMAS SIMPSON.

UNITED STATES CONSULATE,
Puerto Plata, February 27, 1890.

SPANISH WEST INDIES.

CUBA.

HAVANA.

REPORT BY CONSUL-GENERAL WILLIAMS.

With the view of obtaining reliable information upon the subject, I addressed a note on the 26th of last month to Mr. F. K. Sowers, a citizen of the United States established here, he being thoroughly informed both with respect to the importation of refrigerators and the manufacture of ice in this city. Accordingly, I inclose for the information of the Department a copy of the answer of Mr. Sowers, dated the 27th of December ultimo.

RAMON O. WILLIAMS,
Consul-General.

UNITED STATES CONSULATE-GENERAL,
Havana, January 13, 1890.

Mr. Sowers to Consul-General Williams.

In reply to your esteemed favor of yesterday with copy of circular from the Department of State asking for information regarding the use of refrigerators and how ice is obtained in this city, I take pleasure in answering the five questions therein contained, to the best of my ability, thus:

Refrigerators are used in this city, but to no great extent.

There are no peculiar features required in their construction for use in this place; still I will say that some people prefer those prepared with separate compartments for water, as many like cold water, but do not want ice put in it.

Most of the refrigerators used are imported from the United States, some few from France, and still a smaller number made here.

Different sizes are used, say for families, 24 inches front by 36 inches height up to 40 inches front by 50 inches height, up to 75 inches front by 65 inches height; the class known as "upright" are generally preferred to the "chest." Prices from $20 to $150, according to size, class, material used, and fancy work.

Ice is manufactured here, and price at present from 60 to 80 cents per 100 pounds, according to quantity and location of delivery.

I would also add that I am inclined to think the use of refrigerators would become more general if they could be delivered here cheaper. The high freight and duties increase the cost beyond the means of many people. Possibly it might be an object to large manufacturers in our country to ship them in the "shook" form and then erect or put them together here; but in this case it would be necessary to send down an experienced man to do the work.

F. K. SOWERS.

Havana, December 27, 1889.

MATANZAS.

REPORT BY CONSUL PIERCE.

Refrigerators are used in my consular district to the extent of about fifty per year.

There are no peculiar features in their construction and all are manufactured in the United States. The prices vary from $10 to $70, according to sizes and formations, which also differ to suit the wants of the purchasers. The ice used in this consular district is supplied from Havana, and the price is $6, Spanish gold, per 100 pounds.

The best manner of introducing refrigerators is through commission houses.

FRANK H. PIERCE,
Consul.

UNITED STATES CONSULATE,
Matanzas, January 14, 1890.

SAGUA LA GRANDE.

REPORT BY COMMERCIAL AGENT MULLEN.

Refrigerators are almost unknown in this district, there being but one in use here.

The ordinary American refrigerator would fill all the requirements necessary.

Ice is secured in home-made chests consisting of two ordinary boxes, the inner one lined with zinc and the intermediate space between both boxes packed with ordinary salt. There are two deposits of this kind in this district, each one capable of storing about five tons of ice. This ice, which is artificial, is purchased at $16 per ton and sold here at $3 per hundred-weight.

At a first glance it would seem that a refrigerator of some kind would be an absolute necessity in this climate; but when it is understood that the meat intended for daily use is slaughtered every day, it will be apparent that the necessity is not so urgent. Meat killed at 2 p. m. is in some instances placed on the table for use at 6 p. m., and, as a general rule, is tough and unpalatable. During the warm summer months meat becomes tainted inside of twenty-four hours. At the hotels and restaurants meats are kept in an ordinary ice-chest and in direct contact with the ice. Have consulted various persons regarding their opinion, and the general verdict is that the refrigerators are too large and costly. I would therefore suggest for the use of this district a plain, medium-sized refrigerator, the cheapness of which will recommend it to the public in general. The best manner of introducing this and all other manufactures would be through an agent who thoroughly understands the business, and who has a good knowledge of the Spanish language. The sending of agents to this country who do not understand the language is a failure, as all their business must be done through an interpreter who is not well informed on the subject and fails to convey the ideas of the agent. In cases where it is impossible to send a special agent, would recommend the appointing of a resident in the various towns and cities. Printed circulars in English is money thrown away.

D. M. MULLEN,
Commercial Agent.

UNITED STATES COMMERCIAL AGENCY,
Sagua la Grande, January 22, 1890.

SANTIAGO DE CUBA.

REPORT BY CONSUL REIMER.

The fact that on an average only 3 tons of ice per day are consumed in the city of Santiago de Cuba, boasting of a population of nearly 48,000 souls, is conclusive proof that the resources of the people do not permit a large consumption of ice. The exorbitant prices charged by the local company manufacturing artificial ice—$2.50 Spanish gold per 100 pounds wholesale, and $5 Spanish gold per 100 pounds retail—is no doubt, to a great extent, to blame for this, but not altogether. It seems that the colored element, which composes two-thirds of the population, consumes no ice at all, and this, in many instances, because they are not used to it, and I am convinced that even were ice cheaper they would not use it. Almost all the ice consumed here is used by Spaniards and foreigners. The twenty-two to thirty head of cattle killed daily to supply meat to the city are consumed the day following, and are brought from the slaughter-houses direct to the market. Poultry is all sold alive, and killed just before preparing for the table.

The only refrigerator in use here is an old one of American manufacture at the restaurant "La Venus," the largest restaurant here. At the high prices of ice private families use no ice-boxes, but buy their supply to cool beverages daily before meals, and in pieces of 1 to 5 pounds.

It is my opinion that before refrigerators can be introduced here the price of ice must be reduced. I have been requested by people whom I have interviewed in reference to the circular to procure for them circulars of large ice-machines and small ones for family use. As soon as competition can put the price of ice on a basis so that the public can be large consumers, I believe there is a field for the sale of refrigerators of American manufacture.

OTTO E. REIMER,
Consul.

SANTIAGO DE CUBA, *January 10, 1890.*

CONTINENT OF ASIA.

BRITISH ASIA.

BOMBAY.

REPORT BY VICE-CONSUL BODE.

Refrigerators have very little demand in my consular district. It is very difficult to sell, say, thirty or thirty-five of them in a year. They are only used in some hotels and clubs and not in every family, because they have not adopted the system of preserving food and liquids. When people want to preserve ice in summer they have large wooden boxes lined with zinc or tin-plate, which only cost them 10 rupees (1 rupee equals 32.2 cents), while the English-made refrigerators are sold from 50 to 100 rupees.

There are factories established in Bombay since 1872 and up-country for the manufacture of ice, which is remarkably cheap. Price for 100 pounds is only 3 rupees, equivalent to $1.

H. E. BODE,
Vice-Consul.

UNITED STATES CONSULATE,
Bombay, February 28, 1890.

CALCUTTA.

REPORT BY CONSUL-GENERAL BONHAM.

Refrigerators are quite extensively used in this consular district by hotel and boarding-house keepers, as well as by many private families.

The only peculiarity or requisite in the construction of refrigerators for use in this climate is, that they should be made of lumber that is the least susceptible to shrinkage during the dry season and to expansion or swelling during the rains, and which is not subject to ravages by the white ant. The form of construction is substantially the same as of those in common use in the United States. In fact, I was told by a member of a large and reliable firm in Calcutta (Messrs. T. E. Thompson & Co.), who, amongst other things, manufacture refrigerators for the Calcutta and surrounding markets, that some years ago they procured some refrigerators from the United States which were satisfactory in the form of construction but which were defective in the quality of the lumber on account of its susceptibility to shrink and swell. During the dry hot weather (my informant stated) the joints would open so as to let in the hot air, and during the wet weather the wood expanded so that the doors could not readily be opened or shut. Said firm then ordered another consignment of refrigerators from the United States made of hard wood, and these worked better, but were not entirely satisfactory in the respects above named.

Messrs. Thompson & Co. then turned their attention to the manufacture of refrigerators from Indian teak-wood, which is used very extensively in this country in the manufacture of furniture and for various other purposes, and is said to be less liable to shrink and swell than any other wood that is generally obtainable in this country. It should also be understood that the white ant of India, which bores into honeycombs, and destroys most kinds of soft woods, very seldom disturbs teakwood.

The refrigerators in use in this district are manufactured in this country. The labor of a native carpenter (without board or lodging) is from 12 to 15 rupees per month ($4 to $5), and that of a good native cabinet workman about double that of the carpenter. Of course the native mechanic works by hand and his tools and other mechanical appliances are of very simple construction. But, considering the great disparity in the price of mechanical labor between this country and the United States and the superiority of the Indian teak-wood for climatic and other reasons stated, I am afraid that the outlook for building up a trade in refrigerators in this country is not very encouraging. I also find that the few American carriages which have been brought to Calcutta do not stand the climate here so well as those manufactured in the country of teak and other hard Indian woods.

From Messrs. T. E. Thompson & Co. (above referred to), I learn that the common sizes manufactured by them are as follows: 36 by 26 by 21 inches on stand and 30 by 22 by 19 inches on stand. They retail the larger size at 110 rupees (about $36.33) and the smaller at 100 rupees (about $33.33).

The refrigerator above referred to has a zinc ice-box in the top, with with a small lead pipe leading from it to the lower part of the main box, which is also provided with a zinc basin in which wines, etc., may be placed for cooling, and upon which the ice-water trickles through the small pipe referred to. The intervening space between the ice-box and wine-basin is provided with the ordinary gridiron shelves (usually one or two) as receptacles of such articles of the cuisine as it is desired to keep cool.

All the ice we have here (nearer than Kunchinginga) is manufactured and sells at about $1 per 100 pounds.

Prior to the discovery of the art of manufacturing ice, I believe the principal supply of that luxury was shipped here from the United States.

                   B. F. BONHAM,
UNITED STATES CONSULATE-GENERAL,   *Consul-General.*
   Calcutta, February 4, 1890.

STRAITS SETTLEMENTS.

REPORT BY VICE-CONSUL LYALL, OF SINGAPORE.

Refrigerators are not used in this country to any great extent. Most private residences of the better class have an ice-box of some kind, but ice is cheap and generally is kept by the servants in a gunny bag, blanket, or wooden box with saw-dust, washed at meal-times and put into the drinking-glass. Meat in this country must be cooked within twenty-four hours, all the year round, after being killed, so that refrigerators on a large scale, if kept by butchers, would be most useful and one would suppose very profitable, but there is nothing of the kind here.

The sketch attached to query No. 4 gives an idea of the refrigerators used here.

The refrigerators in use in this district come chiefly from England and Germany, occasionally from the United States, and are also made on the spot.

A German mercantile firm, who say they receive consignments of refrigerators from Germany in invoices of half a dozen at a time, give the following prices (wholesale), viz: 30 by 24 by 24 inches, $20 each; 42 by 24 by 24 inches, $30 each.

A retail shopkeeper (the principal shop in the place) reports as follows: 25 inches square, $15; 28 inches square, $18; 31 inches square, $24. Kent's refrigerator, 22 by 20 inches, $40.

The sketches attached hereto show the Kent boxes.

REFRIGERATORS IN FOREIGN COUNTRIES.

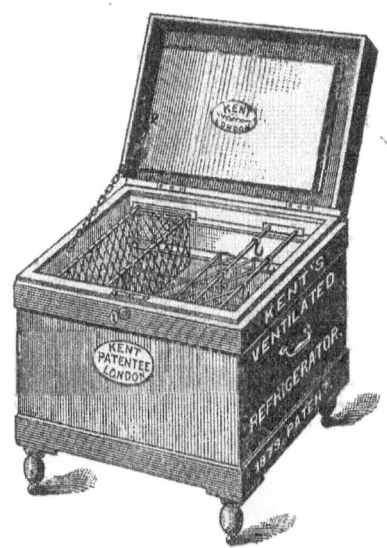

Ice is made daily to meet the current demand, and is taken from the manufactory, as required, by the servants of consumers. The retail price is one cent per pound. For large quantities some abatement would be made.

An efficient and well kept refrigerator every one acknowledges in tropical countries to be a great boon, and if asked why in that case they are not more in use in this district, I think the reason is mainly that the native servants do not properly understand them or will not take the trouble to handle them; and perhaps also it may be due in some degree to the inefficiency of the refrigerators in use.

A refrigerator which will keep its contents really cool with little trouble should become popular in this place.

The best mode of introducing American refrigerators into this district would be the usual one of a trial consignment, with full information as to the mode of handling them. It must be kept in mind that the European community, who are the only users of refrigerators, is comparatively small, and a trial consignment of half a dozen boxes would be ample.

J. LYALL,
Vice-Consul.

UNITED STATES CONSULATE,
Singapore, March 4, 1890.

CHINA.

CHINKIANG.

REPORT BY CONSUL JONES.

The refrigerators in use in this district are very few and are simple ice boxes or chests about 2½ feet square in area at the top and 3½ or 4 feet high. They have two compartments, the top one for the ice and the one below, divided by an open shelf, for meats, butter, etc. They are made of pine wood, lined with zinc, and filled in with charcoal, are of American manufacture, and cost from $12 to $15. They answer the purpose for small families, but are entirely inadequate for anything beyond this.

The winters in this climate are never very severe. The ice is secured from ponds of water, some of them made for the purpose, and is rarely over an inch in thickness. It is stored in ice houses constructed very like the old fashioned ice houses in the United States, by digging a chamber in the earth, lining the sides and floor with planking, and covering with a straw roof.

The water in the ponds can not be said to be of the purest, as it is used by all the families in the neighborhood, who wash their clothes in it, and is also the resort of all their ducks, geese, and buffalo. The ice, therefore, can never be used by mixing it with liquids. Bottles of water, etc., for table use, are kept cool by burying them in it.

The cost of ice in the summer is about 60 cents per picul (133½ pounds). The Chinese do not use it and seldom drink water. The common beverage is tea, which is drank hot and without milk or sugar. This tea is a weak infusion of the common leaf, the cheapest possible commodity, and is accessible to all.

As ice is expensive and often difficult to secure, moderately cheap and easily managed machines for the manufacture of ice would find a ready market in this country. At several of the ports of Japan ice-machines are in use, but they are, I believe, of English manufacture, and too expensive for small communities or family use.

The best method of introducing modern American refrigerators into this district would be for a manufacturer to send one as a sample, that the people may see and understand its use.

A. C. JONES,
Consul.

UNITED STATES CONSULATE,
    Chinkiang, March 18, 1890.

HONG-KONG.

REPORT BY CONSUL SIMONS.

Refrigerators are in use in every house, with the exception of those occupied by Chinese, in all hotels, restaurants, clubs, stores, and on steam-ships. The temperature rarely falling below 60° Fahrenheit during the winter months and for the other eight months of the year rarely below 80° Fahrenheit, with the maximum of moisture in the atmosphere, which, quite as much as the long continued high temperature, facilitates decomposition and fermentation, refrigerators become a necessary appliance toward securing the ordinary comforts of life.

No peculiar features of construction are required in addition to securing the greatest cold with a given quantity of ice for the longest time, a purpose arrived at doubtless in the construction of refrigerators for use in any country.

With scarcely an exception, those in use are manufactured by Chinese cabinet-makers after the patterns of those brought to the colony by Europeans many years ago.

These people imitating everything, while practically originating nothing, makes it extremely likely that, should refrigerators of an improved American pattern be brought to this market in such numbers as to enter into competition with them, they would soon begin the manufacture of them at prices so low that competition would be impossible, the wages paid for such work not exceeding 30 cents a day. Sizes range from 3 feet, costing from $8 to $20 Mexican. Those used on board coasting steamers are much larger, costing in proportion. They are made in wardrobe shape, not unlike those in use in the United States; the outside of wood, 1 inch in thickness, lined with zinc or tin, with a box for the reception of ice at the top. None that I have seen are filled with non-conducting materials or substances.

Ice is manufactured by the usual ammonia and damp-air machines and sold at $1.50 per hundred pounds. I inclose the annual report of the ice company, which indicates a prosperous condition of their affairs.

As to the best manner of introducing refrigerators of American make, which are no doubt greatly superior to those now in use here, a difficulty presents itself already stated, the certainty of their being imitated by Chinese workmen; another, the absence of any tradesman engaged in in selling goods of American manufacture; so that there is no one to whom a consignment could be made with a reasonable hope that merit alone would be sufficient to create a demand. Considering the number of places on this coast where refrigerators are used it is likely the sending of an agent capable of setting forth the advantages of the thing he sells, after the manner of the commercial traveler, while at the outset attended with considerable expense, would, in the end, secure the most substantial results.

O. H. SIMONS,
Consul.

UNITED STATES CONSULATE,
Hong-Kong, February 11, 1890.

[Inclosure in Consul Simons's report.]

THE HONG-KONG ICE COMPANY, LIMITED.

The following is the ninth annual report:

The general managers beg to submit to the share-holders a statement of the company's accounts for the year 1889:

The business of the company has continued to improve, and the result of the year's operations, inclusive of balance from last account, is a profit of $37,896.78.

On the 2d August last an interim dividend of 7 per cent. was paid, which absorbed a sum of $8,750, and there is now a balance to be dealt with of $29,146.78. This will admit of the payment of a further dividend for the year of 17 per cent., or $4.25 per share (making 24 per cent. in all) $21,250.00, and an addition to reserve and depreciation fund of 7,500.00, leaving to be carried forward to new account 396.78; total 29,146.78.

In order to meet the increased demand upon the company it has been found necessary to substitute for the old dry-air machine, which is now obsolete, a modern one, and the order has been placed in the hands of Mr. Bain, the late manager. The cost of the new machine, together with the extension of the present buildings, it is estimated will amount to about $25,000.

The ammonia and damp-air machines were continuously at work day and night during the summer months.

The accounts have been audited by Mr. Thomas Arnold, and the general managers recommend that he should be re-elected auditor.

JARDINE, MATHESON & CO.,
General Managers.

HONG-KONG, *February* 3, 1890.

ASSETS.

Property account	$161,368.05
Invested in Hong-Kong Fire Insurance Company's share	345.00
Cash on hand	281.78
Hong-Kong and Shanghai Bank, current account	27,676.88
Hongkong and Shanghai Bank, deposit account	9,000.00
Outstanding accounts	1,715.83
Accounts receivable	393.29
Ice on hand	180.00
Stores on hand	84.00
Extension account	2,464.26
	203,509.09

SHANGHAI.

REPORT BY CONSUL-GENERAL LEONARD.

There are about eight hundred foreign houses in Shanghai, and it is doubtful if there is one wherein a refrigerator or ice-box is not in use seven or eight months of the year.

There are no peculiar features required in the construction of refrigerators for this district, except that the ice-chamber should be larger than usual, to hold the ice as frozen and gathered as described in No. 5.

The refrigerators in use in this district are manufactured here with the exception of a few imported from the United States.

The common-sized ice-box ranges to meet the wants of the family. Ice-chambers are on top or side, and the cool chamber adjoining. Price from $15 to $50.

Ice is gathered from rice fields flooded with dirty water pumped from stagnant ditches and ponds, the temperature at which it is frozen is seldom lower than four or five degrees below the freezing-point. It is stored in houses built on the level ground, having mud walls 10 or 12 feet high and covered with straw or tiled roofs. The ice frozen at such a high temperature melts very rapidly, so that refrigerators have ice-chambers larger than usual.

In addition to the natural ice, there is a small ice-machine, but its limited power and the cheapness at which the natural ice can be purchased from the native dealer leaves but little room for its business.

The average price of the natural ice is 50 cents per 100 pounds.

J. A. LEONARD,
Consul-General.

UNITED STATES CONSULATE-GENERAL,
Shanghai, February 24, 1890.

TIENTSIN.

REPORT BY CONSUL BOWMAN.

Refrigerators in this consular district have a very limited use among the American and European residents and among a few of the wealthier Chinese families.

No peculiar features are required in their construction as far as I know.

Those in use here are made by individual carpenters.

The kind used among the Chinese are simply tin-lined boxes, with holes below for draining off the water. There are no regular sizes or prices.

The kind used by the foreign residents are also manufactured on the spot by Chinese carpenters, and vary in size and price according to the caprice of the person ordering.

Ice is obtained from rivers and ponds, and is usually sold at about 25 cents per 100 pounds.

I regret that owing to the nature of the case my replies to the questions asked have been rather indefinite.

WILLIAM BOWMAN,
Consul.

UNITED STATES CONSULATE,
Tientsin, March 7, 1890.

JAPAN.

OSAKA AND HIOGO.

REPORT BY CONSUL SMITHERS.

Refrigerators are used in this district by foreigners, but not by the Japanese. The demand for them, therefore, is limited. The greater part of those in use are made in the country by the native mechanics and have no peculiar features in their construction. They are wooden boxes, made as far as possible air-tight and lined with zinc, with an open lattice-work partition, below which the ice is placed. These iceboxes, as they are called, cost from $10 to $15.

Large quantities of ice are used by the Japanese as a beverage, but not to preserve meats or liquids. This ice comes from Hakodate and costs $1\frac{1}{2}$ cents per pound. Large factories at Osaka and Hiogo are now manufacturing ice, which retails in small quantities at about the same price as the natural article.

E. J. SMITHERS,
Consul.

UNITED STATES CONSULATE,
Osaka and Hiogo, March 6, 1890.

NAGASAKI.

Refrigerators are only used in this district by private foreign families; and they have no features different from those in use in America, as to size, formation, or price.

Ice is secured in this district by importation from Tientsin, China, and within the last year a limited quantity has been manufactured by a Japanese company operating an ice-machine.

Price per 100 pounds, Tientsin ice, about $2.50; manufactured ice, $1.

JOHN M. BIRCH,
Consul.

UNITED STATES CONSULATE,
Nagasaki, June 18, 1890.

PHILIPPINE ISLANDS.

REPORT BY CONSUL WEBB, OF MANILA.

In a climate where the thermometer averages 90° the year round, an ice-box or cooling apparatus of some kind is considered a necessity by those who have the means to procure the comforts of life. Hence in Manila, Iloilo, and Cebu, the leading cities of the Philippine Archipelago, an ice-box may be found in the house of almost every foreign resident and in those of most of the well-to-do Mestizos. In Manila there are three ice-machines, one American (the De la Verne), one Swiss, and one German, which make about 18 tons of ice per day. Iloilo has one German machine and Cebu another. Families are supplied at 1 cent per pound and a single ton sells for $25;* special rates are made for larger quantities. The ice is produced in blocks weighing from 800 to 900 pounds and is then cut into oblong blocks weighing 10 and 25 pounds each for delivery to families. Twelve or fifteen carts are used for the purpose of delivery and there are as many more small depots in various parts of Manila where ice is retailed in quantities of 1 pound and upward. As a rule the ice is of excellent quality, being as clear as crystal, although occasionally a lot slightly clouded is turned out. Until about a year ago the product was usually like frozen snow and was always more or less clouded, but Señor Don E. M. Barretto, who has a monopoly of the ice business in Manila, has invented an improvement in the process of molding the blocks which clarifies them perfectly.

Owing to the prevailing system of supplying the family cook in the morning with the money necessary for each day's provisions there is little or no accumulation of food to be preserved from one day to another, and hence the ice is used principally for cooling drinks. The native method of preserving meats and fish is by drying or smoking them; the cooks buy these articles at the markets fresh every morning and, as the native rather prefers his meat a little tainted, the butchers usually get rid of all their stock in trade at a fair price. The native method of preserving meat and fish is to cut long gashes in it about an inch apart and hang it in the sun. Sometimes he salts it, and salt meats may be found in most of the markets.

The refrigerators are, as a rule, plain, double-walled, wooden boxes of various sizes, made by the Chinese cabinet-makers here and sold for from $10 to $18. The spaces between the walls are filled with sawdust, and the box inside is lined with zinc, with a half-inch hole in the bottom for an escape for the water. Midway between the top and bottom of the

---

*An evident error, but just as the consul wrote it. It should, perhaps, be a cent and a half per pound.

inner space and extending half way across it, is a zinc shelf, on which the ice rests, and the space around it is usually utilized for the storage of bottles of wine, beer, liquor, etc. The idea prevails generally that putting ice into the water is injurious to health, and the latter is therefore put into clean bottles, which are laid on the ice; but Señor Barretto tells me that since he has been producing clear ice there has been a largely increased amount of it put into beverages of all kinds. Should this practice become general, there would undoubtedly be a demand for the refrigerators with the zinc or iron water tanks in general use in the United States and the plain ice-boxes now in vogue would be discarded by those who could afford something better. But at present the latter fills all the requirements of domestic use and, as $15 and $18 are considered the highest prices that ought to be paid for such an article, when provisions and the other necessaries of life cost as much as they do here, it would, in my opinion, be difficult to find a profitable market here for the better class of American refrigerators.

The best manner of introducing American refrigerators would be to have an active, energetic salesman here who could speak the Spanish language. The next best method would be to induce one of the English, German, or Spanish houses to accept the agency for the manufacturers and make a special feature of American refrigerators. There are no American dealers here, and extra inducements would probably be necessary to stimulate interest in the making of sales. Indifference and even opposition would be met with at first, but perseverance and tact would undoubtedly secure satisfactory results.

The duty on refrigerators is 10 per cent. of the declared value, 20 per cent. on the duty for port tax, and $1 per ton.

ALEX. R. WEBB,
Consul.

UNITED STATES CONSULATE,
    Manila, January 24, 1890.

SIAM.

REPORT BY CONSUL-GENERAL CHILD, OF BANGKOK.

Only a small number of refrigerators are used here.

There are no peculiar features required in their construction, except that they are almost exclusively used to cool bottled aerated waters and liquors.

They are of local Chinese make.

They are generally box-shaped, lined with zinc, and vary in price according to size and contract with the maker.

Artificial ice at $2.50 per 100 pounds.

JACOB T. CHILD,
Consul-General.

UNITED STATES CONSULATE-GENERAL,
Bangkok, February 26, 1890.

TURKEY IN ASIA.

ASIA MINOR.

REPORT BY CONSUL EMMETT, OF SMYRNA.

The use of refrigerators is so limited as to warrant me in saying as a household convenience they are unknown. Less than a dozen are in use in this city, and those are in beer saloons.

I should judge that a good cheap article would be the only one to find sale; and owing to the extreme carelessness of servants one fed from top with ice compartment separate from food closets would be most likely to find favor and do good service.

The refrigerators in use in this district are manufactured in Germany. The sizes are large, for holding beer kegs.

There are two factories for the manufacture of ice which run six months in the year and have very moderate success. A supply of snow is gathered in the mountains during severe winters and stored in large holes. This is covered over with some rock salt and pine leaves. During the summer this snow is brought to the city in thick felt bags and disposed of mainly to confectioners. The use of ice is by no means general and is considered very unhealthy in this climate. Since the artificial-ice factories have been established, the use of snow for refrigerating purposes has diminished. The price of either is about $1 per 100 pounds.

The practice of hanging meats, poultry, etc., to ripen is unknown here and meat is generally used within twenty-four hours after killing. As to poultry the time is much less, unless the same is to be consumed by Europeans.

I have great doubts as to the feasibility of introducing American refrigerators into this market with success. Such a thing is not to be found for sale nearer than Constantinople, and the demand there is very limited.

The only firm in Smyrna who deals in American inventions is Jacob Balladur & Co. If any trade can be established for refrigerators here, they can give definite information as to size, prices, and terms upon which the goods can be sold.

W. C. EMMETT,
Consul.

UNITED STATES CONSULATE,
Smyrna, January 15, 1890.

JERUSALEM.

REPORT BY CONSUL GILLMAN.

Refiigerators are not used in this consular district.

No peculiar features, however, would be required in the construction of refrigerators to adapt them for the use of this district.

Ice is not secured in this district, as it rarely forms, and then in insufficient quantity for the purposes referred to. About two years ago a company was formed at Jaffa for the manufacture of ice, but though the artificial article was of excellent quality the enterprise was not sufficiently patronized to prove remunerative, and after a few months' existence was, in consequence, abandoned. Underground cisterns abound in this country and where the preservation of foods and liquids is required they are let down into them and so can be kept for a sufficient time. The thick stone walls of the houses, keeping out the heat, also render refrigerators less necessary than in other warm countries. It is scarcely necessary for me to add that in the present state of things I could not recommend the introduction of refrigerators into this district.

HENRY GILLMAN,
Consul.

UNITED STATES CONSULATE,
Jerusalem, January 20, 1890.

SYRIA.

REPORT BY CONSUL BISSINGER, OF BEIRUT.

Refrigerators, in the American sense of the term, are not used in Syria, and until within about a year ago, were practically unknown.

Recently the Beirut Gas Company utilized part of its capacious plant in manufacturing artificial ice. The great heat in the summer and the distance of the works from the city suggested the necessity of providing some means of preserving the ice from too rapid evaporation or melting in transit and during delivery. A small number of wooden boxes were therefor constructed having two compartments, or rather one box placed inside the other with a vacuum of some six inches between the two; this space or vacuum is filled with either sawdust or cork, or both, the inside box—lined with zinc—containing the ice; it is perforated at the bottom to permit the escape of the water from the melting ice.

The dimensions of these boxes are about $4\frac{1}{2}$ to 5 feet long, $2\frac{1}{4}$ feet high, and $1\frac{1}{2}$ feet wide.

A small number of similar boxes, but of more diminutive size, were also made for the customers of the company and were either presented to them gratis to induce them to become clients or sold for a mere trifle; their cost, the director of the gas company says, does not exceed from, say, 50 cents to $1 for each box. By this authority and others who are most competent to speak on such matters, I am assured that expensive refrigerators would not find a market here, and that anything costing over $1 or $2 could not be disposed of.

Foods and liquids are preserved in the most primitive manner by simply exposing them to the air, as houses are not provided with cellars.

The price of ice per 100 pounds is about $1, the competition with snow, which is a trifle cheaper, having forced the company to establish a low tariff.

Before the introduction of artificial ice, snow was exclusively used in this country and sold at much higher prices than ice does now; but, as people begin to prefer ice, its price has been forced slightly below.

The sale of both ice and snow is, however, very limited, the former not exceeding about 2,750 to 3,000 pounds daily during a period of about five or six months per annum.

From what precedes, it is obvious that American refrigerators could not be sold in this market, nor even so modified as to meet the local requirements of the immediate future.

ERHARD BISSINGER,
Consul.

UNITED STATES CONSULATE,
  Beirut, January 20, 1890.

AUSTRALASIA.

REPORT BY CONSUL GRIFFIN, OF SYDNEY.

FOOD PRESERVATION.

Although much attention has been given for some time past by the Government and people of New South Wales to refrigeration and the various methods and appliances for the preservation of food, but little progress was made in the industry until about two or three years ago. In 1886 the New South Wales Government obtained information from the United States as to the methods and processes in use there for the preservation of food, and especially in regard to the transportation of fresh meat in refrigerating cars. Much of the information was obtained from the Department of Agriculture at Washington, and wide publicity was given to it by the New South Wales Government through the public press. Since that time several meat-preserving companies have been established with more or less success, and the governments of all the Australasian colonies have taken deep interest in the subject. The Government of Victoria, not long since, offered a premium of £300 ($1,460) for the invention of an economical means of cooling a chamber for the preservation of milk, cream, and butter, to be used on farms and at factories, and such as would reduce the temperature during hot weather to 50° Fahr. for ten hours without the aid of ice, chemicals, or machinery when the outside temperature would be not less than 120° Fahr. The Government also offered a premium of £300 ($1,460) for a machine of a cheap character which would produce like results; a premium of like amount was also offered for the invention of a chemical means to produce like results, such means to be of a cheap character readily applied. The same Government has also undertaken the erection of a number of cool stores for perishable produce at the various railway stations. Thirty of these stores are now in operation and forty-three others are in course of erection. Several methods were tried with the view of finding out the best design and materials. Trials were made in which terra-cotta lumber was largely used, but the result was not satisfactory. Finally it has been decided that the stores shall be built of wood, with double lining filled with charcoal for the walls, and shingle roof with charcoal ceilings. They are substantially built, and are fitted with thick doors, beveled and padded all round to make the openings air-tight. It is said that the temperature inside the sheds is from 20° to 30° less than ordinary shade heat outside. The stores cost between £300

($1,460) and £400 ($1,945) each, and already about £10,000 ($48,665) has been expended for this purpose. The question of artificial cooling in the storage sheds is under consideration, but the first object has been to create an insulated storage, where perishable products can be placed while waiting for carriage by railway in the refrigerating cars.

The cars that have been built in these colonies for refrigerating purposes can hardly be said to have passed more than the experimental stage, and there is, I think, a splendid opportunity for the introduction of refrigerating cars like those in use in the United States.

The use of ice in private houses in Australasia is comparatively of recent date. American processes for its manufacture have been adopted, and the industry may be said to be fairly started in all the large cities of these colonies. The cost of ice, until recently, was very high, but with the introduction of improved facilities for its manufacture the prices have been considerably reduced. The following are the present quotations: $0.73 to $1.22 per 100 pounds.

The Fresh Food and Ice Company, of Sydney, have recently erected a machine capable of turning out 60 tons of ice per day. Previously their ice plant, which was the largest in the colonies, turned out 20 tons per day. The ice is made on the ammonia-compression principle. This company's new machine has three 20-inch pumps, which draw sea-water from Sydney Harbor at the rate of 100,000 gallons per hour. The company's works include spacious cool-air chambers for preserving meat, fish, and dairy produce, and they have arranged for the sale of fresh fish in Sydney brought in the cool rooms of the Union Steamship Company's steamers from New Zealand. The following list will show the cost of the fish per pound in the Sydney market:

	Cents.
Blue cod	16
Butter fish	24
Flounders	18
Gurnard	18
Kippers (smoked)	18
Soles	24
Salmon	61
Salmon trout	61
Schnapper and bream	12
Trumpeter	24

The New South Wales Co-operative Ice and Cold Storage Company is another of the ice-making companies in Sydney. It was formed to purchase the plant of the Sydney Ice Company, which commenced business five years ago, having erected a machine upon the American Bath-Tevis patent. This machine, however, did not turn out well, and the company, after spending £30,000 ($145,995) was wound up voluntarily. One cause of failure has been put down to want of skill in the erection of the plant, another cause to unsuitable material having been used, the company having, as the secretary reports—

To save money, bought tubing and fittings in London, and the wrong kind of joints were obtained, namely, running sockets instead of tapering, and the black iron tubes butt welded (although they will stand a pressure of from.180 to 200 pounds, and are good of the kind, will not stand the extreme temperature) instead of double lap welded best steam tubing."

The secretary further states that the original company had imported a 6½-ton Guide machine, had altered the Bath-Tevis machine by applying it to ice-boxes, and had converted the large room used under the Bath-Tevis process into storage chambers. The new company has this season imported a third machine on the compressor principle. The ice supplied by this company is in 10-pound blocks, 9 inches square by 5 inches thick, and larger sizes as desired. The cold-storage rooms are largely used by butchers and others, who find it more convenient to send their goods into them instead of keeping refrigerators on their own premises.

An American machine called the "Picket" has been successfully introduced into Melbourne, and it is said several have been ordered for Sydney. It works extremely well. The only objection to it is that certain chemicals required for its use have to be imported here in copper vessels, the whole having to be prepared in the United States. No ammonia is used, the principal ingredient being sulphuric acid. The fact that the chemicals have to be prepared in the United States not only adds to their cost but renders it difficult to keep a regular supply on hand.

REFRIGERATORS FOR DOMESTIC USE.

Refrigerators were introduced in Sydney from the United States. The people were slow to take hold of them, but in time their use became more general. The number sold annually in Sydney is not large and does not probably amount to more than 500 or 600 per annum, one half of which are made in this colony and the remainder imported, chiefly from the United States. American manufacturers have some difficulty in competing with the locally made article on account of the cubic space occupied in transit to Australia, the cost of freight being thus rendered very heavy. If a refrigerator could be made so as to ship in what is called a knock-down condition it could be sold in these colonies at a much lower price. A machine for the manufacture of ice in small quantities is said to be greatly needed in Australia, especially in the smaller inland towns. Such a machine, however, ought to be supplied at a moderate cost. The refrigerators made here vary in size from 2 feet to 4½ feet in height and from 1 foot to 2 feet in depth and from 1 foot 9 inches to 3 feet 10 inches in width.

The following table shows in detail the sizes and kinds of refrigerators on sale here by one of the largest firms. The retail prices are also given in British and United States currency.

REFRIGERATORS IN FOREIGN COUNTRIES.

No.	Description	Sizes.			Price.	
		High.	Deep.	Wide.	British currency.	United States currency.
		Ft. in.	Ft. in.	Ft. in.	£. s. d.	
1	1 cupboard, with shelf; also compartment for ice	3 0	1 9	1 9	3 0 0	$14.65
2	...do	3 0	1 8	2 0	3 15 0	18.25
3	1 cupboard, with 2 shelves; also compartment for ice	3 10	1 9	2 1	4 10 0	21.90
4	1 large cupboard, with 2 shelves; also compartment for ice	3 9	1 10	2 4	5 0 0	24.33
5	...do	4 0	1 11	2 10	6 5 0	30.42
6	2 cupboards, with shelves in each; also compartment for ice	3 4	1 8	3 3	8 15 0	42.58
7	2 cupboards, with 2 shelves in each; also compartment for ice	3 8	1 8	3 6	10 15 0	52.31
8	2 large cupboards, with 2 shelves in each; also compartment for ice	4 6	2 0	3 10	12 10 0	61.83
9	1 large cupboard on one side and 2 smaller ones on the other, both with shelves complete; also large compartment for ice in which can also be stored æerated waters	4 8	2 0	4 0	15 0 0	73.04

English manufacturers recommend a consumption of 40 pounds of ice weekly for their smallest refrigerators, ranging up to 150 pounds of ice weekly for the larger sizes.

In 1887 the firm of John Matthews, of New York, manufacturers of carbonated beverage apparatus and supplies, instructed Mr. I. B. Millner to place their refrigerating goods upon the Australasian markets. The portability, strength, and resultant purity of the "block-tin-lined steel fountains" made by this firm was apparent from the first and gained for them a place without difficulty. The introduction of their "draught apparatus," with its ice-box, coolers, etc., met with less favor until its peculiar features became known, when the economy of its working, in connection with reliability of its glass tanks, made it a favorite with the dealer, while his customer readily appreciated the pure, fresh coolness of the beverage produced.

These apparatus are now largely in use in each colony, while the steel fountains are to be found in the leading hotels and many private families, and are growing in favor as a means of developing a popular taste for the natural mineral waters of these colonies. The increased popularity of iced beverages is best shown by the numerous places opened for the sale of such, and the action of Mr. Milner in placing the waters of colonial springs before the public by means of apparatus especially adapted for the purpose can not fail to develop commercial value in what is now an idle element of wealth.

The locally made refrigerators are much heavier and not so well put together as the imported ones, but they appear to answer the purpose fairly well and sell at low prices. Indeed, it is often said that the high cost of the imported machines operates against their use. One firm of manufacturers at Adelaide, South Australia, are said to have succeeded in making a refrigerator at a cost of about one-fourth less than the least expensive of the ones imported. It occupies very little space. The air is received in a compression-cylinder, subject to a pressure of 60 pounds, and is compressed to about 50 pounds to the square inch and forced through cooling pipes surrounded by water. It is reconveyed into an expansion chamber whence it is emitted at a temperature as low as 23° Fahr. above zero or 10 degrees below freezing point. The cool air is very dry and any snow that may be formed is collected in a snow chamber. The makers propose that this refrigerator shall be used on the railway cars and it can be run by a belt attached to the axle of the car.

The manager of the New South Wales Co-operative Ice and Cold Storage Company, in Sydney, informs me that a refrigerator suitable for the preservation of fish is greatly needed. He states that quantities of fish are regularly brought to the Sydney market packed with ice. They are generally in the boxes about forty-eight hours, but the boxes used are very clumsy and difficult to handle. The kind of refrigerator box which is needed is a portable one, suitable to convey the ice to the different fishing centers and be returned filled with fish. The sides of the box, he states, should be lined with some non-conducting material. It is said, however, that a still better plan would be to introduce American machines for the manufacture of ice in suitable quantities, on the spot, so that the fish and ice could be put into the boxes at the same time and place and conveyed to Sydney, instead of shipping the ice from Sydney and back again.

Several kinds of refrigerators, manufactured by L. H. Mace & Co., of New York, have been introduced in these colonies, the best known of which are the upright refrigerators. There are three sizes of this refrigerator: No. 1 is 19 inches long, 14½ inches wide, and 35 inches high; No. 2 is 25 inches long, 18¼ inches wide, and 40 inches high; and No. 3 is 31 inches long, 22 inches wide, and 45 inches high. The three sizes when nested and boxed for shipment occupy 19 cubic feet. The other styles are called the chest refrigerator and the excelsior chest refrigerator. The retail price is from £3 ($14.60) to £10 ($48.67).

Messrs. Hudson Bros., of Sydney, manufacture several kinds of refrigerators, chiefly from American designs. I am informed, however, that at present there is no large demand for them.

COOLING CHAMBERS.

Several cooling chambers, the invention of Mr. J. B. Witt, chairman of the Australian Ventilating Company, limited, have been erected, and they are in use at the Federal Coffee Palace in Melbourne, and at the Grand Central Coffee Palace in Sydney. They have given very general satisfaction. They are constructed on the dry-air principle. A fan or air-propeller is used, which draws the air from any given point and distributes it in the room at the ceiling. The air is distributed in a circular manner, so that there is a total absence of draught. The mechanism of the rotary fan is simple and inexpensive. Mr. Witt has also invented a contrivance for cooling the atmosphere by evaporation, and by this invention, when connected with the pipe attached to the air distributer, a low temperature is obtained. The dimensions of the cool chamber in the Grand Central Coffee Palace, Sydney, are 9 feet by 9 feet, and nearly the same height. The air in this chamber is cool enough to keep meat fresh. When it is desired to lower the temperature to 40° Fahr. or 45° Fahr., a small quantity of ice is placed in the refrigerator, through which the supply of air for the cool chamber is drawn. Mr. Witt claims that the superiority of this dry-air refrigeration system over the ordinary ice method is shown in the appearance of the meat, it being as bright and fresh looking as when placed in the refrigerator. Mr. Witt has successfully introduced his ventilating and cooling system in several churches, theaters, and other public buildings. He states that the means heretofore used to carry off vitiated air at or near the ceiling while introducing fresh air from below does not accomplish the desired results, for the reason that carbonic acid gas is much heavier than the outside atmosphere, its specific gravity being 1.524, or half as heavy again, and if an analysis were made the foul air would be found near the floor, owing to its specific weight. Under his system the fresh air is brought from the ceiling and forces out the vitiated mixture at the bottom. The pipes connected with the air distributer are carried through a chest containing ice and salt, which cools the air in transit and at the same time keeps it perfectly dry.

CHILLED-MEAT EXPORT.

The export of chilled meat, which for several years has been conducted at a pecuniary loss in most parts of the Australasian colonies, now seems likely to become a very profitable industry. The trade has made extensive strides during the year 1889, especially in New Zealand. Twenty-seven steamers and ten sailing vessels are now employed in the frozen-meat trade of that colony. Of the steamers, eight are under the flag of the New Zealand Shipping Company. The Shaw, Savill and Albion Line have built three new steamers especially for the trade, and these are marked with an asterisk in the following list :

List of vessels, with names and tonnage of each, engaged in the meat export trade of New Zealand:

Shaw Savill and Albion Line. —*Coptic*, 4,448 tons, 36,000 carcasses ; *Ionic*, 4,753 tons, 36,500 carcasses; *Doric*, 4,784 tons, 36,500 carcasses; *Tainui*, 5,031 tons, 36,500 carcasses; *Arawa*, 5,026 tons, 36,500 carcasses; **Mamaria*, 3,583 tons, 36,000 carcasses; **Matatua*, 3,000 tons, 36,000 carcasses; **Maori*, 2,790 tons, 36,000 carcasses; total, 33,415 tons, 290,000 carcasses. The estimated voyages give this line of steamers 798,-400,000 carcasses per annum. New Zealand Shipping Company.—*Tongariro*, 4,163 tons, 30,000 carcasses; *Aorangi*, 4,163 tons, 30,000 carcasses, *Ruapehu*, 4,163 tons, 30,000 carcasses ; *Kaikoura*, 4,474 tons, 36,000 carcasses; *Rimutaka*, 4,474 tons, 36,000 carcasses; *Duke of Westminster*, 3,726 tons, 35,000 carcasses ; *Duke of Buckingham*, 3,123 tons, 35,000 carcasses ; *Duke*, 3,100 tons, 35,000 carcasses; total, 31,386 tons, 267,000 carcasses. The estimated voyages will give this line 728,400 carcasses per annum.

Tyser Line.—*Balmoral Castle*, 3,050 tons, 39,000 carcasses; *Ashleigh Brooke*, 2,863 tons, 38,000 carcasses; *Bayley*, 2,607 tons, 37,000 carcasses; *Star of Victoria*, 3,240 tons, 39,000 carcasses; *Star of England*, 3,511 tons, 41,000 carcasses; *Maori King*, 3,700 tons, 40,000 carcasses; *Celtic King*, 3,700 tons, 40,000 carcasses; total, 22,671 tons, 274,000 carcasses. This line also runs to Queensland, and the estimated voyages are reckoned to be equal to 348,000 carcasses from New Zealand per annum.

Martin Line.—*Elderslie*, 2,761 tons, 28,000 carcasses; *Fifeshire*, 3,720 tons, 28,000 carcasses; *Morayshire*, 3,720 tons, 28,000 carcasses; *Nairnshire*, 3,720 tons, 28,000 carcasses; total, 13,921 tons, 112,000 carcasses. This line is estimated to carry 224,000 carcasses per annum.

Of the ten sailing ships engaged in the frozen-meat trade, seven belong to the Shaw Savill and Albion, of the aggregate of 9,998 tons, with capacity for carrying 87,500 carcasses per annum, while only three belong to the New Zealand Company, carrying 34,000 carcasses per annum. The total carrying power affected to New Zealand, summarized from the above, provides for the transport to England in a single year of 2,220,300 carcasses.

The New Zealand meat export trade began in 1882, when she shipped 8,839 carcasses of mutton. In 1883 the exports rose to 120,893 carcasses; in 1884, to 412,349 carcasses; in 1885 they were 492,269 carcasses; in 1886, 655,888 carcasses were exported; in 1887, 766,417 carcasses, and in 1888, 939,231 carcasses; while in 1889, 1,063,506 carcasses were exported. Thus in eight years New Zealand sent to London no less than 4,459,392 carcasses of mutton, averaging in weight 85 pounds each. The result of the expansion of the frozen-meat trade has been to increase the price of mutton in New Zealand $0.61 per 14 pounds to $1.46 per 14 pounds weight. The Gear Meat Freezing and Export Company, of Wellington, New Zealand, paid a dividend last year of 10 per cent., increased its reserve fund by £2,500 ($12,166), and carried forward, after making large reduction in value of plant, £4,800 ($23,359). During 1889 upwards of 200,000 animals were slaughtered.

The supply of beef and mutton in the seven Australasian colonies is practically inexhaustible. The number of cattle in the entire group is about 11,000,000 head at the present date.

The subjoined table shows the number of sheep, horned-cattle, horses, and swine in the entire group of these colonies for the year 1888:

Colony.	Sheep.		Horned cattle.		Horses.		Swine.	
	No.	Per cent.	No.	Per cent.	No.	Per cent.	No.	Per cent.
New South Wales	46,503,469	48.15	1,622,907	17.49	411,368	27.35	248,583	21.80
Victoria	10,818,575	11.20	1,370,660	14.77	323,115	21.48	245,818	21.56
Queensland	13,444,005	13.92	4,654,932	50.17	324,326	21.56	68,994	6.05
South Australia	7,150,000	7.40	430,000	4.64	170,000	11.30	170,000	14.91
Western Australia	2,112,392	2.19	95,822	1.03	41,390	2.75	25,083	2.20
Tasmania	1,430,065	1.48	142,019	1.53	29,238	1.95	43,227	3.79
New Zealand	15,122,133	15.66	*962,200	10.37	*204,700	13.61	*338,500	29.69
Total	96,580,639	100.00	9,278,540	100.00	1,504,137	100.00	1,140,205	100.00

NOTE.—The figures for all the colonies, with the exception of New Zealand, are for the year ended March 31, 1889. In the case of New Zealand the number of sheep is for May, 1888.
* Estimated.

The estimated value for the same period of sheep, cattle, and swine in the seven Australasian colonies is given by Mr. T. A. Coghlan, government statistician for New South Wales, at £33,068,000 ($160,925,422), of which £21,488,000 ($104,571,352) represents the value of sheep; £6,200,000 ($30,172,300) cattle for meat; £4,144,000 ($20,166,776), dairy cattle, and £1,236,000 ($6,014,994) of swine. It should be understood, however, that the greater part of the value of the stock returns is due to wool. Thus, out of the total quoted, about £17,100,000 ($83,217,150) is the value of wool. If the cost of freight, handling, brokerage, etc., were added the value of clip would amount to about £2,000,000 ($9,733,000) more. Mr. Coghlan, in referring to the food supply of the colonies, mentions that the meat consumed is greater in Australasia than in any other country in the world. He gives the consumption of meat in the colonies at 276 pounds per head of the population against only 69 pounds in Germany, 74 pounds in France, 115 pounds in Great Britain and 120 pounds in the United States; or, in other words, Australasia consumes four times as much meat per inhabitant as Germany and nearly three times as much as Great Britain, and more than twice as much as in the great wheat and meat exporting country, the United States. The surplus exported from Australasia forms only a small fraction of the quantity produced. The increase in cattle and sheep averages about 10.4 per cent. per annum. Of this, Mr. Coghlan states there is needed for the ordinary requirements of food supply, excluding exports, 9.4 per cent. of cattle and 6.8 per cent. of sheep, so that the net increase of the herds of Australasia is about 1 per cent. per annum, and of the flocks about 3.6 per cent. per annum. He says:

Under the most favorable conditions—that is, if there were no losses from failure of food or water—the increase of sheep would be about 24.3 per cent., and of cattle 24.9 per cent., giving a net surplus of 17.5 per cent. and 15.5 per cent., respectively.

Mr. Coghlan, however, states that the frequency of droughts renders the increase of sheep only about 20 per cent., and that if steps are not taken to mitigate the effects of drought and to save part of the unnecessary waste of animal food, the demand for beef will eventually exceed the supply, but that the case is different with regard to sheep, as the supply is never likely to be seriously trenched upon, and a large surplus will always be available to meet the requirements of markets outside of Australasia.

In regard to the machine employed on steam-ships and sailing vessels for the export of meat, the Bell-Coleman and Haslem process appears to be most generally in use, although it is said that the Goodfellow machine is likely to take its place as it does not require to be kept running one-third the length of time. The American De La Vergne machine has also been successfully used, and is said to give very general satisfaction.

The new steam-ship *Matautis*, of the Shaw, Savill and Albion Line, is fitted up with Blythe & Passios refrigerators. There are three of these machines, two forward and one aft. The two forward are of 60,000 cubic feet and 40,000 cubic feet, and the aft machine is of 70,000 cubic feet capacity. The refrigerating rooms have a capacity for 30,000 carcasses of mutton, averaging 80 pounds each.

A considerable portion of the colonial frozen meat passes into consumption in the London market as prime English or Scotch mutton. It is found to be in a thoroughly sound and firm condition and would readily pass for the best home product. Objection is, however, being made to the article being sold as fresh meat. A bill has been introduced into the British Parliament to prevent its sale as such. The proposed bill provides that it shall not be lawful for any person to sell or expose for sale any foreign or colonial meat unless a conspicuous notice is placed over the shop indicating that foreign and colonial meat is sold there. It is further provided that no foreign or colonial meat shall be sold elsewhere than at these labeled shops unless notice is first given to the purchaser in writing to the effect that such meat is foreign or colonial, or unless the purchaser shall have expressly ordered or asked for colonial or foreign meat. Carts used for the conveyance or sale of such meat must also be marked, and there are other clauses of a similar nature.

In most of these colonies one of the principal obstacles to the successful development on a large scale of the frozen-meat export trade is the absence of a safe and convenient mode of bringing the meat to market in the dressed state. The cattle are usually driven through the country to a railway station, where they are shipped on the cars to Sydney; thence they are taken to the abattoirs on Glebe Island, situated not far from the city and sufficiently isolated and open to every breath of air.

The great attention now being given to the meat export trade of these colonies will unquestionably open up a wide and profitable field for manufacturers in the United States of processes and machines for the refrigeration and cool storage of meat, fish, and dairy produce.

Mr. Alexander Bruce, the chief inspector of stock for New South Wales, has favored me with an exhaustive report, under date of May 5, on the chilled-meat trade. From this valuable document I learn that it is now some eighteen years since the late Mr. T. S. Mort, of Sydney, to whom the Australian colonies and New Zealand are indebted for the establishment of the frozen-meat trade, endeavored to form a fresh-meat depot at Lithgow, 96 miles west from Sydney, and although himself unsuccessful in that enterprise, the trade in chilled meat has, in America, become firmly established, and is there supplanting the live-stock trade, as it will before long do in Australasia and throughout the civilized world. Mr. Mort's theory was that with the aid of artificial cold properly applied there need be no more waste, and the correctness and practicability of his proposals are fully borne out in the success of the chilled-meat trade, but more especially in that of the frozen-meat export from the Australian colonies, New Zealand, and America.

Mr. Bruce states that he has for the past ten or twelve years constantly advocated the establishment of a fresh or chilled meat trade, both on account of the numerous evils which attend the existing livestock trade and the advantages which must accrue from the change, and he very fully describes the evils of the live-stock trade and the suffering and cruelty inflicted on the stock. He says, speaking of New South Wales, that leaving out of view the hardships stock undergo in the outlying districts (where, as a rule, the feed is comparatively good) when traveling to the nearest railway station, and following them from the time they are yarded there till they are killed at the abattoirs, the treatment they receive in reaching Sydney from an outlying station like Bourke, 503 miles west from Sydney, is cruel and wasteful in the extreme, for they are between seven and eight days without any food, made up as follows:

In yarding, trucking, and despatching, say, from Bourke, 10 hours; on the cars to Homebush, near Sydney, unloading there and yarding, say 40 hours; lotting, selling, and removal to paddocks at Leichhardt, a suburb of Sydney, 15 hours; in waiting paddocks there (for as a rule the cattle purchased at one sale remain in these paddocks until next sale day, and a fresh lot have been purchased, before they are sent to the abattoirs), say, 84 hours; at the abattoirs waiting slaughter, say, 24 hours; total, 173 hours; that is, 173 hours, or 7 days 5 hours without any food, and sometimes without water.

It thus appears that a considerable portion of some 1,500 head of cattle and 15,000 sheep are week after week subjected to the terrible torture of five, six, seven, or even more days' starvation, till the cattle may be seen at the abattoirs with their heads hanging down, their bellies tucked up to their backs and looking utterly miserable and wretched. Nor is this all. The poor animals in trucking are terrified, beaten, and bruised, and when in the cars they push and horn each other, while the stopping and shunting often throw them down, and some are not infrequently trampled to death. The losses of cattle on the cars and the bruises so noticeable on their bodies when killed show conclusively the cruelty now inflicted on the animals under the live-stock trade and, as Mr. Bruce says, "with the terrible starvation which that system entails, cries aloud for a thorough change."

With reference to the waste and deterioration of the meat Mr. Bruce says that the shrinkage in weight alone is a serious matter; for if quiet, fat cattle in England, carefully driven short distances, and fed two or three times a day waste, on an average, over 8 pounds in twenty-four hours, it is certain that the loss in weight on the comparatively wild fat cattle of New South Wales must, till they reach the killing-pen, subjected as they are to the barbarous treatment and starvation from which they now suffer, waste nearly double that amount, and that the shrinkage in their case will amount to 12 or 14 pounds a day, which again for seven or eight days would on an average be at least 100 pounds per bullock, i. e., one-eighth of the whole weight and the very best of the meat.

As to the deterioration in the quality of the meat, I learn from the report that it is notorious the meat supplied in Sydney is, as a rule, inferior, tough, and void of flavor, especially in bad seasons. It is, in fact, after the cruelty and starvation to which the cattle are subjected, simply hard, well-trained muscle, with all the primest and most nutritious part of the meat gone, which not only renders it dear and innutritious to the consumer, but, so far as the beef is concerned, utterly unfit for export to London; while, as regards the frozen mutton now sent from Sydney to London, it on an average brings two-thirds penny per pound less than the mutton from New Zealand.

Mr. Bruce says the remedy for this unsatisfactory state of things is simple. It lies in the preservation of the quality of the meat by artificial cold, which can be obtained at a comparatively trifling cost. On or near its own pastures the meat is as good as any in the world, and if only conveyed from the pastures to market without deterioration it is an article in every way fit for local consumption and can be offered with confidence in any market, either in a fresh, frozen, chilled, tinned, or salted state.

Mr. Bruce's recommendations are:

(1) To kill the stock at the main centers of the stock traffic on the railways, as near the pastures on which they are fattened as possible; or, if they have traveled any distance, to keep them in paddocks near these centers where they can get plenty of good grass and water for six, eight, or even more days, till they are well rested and cooled down and thoroughly free from fever.

(2) To send the meat, with as little handling as possible, to a chilling-room cooled down to 36° F. in winter and moderately cool weather; and in the summer time down to 33° F. (just above freezing), in order to have a good surplus of cold to meet the loss which takes place in the transit when the weather is warm, and thus do away as far as possible with the necessity for providing ice by the way. The meat for consumption in Sydney could in this way afford to lose, say, 30° F. (the car would then only be 53° F.), and arrive perfectly safe. The cost of chilling would in the height of summer be, say, 61 cents per body of beef from Bourke or Hay, with the temperature at 100° F. in the shade.

(3) To put it late in the day into non-conducting meat cars (which would also be cooled down to the temperature of the meat, and send it by train at a speed of at least 20 miles an hour to market; and

(4) To run the cars, on reaching Melbourne or Sydney, into a meat market provided with the necessary appliances for cooling and keeping the meat, and there, according to the state of the market, either dispose of it to the retail butchers, send it to the chill-room (where it can be kept perfectly sound for a fortnight) to wait a better market, or prepare it for exportation as frozen, chilled, tinned, or salted meat.

A proper chilled room to protect the meat should it not be sold on arrival is a *sine qua non*. It was the want of this that was one of the principal causes of the failure of the Orange Company to establish a fresh-meat trade, for as the company had no means of protecting the meat when not sold, they had to take the price offered by the retail butchers or allow it to stink. They were, in fact, largely at the mercy of the trade; whereas with a proper chill-room the salesman could put the meat in and wait a fortnight if necessary for better prices, to say nothing of the other outlets secured by a proper system of artificial cold.

In reporting on the success of the fresh-meat trade in the United States Mr. Bruce acknowledges the assistance the project derived owing to information obtained from America in the following words:

> Mr. Gilderoy W. Griffin, consul for the United States, who has done so much to make our resources known there and to promote trade between the colonies and America, kindly obtained from the Commissioner of Agriculture, Washington, an exhaustive and very valuable report on the fresh-meat trade in the United States, which showed that the fat-stock trade in America, in spite of the powerful vested interests which exist there, was fast becoming a fresh-meat one. In the short space of six years the volume of the fresh-meat trade from the Western to the Eastern States of America, which only began in 1880, had increased with great rapidity, and has by this time overtaken and passed that of the live-stock trade; and the Commissioner of Agriculture in reply to the question whether the fresh-meat trade is likely to increase very tersely observed that, "it must continue to increase unless there should be a revolution in trade affairs and in the desire of the people to obtain the best meat for the smallest outlay," a contingency which it would be simply absurd to suppose would ever arise.

I learn that during the five years from 1881 to 1885 the growth in dressed meat was: From 1881 to 1882 the increase was 42.5 per cent. over the trade of 1880; in 1882 the gain was 52.3 per cent.; in 1883 it was 127.5 per cent.; in 1884 it declined to 23.6 per cent.; and in 1885 it was 25.2 per cent.

The Mark Lane Express, London, in January last, says:

> The dressed-beef business has driven the carcass-butcher out and is the coming method of handling beef in America.

And the Daily News, London, says:

> There are enormous numbers of us able to regale ourselves on the roast beef of old England brought straight from Chicago.

As to the success of the fresh-meat trade in Australia in 1889–'90, Mr. Bruce says that it is still asserted by some in the meat trade that though the system has proved a success in America it may not answer in Australia, but that fortunately it is not necessary to be dependent on American experience, for through the energy and enterprise of Mr. Robert Hudson, of the firm of Messrs. Hudson Brothers, of Sydney and Melbourne, the reports of the success of the fresh-meat trade in America have been fully confirmed by the experimental trips he has made with his refrigerating cars from Narrandera and Narrabri to Sydney, which were thoroughly successful, not only as regards the condition of the meat on its arrival in Sydney, but also as regards expense and the owners' net returns.

With the view of showing the advantages still more clearly Mr. Bruce supposes a case where two fat bullocks of the same weight at Bourke are sent to Sydney. One of them is sent alive and sold at Homebush, and the other killed and chilled at Bourke and the carcass sent, with the profitable offal, by refrigerating car to the meat market, Sydney, by which means, he states, there is a saving of at least 10s. ($2.43) per bullock to the owner, while the indirect advantages to the stock-owner, owing to the superior quality of the meat and the price it will bring in the London market if frozen and shipped, are of great moment.

KILLING AND CHILLING DEPOTS.

With regard to who should erect killing and chilling depots Mr. Bruce advocates the construction of these depots by joint stock companies, formed to a considerable extent by trades-people in the towns near which the depots are to be established, but principally by the stock-owners in the areas from which the stock would be brought to the depots for slaughter and chilling. He would have these companies to act as agents for the stock owners and dealers, take delivery of the stock and kill and chill them, forwarding the carcasses on owners' account to market in the refrigerating cars, for which they would supply the ice when required, charging a moderate amount for their services, which would to some extent be paid for in offal.

Mr. Bruce has consulted one of the leading mechanical engineers in Sydney, who has given the question of cost special study both in Australia and in America, and he understands that the cost of the necessary buildings and of a complete chilling and ice-making plant, together with yards, slaughter-houses, land, etc., for an establishment capable of dealing with, say, 120 cattle or 1,200 sheep a day, and supply the necessary ice for transit, would be £12,000 ($58,398), while the working expenses of such a depot, including interest on cost of plant, wages, coal at £2 per ton, water, ammonia, sundries, etc., would bring the cost of chilling a body of beef weighing say, 800 pounds, to 48 cents.

On the question as to who should provide the refrigerating cars Mr. Bruce says, while it is taken for granted that the trades-people in the more important towns will co-operate with stock-owners in the surrounding country to form companies for the erection of killing and chilling depots, he believes that the Government railway commissioners are the proper body to supply refrigerating cars, the companies not only supplying the cold for chilling the meat, but also the ice for keeping the cars cool. He states that an endeavor was made to form a metropolitan company to rent the meat market and chill-room in Sydney from the railway commissioners and, where necessary, to assist the up-country killing and chilling companies in the construction and working of their depots.

The promoters of the Metropolitan Company also proposed that they should find the refrigerating cars, that the cars should be hauled by the railway authorities at a stated rate per ton, and that the railway commissioners should have the use of the cars for back loading.

Mr. Bruce, however, points out several objections to this arrangement and among others mentions the following:

(1) It would take a great deal of capital to provide the necessary cars, and shortness of funds is one of the principal drawbacks to the formation of the proposed Metropolitan Company.

(2) The question of who should make the repairs to the cars would be a difficult one to settle, and it would, I am afraid, be at times impossible to say who should do so.

(3) The Commissioners would be able, besides conveying the fresh meat, to make much more use of the refrigerating cars than the company in carrying milk, dairy produce, fruit, and game to Sydney, and fish and other perishable articles up country.

REFRIGERATING CARS.

Mr. Arthur G. Kenway, superintendent engineer in charge of the New South Wales Government works connected with the meat trade, has furnished me with an account of an experimental trial of a refrigerating car designed by him. He states that his method consists in placing meat chilled in simple insulated cars, without ice or other artificial cold-producing agents, trusting simply to the insulation of the cars and the cold stored in the meat to effect the purpose for the shorter distances, and for those longer to recharging the cars with cold air at intervals from stationery machinery if found necessary.

The car which Mr. Kenway designed was divided into three sections, the first containing the refrigerator; the second was the insulated chill-room; the third section contained a tank of a capacity of 750 gallons. The refrigerator was one of the Bell-Coleman and Hastem pattern, dry cold-air machines, capable of discharging 5,000 cubic feet of cold air per hour. It was connected with the boiler of the locomotive by a flexible rubber steam-pipe, and it discharged its cold air into the insulated chill-room, the walls, floor, and ceiling of which were built in the manner Mr. Kenway proposed should be done for the permanent insulated cars, with 5 inches of woolen flock packed between two inner and two outer thicknesses of 1-inch tongued and grooved pine boards which had a layer of paper felt between them, except on the floor, which had a layer of waterproof paper instead.

If chilled meat had been procurable up country, Mr. Kenway states, a simple insulated car would have been all that was necessary for the experiment. The meat, namely, six quarters of beef and five bodies of mutton, was previously chilled by the cold-air process at a private establishment in Sydney in order to economize time, and was put into the car shortly before leaving Sydney on Sunday night, the 17th of March. A start was made at 9 o'clock, and the refrigerator in the car was kept at work for a period of sixty-five minutes. The meat and the room then showed a temperature of 30° Fahr. The machine was then stopped until Nyngan was reached, a distance of 343 miles. This portion of the journey occupied twenty-two and one-half hours. A number of delays occurred before the car reached Bourke, 503 miles from Sydney, where the temperature was found to stand at 50° Fahr. The temperature outside the car during the greater part of the trip varied from 57° Fahr. to 80° Fahr., and while traversing the plains the thermometer ranged from 80° Fahr. to 98° Fahr. on the sides of the car, in the shade, while in motion. On the return journey the temperature was reduced to 30° Fahr. before leaving Bourke, and from that time until Sydney was reached the machine was never used. The meat when removed from the car was found to be in prime condition, firm and cool, its temperature being 46° Fahr.

The most desirable temperature for meat to stand at when delivered is believed to be 60° Fahr., so that the journey might have been continued eight or ten hours further with safety. Mr. Kenway states that the results of the experiment show that it is possible to convey chilled meat in simple insulated cars for the longest journeys in New South Wales without the aid of any refrigerating appliances during the hottest weather if the meat is properly chilled before being placed in the insulated cars, the temperature in which being reduced to 30° Fahr., the explanation being that sufficient cold is stored up in the chilled meat to answer all requirements on the journey.

It is doubtful whether the Government will construct cars on this pattern, as it is believed they are too heavy and expensive.

The Messrs. Hudson Brothers, who have constructed several refrigerating cars for the Government railways, are taking steps to introduce into Australia refrigerating cars made by the Wikes, the Zimmerman, and the Riordan Manufacturing Companies, of Chicago, Ill. The Messrs. Hudson Brothers had on exhibition at the Metropolitan show near Sydney on the 7th April last, a chill-room similar to those they propose to erect in the country districts. A number of sheep killed at Bourke seven days previously were brought to the Metropolitan show and hung up in this chill-room. The fine condition of the meat and the ease with which it was conveyed to Sydney were subjects of commendation by those interested in the exhibition. The Messrs. Hudson Brothers state in a communication to me that they have had much difficulty in selecting a suitable machine for the manufacture of ice; that they have visited every place where these machines could be procured in Europe and America, but up to the present time not one seemed to answer their purpose. They state:

Our great effort has been to find an economical machine which we could use in connection with the chill-room. The machines with which we are most pleased are the Goodfellow and the Kilbourn & Co. The latter is an American machine and will probably be adopted by us.

The Messrs. Hudson Brothers state that the De la Vergne machine is a good one, but very costly and scarcely suitable to take a long distance into the interior of this continent.

G. W. GRIFFIN,
Consul.

UNITED STATES CONSULATE,
Sydney, May 6, 1890.

NEWCASTLE, N. S. W.

REPORT BY COMMERCIAL AGENT DAWSON.

The majority of freezers in use in this consular district are of American make. There is no great quantity of them nor any great demand for them, but the leading hotels and restaurants have them, and some private families. Their size varies from 3 feet 6 inches by 2 feet 6 inches, to 5 feet by 3 feet 6 inches, *i. e.*, the size of the box. Those used in restaurants have cooling ovens with ice chambers at the top and water chambers at the sides. Those in hotels are shelved off for holding liquids, bottles, etc. They cost from $25 to $75. Ice is imported from Sydney at present, and retails in 14-pound blocks at 36 cents per block. It probably costs the importers 75 cents per 100 pounds in Sydney. There was an ice manufacturing establishment here, but it collapsed. There is room for another. Refrigerators are brought here from Sydney, but there is no reason why they should not come direct from the United States.

THOMAS M. DAWSON,
Commercial Agent.

UNITED STATES COMMERCIAL AGENCY,
Newcastle, February 13, 1890.

NEW ZEALAND.

REPORT BY CONSUL CONNOLLY, OF AUCKLAND.

The subject of refrigerating machines is one of considerable magnitude in New Zealand, embracing as it does one of the most important industries of the colony. I found at the outset that in order to obtain thoroughly reliable information I must visit a few of the great "freezing works" in several localities throughout the country.

All the refrigerating machinery used in New Zealand is manufactured in England, and is known as the "Haslam dry-air refrigerator," and is used exclusively for freezing beef and mutton for export to the London market.

Owing to the fact that there are no small freezing machines in use in this colony, the people are of course unfamiliar with the benefits to be derived from the use of the smaller refrigerators as used in the United States.

As to the best means of introducing American refrigerators, I find is a most difficult matter to suggest a practical method of doing so successfully, for many reasons. The American refrigerators are comparatively unknown in this colony, and until their superiority is established beyond any possibility of doubt the people would be slow to favor them, especially as there is an impression prevalent here that American refrigerating machinery is not adapted to the use most required here, viz, meat freezing. Those who are engaged in this business, and presume to be familiar with all the necessary requirements of the trade, claim unhesitatingly that the American refrigerators could not be utilized as economically or as advantageously as the English-manufactured machine. Consequently, in view of the prejudice that already exists against the American machines, it would, as I have already stated, be difficult to advise intelligently concerning the successful introduction of our American-made refrigerators.

Perhaps the most economical manner of introducing some of the smaller refrigerating machines for the preservation of food and liquids would be for some of our American merchants who have correspondents in this colony to ship a few sample machines to such correspondents with full and complete instructions. This I have no doubt would be much the cheapest and least expensive way. But a far more satisfactory method would be to send a duly authorized agent with the machines one who would be capable of publicly demonstrating the capacity and utility of our American refrigerators. This would undoubtedly be far the most desirable and practical manner of bringing out machines successfully and satisfactorily before this public. The advantages derivable from an authorized agent presenting the machines as compared with those of a local resident agent are numerous and must readily suggest themselves to the manufacturer. The American agent would thoroughly understand his business, and for this reason would inspire the public confidence while the resident agent would be ignorant of the proper methods employed to produce the most satisfactory results, thus practically destroying in the beginning whatever chance there might be of introducing our American-made machines. No matter how meritorious the machine may be the uninitiated when testing it under the gaze of a prejudiced and critical public might fail utterly. Therefore, if ever an effort is made in this direction, I would strongly urge the unmistakable necessity of sending a thoroughly reliable and practical person to represent the goods, as much will depend on the ability of the representative, presuming, always, the machines are useful and adapted to the requirements of the people of this colony.

The manufacture and sale of ice in this colony is very limited indeed. Machinery intended for the manufacture of ice alone would not in my opinion pay here. Ice is not used in any considerable quantities, as the climate in most parts of New Zealand is mild and equable, and in consequence of this the necessity for ice is correspondingly reduced. Whatever ice is required is procurable from any of the "freezing works" throughout the colony and at very reasonable rates, considering that none are manufacturing it specially for sale. Ice is obtainable at the rate of 1 cent per pound.

The following will afford some idea of the size, cost, and capacity of a few of the refrigerators in use in this consular district.

In the Christchurch district there are two meat-freezing establishments, both of which machines are manufactured by Haslam & Co., Derby, England, as, indeed, are all the machines used for freezing purposes in the colony. I will give the size and power of one of those in use in Christchurch, which will suffice for both. One of these machines is capable of delivering 110,000 cubic feet of cold air per hour. The cost of this machine in England was $18,248.87.

There are also two freezing works in the Wellington district. The Gear Meat Preserving and Freezing Company of Wellington have two machines, each capable of discharging 45,000 cubic feet of cold air per hour. The cost free on board in London was $13,139.55. This company will have an additional machine in about two months hence, with a capacity equal to 150,000 cubic feet of air per hour, which will cost, including condensers, free on board, London, $21,899.

The Wellington Meat Export Company have three refrigerating machines in constant use. Two of these machines deliver 120,000 cubic feet of cold air per hour, at a temperature of about 70 degrees below zero at the point of discharge. The third delivers about 50,000 feet of air at about the same temperature. The two larger machines will freeze 500 sheep per diem, while the smaller will only freeze about half the above number. They are all air-compression machines. The larger ones cost in London $17,032, while the smaller one would be supplied now for about $10,949.32.

This company has been sending away for the last six months an average of 1,100 cattle and 17,000 sheep per calendar month.

It may be said of all the machines used in this colony for meat freezing purposes that no special or peculiar features are required, except that they have to be adapted to freezing large quantities of meat in a short time. None of these machines are used for chilling or storing meat for local consumption.

It may be somewhat interesting to many to get a pen picture of one of these great meat-freezing works and the *modus operandi* of meat-preserving and the disposition made of a sheep from the time it enters the slaughter-house until the final process is gone through with. For this purpose I will select the freezing works of Nelson Brothers, at Tomvana, near Napier, N. Z., commencing with the slaughter-house, which is a long shed where the sheep have arrived at the "sticking point" and come under the hands of twenty butchers who are busily engaged killing, skinning, and dressing them. Through this shed runs a miniature railway, which takes away the fat to the boiling-down house, the skins to the fell-mongery, the intestines in due time becoming fiddle-strings to charm or torture as the fates decree. Overhead are a number of rails on which run friction rollers, to which the carcasses are hooked, and here they begin the long journey which is to end in London. Along these rails they are rolled into the cooling-room, in which they remain till all their animal heat has been expelled, when they are passed into the refrigerating chambers, where they are frozen for thirty-six hours, by the end of which time they give out a bell-like sound when struck. From these chambers (which hold from 200 to 600 carcasses) they are removed to storing-rooms, and in due course are taken away to the port of shipment in specially constructed railroad cars; 1,400 sheep can be prepared per day, and there is storage for 40,000 carcasses.

From the slaughter-house we pass to the boiler-house, in which we find, in addition to four 20 horse-power boilers, a striking novelty in the shape of a 60 horse-power Babcock and Wilcock boiler, in which the steam is generated in groups of tubes between which the heat from the furnace circulates, which tubes depend from a horizontal steam-drum mounted on trunions at its ends, which arrangement allows for an unequal expansion of the parts, the drum being luted to the brick setting inclosing the tubes. The flues of all the boilers lead into one of "Green's Economizers," containing 168 tubes 12 feet long and 4 inches in diameter, for heating the feed-water which is passed through them on its way from the condensers to the boilers, and is thus heated by the waste heat circulating between the tubes.

Adjoining the boiler-house is the refrigerating machine. Here are four Haslam dry-air refrigerators busy at work, in which the air on its way to the freezing chambers is first heated by compression, then cooled by passing through pipes surrounded by cold water, and then passed into a chamber containing dry-air pipes. After passing through these pipes the air is expanded, by which means its temperature is reduced to 80° below zero. It then passes through air trunks into the freezing chambers, and, after doing its duty, passes back through exhaust trunks to the compressors. In the freezing chamber the cold is indeed most intense—frost on the roof, on the walls, on the floor, and here and there a little snow. In this chamber are countless carcasses undergoing the freezing process.

The engine-room and freezing-chambers are lighted at night by a Siemens electric light, the dynamo for which is driven by a 3 horsepower engine.

Leaving the engine-house we pass two large reservoirs, from which 700,000 gallons of water are daily passed through the machines.

Entering the wool-shed, here is an invention which will probably revolutionize all those processes in which wool requires to be dried after being washed, dyed, etc. Sheep-raisers, fellmongers, wool-scourers, and dyers have long sighed for some inexpensive and efficient apparatus which should render them independent of the weather and enable them to do their work with satisfaction, precision, and absolute certainty. This desideratum is at last supplied in these patent wool-drying machines, two of which are here at work, and by which the wool to be dried is exposed to a blast of warm air so that its fibers may be repeatedly acted upon thereby and thus be regularly and rapidly dried, the dried wool being expelled from the machine by means of the blast. Each machine consists of a sparred drum, open at both ends and revolving on friction-rollers in a casing, between the bars of which (drum) air is forced from a longitudinal air-trunk. The interior of the drum is furnished with sparred shelves which, as the drum revolves successively, take up portions of the wool and allow them to fall, and thus expose them fully to the current of air, and also shake out any dust or other foreign substance, which in itself is a great advantage. Both drums are 8 feet in diameter, one being 14 feet long and the other 30 feet. The shorter drum is worked intermittently; that is, a charge of wool is thrown in at one end and when dried is blown out at the other by turning on a blast. In the longer drum the feeding and discharge of the wool are carried on continuously, the wool fed in handfuls through a hopper at one end, and the blast from the air-trunk being directed by means of adjustable "feathers" on to the wool in an oblique direction, so that the blast both dries and propels the wool through the drum. The apparatus, which is exceedingly simple in construction, can in two hours be taken to pieces for transmission, and as readily set up on its arrival at its destination. Upon examination the dried wool is found to be of an extremely silky luster. I have devoted considerable space to this "wool-drying" apparatus in the hope it may be interest to the wool-growers and others interested in the wool industry in the United States.

One noticeable feature around these great meat-preserving establishments is that there is positively no waste. Everything fit for human consumption is utilized and prepared in the most careful and painstaking manner. Thus the skins of the refrigerated sheep are cured for subsequent manufacture into parchment, "morocco," and "roans;" the clippings from the pelts are washed and dried by patent machines already referred to and turned out as short wool; the kidneys, tongues, etc., are tinned, and even the horns and bones of the bullocks are sent to the bone-dust factory to be ground, and thus again assist in the production of additional comforts for mankind. In my description of the cooling chamber I find I have omitted some important details. The cooling-room is constructed with a double ceiling, through which a current of air is drawn by a fan driven by a donkey-engine. In this cooling-room the carcasses are permitted to remain for 10 hours, when all the animal heat has been expelled. The carcasses are then placed in the refrigerating chamber, the walls, floors, and ceilings of which are insulated with a charcoal lining, and the cold-air is supplied through an inlet air-trunk direct from the engine, and afterwards passes back to be cooled down and used over again. By this means there is a constant circulation of cold air thoughout the freezing-chamber.

All the steamers and sailing vessels plying between England and New Zealand and engaged in the frozen-meat carrying trade are supplied with Haslam refrigerators. It is asserted that 95 per cent. of all the frozen meat placed upon the London market is treated by the Haslam process.

There are seven refrigerating machines in the Auckland district, with a capacity ranging from 2,000 to 120,000 cubic feet of cold air per hour.

The cost of the smaller machines is about $3,400 each, while the cost of the larger machines, those capable of discharging 120,000 cubic feet of air per hour, is $17,032 in England.

There are ten large meat-freezing establishments in the colony and about five smaller ones, as near as can be ascertained. The total number of Haslam refrigerating machines in use in New Zealand for meat-freezing purposes are twenty-six. It is asserted by all who are interested in the frozen-meat industry that "the American ammonia machines" are useless for meat freezing, consequently could not be sold here at any price for meet-freezing purposes.

JNO. D. CONNOLLY,
Consul.

UNITED STATES CONSULATE,
Auckland, May 9, 1890.

WEST AUSTRALIA.

REPORT BY CONSULAR AGENT SANDOVER, OF FREEMANTLE.

Refrigerators are not used in this district, ice at the present time not being manufactured here. From my knowledge of the American refrigerators I believe that when ice is manufactured here, which will be when the population becomes larger, these refrigerators will be the most suitable kind for the place.

Regarding the best manner of introducing them, I think the best way would be to instruct the manufacturers to send circulars and prices to this consular agency, and I would see that they were distributed among dealers.

WILLIAM SANDOVER,
Consular Agent.

UNITED STATES CONSULAR AGENCY,
Freemantle, March 6, 1890.

POLYNESIA.

FIJI.

REPORT BY COMMERCIAL AGENT ST. JOHN, OF LEVUKA.

There possibly may have been a half dozen refrigerators brought here from England several years ago when the colony was more prosperous, but on account of the impossibility of getting ice they have gone into disuse.

Ice is at present manufactured in very small quantities and at very irregular intervals. The price demanded for it is 12 cents per pound or $5 per hundred-weight.

As to the conditions which prevail relative to the preservation of foods and liquids, it is the very simple way of placing them in a well-ventilated safe (usually of wire netting) and placed in as cool a shade as possible, either under the shade of the house or of trees as most convenient.

No attempt is made, however, at keeping them for any length of time.

As to whether American refrigerators could be so modified as to meet the local requirements in the absence of ice, I am unable to say.

In consideration of the small trade that could, even under favorable circumstances, be realized in this colony, I could only suggest but one way for the introduction of refrigerators here, and that would be through New Zealand or the Australian colonies. That is, that they be reshipped from houses dealing in such goods in those colonies to this colony of Fiji.

ANDREWS A. ST. JOHN,
Commercial Agent.

UNITED STATES COMMERCIAL AGENCY,
  Levuka, April 9, 1890.

HAWAII.

REPORT BY CONSULAR AGENT FURNEAUX, OF HILO.

Refrigerators are in use by the foreign families resident in this place. The ordinary kind, such as are in common use in the United States, fully meet the requirements of this community. Those in use here are manufactured in San Francisco, Cal., and in Buffalo, N. Y.

The average size is 2 feet 6 inches by 2 feet 10 inches; height, 3 feet 8 inches outside measure.

Ice is manufactured here and furnished at $3 per 100 pounds. The machine in use was made in San Francisco.

CHAS. FURNEAUX,
Consular Agent.

UNITED STATES CONSULAR AGENCY,
Hilo, February 10, 1890.

CONTINENT OF EUROPE.

AUSTRIA.

REICHENBERG.

REPORT BY COMMERCIAL AGENT HAWES.

No refrigerators are for sale here. Owing to the cold climate, they are little needed and are either made in a primitive manner by a carpenter or are ordered from Prague or Vienna. As they are only in the possession of private parties, it is impossible to procure any valuable information on the subject. Reichenberg is too small a city to do any direct importation from the United States, but perhaps if American refrigerators were introduced in Prague and Vienna, a limited number would be ordered here. The demand, however, would be so small that I am convinced that a couple of dozen would meet the demand for a year.

Consignment to responsible firms would be the only way of introducing such articles to the trade in this city.

JNO. B. HAWES,
Commercial Agent.

UNITED STATES COMMERCIAL AGENCY,
Reichenberg, April 11, 1890.

TRIESTE.

REPORT BY CONSUL HARTIGAN.

Refrigerators are used everywhere in this consular district. They are mostly made in Germany, Austria, and a few in Trieste.

The natural ice for local use and export is obtained from the surrounding mountains (Karst), small lakes, rivers, etc.

There is one establishment for the manufacture of ice, that of Heinrich Ritter von Zahony, where the ammonia process is employed; Linde patent.

The population of the Karst being extremely poor, ice is sold by them according to the season, between 20 and 40 soldi per 100 kilos, or an average of about 7 cents for 100 pounds. The artificial ice is considered a purer quality and commands a price one-third higher.

The system in vogue by butchers and others for preserving meats, etc., is somewhat similar to that in the United States.

Verderber & Co. are the principal agents and dealers here in refrigerators; they are enterprising men, and the best way, in my judgment, for the introduction of American make would be through them, if they were furnished with an illustrated catalogue of some large manufacturer, giving full particulars, dimensions, prices, etc. The price, I need not say, is an important consideration to compete with European production.

JAMES V. HARTIGAN,
Consul.

UNITED STATES CONSULATE,
Trieste, January 24, 1890.

BELGIUM.

ANTWERP.

REPORT BY CONSUL STEUART.

Refrigerators are used in this consular district not so generally, probably, as they would be in a city of the same size in the United States, but an appreciation of their convenience seems to be growing, and may increase the demand for them. It is difficult to say about how many are sold, but a dealer who handles more than any other one in the city told me he disposed of say from forty to fifty a year.

Those on sale here are manufactured in Germany, and are constructed similar to those in use with us at home. As they are of comparatively recent introduction, they are, I am sure, imitations or copies of those made in the United States and exported to Germany. The formation, therefore, is almost the same; the sizes range, according to a German price-list that I saw, from 50 by 65 by 76 centimeters to 88 by 185 by 188 centimeters. Then there are extra large sizes made for the use of restaurants and hotels, and also others constructed to hold beer in the keg or barrel, the smaller ones with single door and shelf, the larger ones with double doors—shelves on one side. They are made of wood, painted, and lined with zinc.

The ordinary sizes for family use here range from 50 by 65 by 76 centimeters, to 60 by 100 by 110 centimeters. The cost price of the former is 28 francs or $5.40, and the larger 82 francs, or $15.82 delivered in Antwerp. Extra large-sized ones are sold at from 200 to 275 francs by the retailer.

It is obvious that as price must be the main consideration in the effort to introduce the American refrigerators on this market, it will be necessary for the manufacturer to satisfy himself that he can place his product in successful competition with those now on sale here. It must be done at a price that will enable the dealer to sell as low or lower than he does his German ones, and find as much profit in them. An advance in price on account of any claim for superiority in any particular, however well-founded, will have no effect. They will buy the cheapest and remain true to them until convinced by experience in the use of others that they are as good or better than the ones they have been accustomed to.

In regard to the manner of introducing any goods upon a foreign market, there are several ways—as, for instance, by personal effort of an agent sent for that purpose; by sending a consignment of the goods, if a dealer can be found to receive and offer them; by procuring the names of parties dealing in the goods; and then by means of correspondence and circulars or price-lists printed in the language of the country, inducing them to make a trial. In the latter method the consul can and is often called upon to give the names of parties in his district engaged in the various branches of trade.

The small quantity of natural ice gathered during the winter is of no importance, and manufactured ice is in general use. There is a large company here engaged in that business, and the price is about 10 francs per 500 kilograms or $1.93 per 1,000 pounds. They furnish tickets to families, 25 tickets, at a price of francs, 12.50, each ticket calling for 25 kilograms of ice.

JOHN H. STEUART,
Consul.

UNITED STATES CONSULATE,
    Antwerp, January 28, 1890.

BRUSSELS.

REPORT BY CONSUL ROOSEVELT.

Although the use of refrigerators is yearly increasing in this consular district, the general use of same is considerably less than in any section of the United States.

Refrigerators for this market are of domestic and foreign manufacture, made of various kinds of woods, in all sizes and forms, without any special or peculiar features, but more or less imitations of American refrigerators. Prices for domestic production varies from 46 to 200 francs each, according to size and quality of wood. English refrigerators vary from 45 to 150 francs, and the German article from 46 to 160 francs each.

Different varieties of refrigerators are employed here in breweries for cooling beer. The most popular are the Schmidt, Mennig, and Briggs. The Schmidt patent is most generally used in this consular district.

Upon inquiry at the different establishments dealing in refrigerators I discovered only one firm, C. Duhot & Co., No. 3, Vieux Marcheaux Grains, Brussels, willing to accept an agency for the sale of American refrigerators. Mr. Duhot stated that, some years ago, he introduced American stoves on this market; that he is more than satisfied with the result of the venture, as the demand for this merchandise steadily increases. He is consequently favorably disposed to handle American refrigerators, provided American manufacturers are inclined to furnish said goods at equally advantageous rates as English and German producers.

I would suggest, as the most practical and satisfactory manner of introducing American refrigerators on this market, that manufacturers send samples of goods and arrange to have them presented to trade by intelligent, active agents, having a perfect knowledge of the French language.

ICE SUPPLY.

Ice for domestic consumption is largely procured from natural ponds and lakes in the provinces of Brabant, Hainaut, and Namur, large quantities are manufactured at the several ice-manufactories situated at Brussels, and a small amount is annually imported from Holland.

Price for ice for domestic use, 8 francs ($1.54) per 200 pounds. Wholesale price, 5 francs (97 cents) per 200 pounds.

I inclose cuts of different refrigerators in use here.

Nos. 1 and 2, refrigerators for preserving food. No. 3 Mennig, No. 4 Briggs, Nos. 5 and 6 Schmidt, for cooling beer.

DESCRIPTION OF SCHMIDT PATENT.

The Schmidt refrigerator is manufactured at Bretten, Baden. It has a cooling capacity from 8 to 40 hectoliters per hour. It is made of the best sheet brass, plated with pure tin. This apparatus consists of three parts, as follows: (1) Distribution pan, C; (2) reeded cylinders, D; (3) receiving basin, K.

The distribution pan consists of a round disk slightly curved, supplied with a central basin which receives the regulating stopple. This basin serves to distribute the wort and can easily be removed from the apparatus.

The undulated cylinder is formed of oval pipes, which are soldered in following a curve making the form of a continued screw or spiral; the form of the pipes, as well as their adaptation, is calculated with the view of obtaining the greatest possible cooling effect, so that the surface to be gone over by the wort be as long as possible and the flowing not too rapid. By means of the receiving basin the flowing of the wort is obtained in a regular manner, thus completely avoiding foam and splashing. The receiving basin is attached to the cylinder in the apparatus Nos. 1, 2, and 3, but is movable in Nos. 4, 5, and 6, but if desired can also be fixed to the cylinder of the last-mentioned apparatus. The wort to be cooled is brought into the receiving and distributing basin B by the regulating stopple A. It penetrates into the distributing pan C by the openings in the bottom of the receiving basin; it runs from this basin in a regular manner over the cooler D, and reaches the collecting basin K cold, where, by means of stopple E it is conducted into the fermenting vats.

The cold water is conducted into two separate divisions. For the upper division ordinary water is used, for the lower division ice-water is employed. By means of a communication pipe the apparatus can be supplied with either ordinary or ice-water, as may be desired. The ascension of the cold water is obtained by pumps or pressure. The ice-water enters the apparatus by F and circulates through the pipes surrounding the cylinder and flows out by stopple G. Ordinary water circulates likewise in the pipes; it enters by H and flows out by J. The apparatus reduces the temperature of the beer in an hour from one-half to 1 degree above ice-water temperature. If only ordinary water is used the temperature of the beer is reduced to that of the water.

Model B has two cooling surfaces, external and internal.

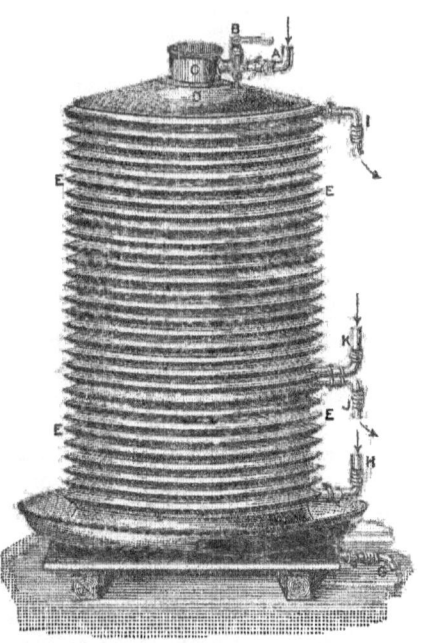

No. 3.—Mennig. (Imitation of the Schmidt patent.)

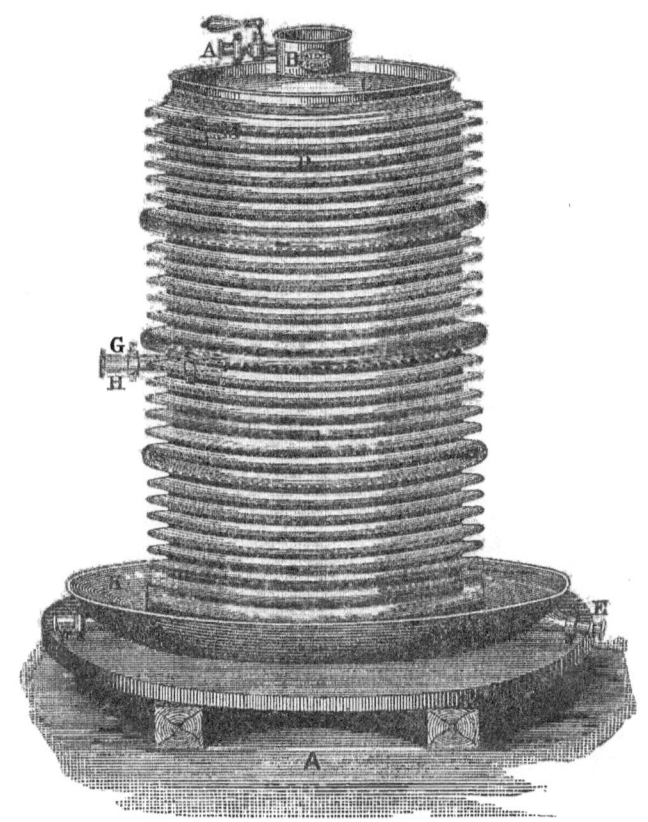

No. 5.—Model A.

A. Regulating stopple.
B. Basin of reception and distribution.
C. Pan of distribution.
D. Reeded or fluted cylinders.
E. Stopple for drawing off the wort.
F. Ice-water inlet.
G. Ice-water outlet.
H. Ordinary cold-water inlet.
J. Ordinary cold-water outlet.
K. Receiving basin of the cooled wort.

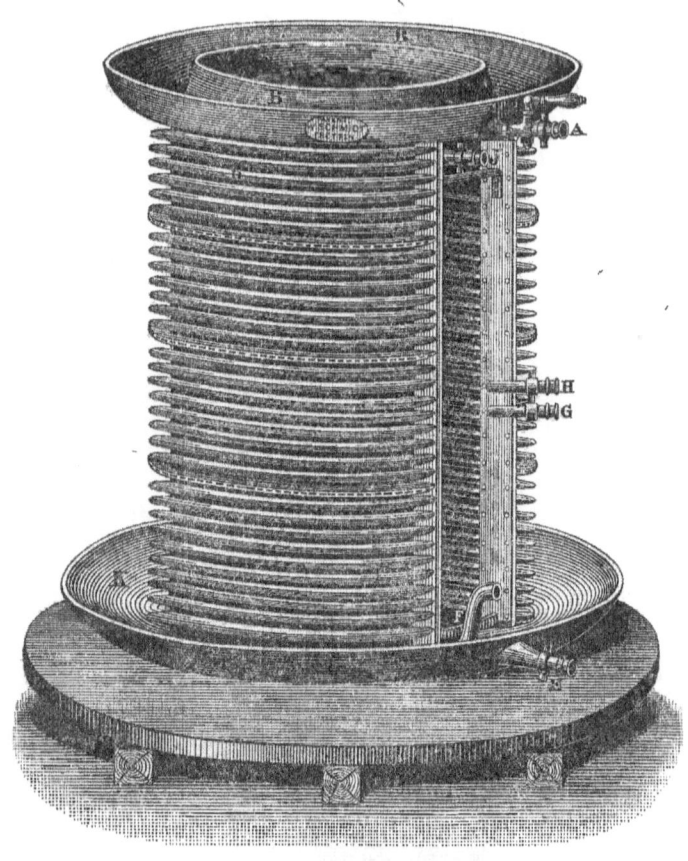

No. 6.—MODEL B.

A. Regulating stopple.
B. Basin of reception and distribution.
D. Reeded or fluted cylinders.
E. Stopple for drawing off the wort.
F. Ice-water inlet.
G. Ice-water outlet.
H. Ordinary cold-water inlet.
J. Ordinary cold-water outlet.
K. Receiving basin of the cooled wort.

This apparatus can cool from 50 to 120 hectoliters per hour.

PRICE AND DIMENSIONS OF MODEL A.

Number.	Full height of apparatus.	Diameter of cooling cylinder.	Number of flutings.	Extent of the cooling surface.	Cooling power per hour.	Price of apparatus.
	Meters.	Meters.		Sq.meters	Hectoliters.	Francs.
1	1.30	.48	27	3.50	7	325.00
2	1.40	.59	28	5.00	10	437.50
3	1.50	.75	28	7.50	15	562.50
4	1.60	.92	29	10.00	20	750.00
5	1.65	1.08	30	12.50	25	937.50
6	1.75	1.27	29	15.50	30	1,125.00
7	1.80	1.41	30	18.00	35	1,312.50
8	1.85	1.55	31	20.50	40	1,475.00

PRICE AND DIMENSIONS OF MODEL B.

9	1.07	1.44	30	33.00	50	1,750.00
10	1.77	1.59	32	39.50	60	2,075.00
11	1.87	1.74	34	46.50	70	2,425.00
12	1.87	1.92	34	52.50	80	2,775.00
13	1.07	2.04	36	59.50	90	3,125.00
14	1.07	2.22	36	65.50	100	3,475.00

GEO. W. ROOSEVELT,
Consul.

UNITED STATES CONSULATE,
Brussels, February 21, 1890.

LIEGE.

REPORT BY CONSUL PRESTON.

Refrigerators are scarcely ever used; I have never seen one here. The weather is never so warm but that the butchers hang their meat in the open air, and in private houses there is no need for them.

Very little ice is used, or is necessary here, except in the restaurants or bakeries where they make ices and ice-cream. Ice has been brought for these purposes for the last two years from Norway, via Ostend, at prices ranging from $2.90, $3.87, to $3.96 per 1,000 kilograms, in carloads of 10,000 kilograms. There are two manufactories for making artificial ice in Liege. It is now selling at $39.60 for 10,000 kilograms; $5.79 for 1,000 kilograms; $3.96 for 500 kilograms; 96.5 cents for 100 kilograms; 58 cents for 50 kilograms.

I may add that the river never freezes here, therefore all the ice used is artificial or imported.

WM. S. PRESTON,
Consul.

UNITED STATES CONSULATE,
Liege, January 14, 1890.

DENMARK.

REPORT BY CONSUL RYDER OF COPENHAGEN.

Besides the use of ice in the numerous home industries, such as breweries, dairies, slaughter-houses, etc., where the ice is preserved in underground cellars and placed in tanks constructed according to its special use for cooling of large stock rooms and milk rooms, refrigerating boxes are used here in large quantities in all the hospitals, hotels, restaurants, beer saloons, bakeries, butcher, fish, milk, and provision shops, as well as in many private establishments.

The boxes so employed, and which are almost entirely of home manufacture, are of different systems; of which the first consists of two wooden cases, the one contained within the other, the interstices between of $1\frac{1}{2}$–2 inches in width being filled with cork shavings, the doors being quite tight, with one or two air valves to the inside. The interior of the boxes is cased with zinc sheathing and the shelves placed therein are of grating form. From the top plate of the box, a tank, also of zinc sheathing, to contain the ice, extends down the middle of the box or is attached to one side of the cooling-chamber, the ice being placed on a grating in the tank, the lower part of the tank receiving the escaping water. The most of the refrigerators sold here would appear to be of this pattern; but experience has shown that the system is faulty in many respects. The keeping clean of the zinc casing is attended with much trouble, and a deposit of zinc white is found to be left on the sheets; the inside wooden case is also found to be very prone to decay underneath the zinc.

The other system is also constructed of two wooden cases and the interstices are filled with cork waste, but has no inside casing of zinc. The interior of the box is on the other hand painted with a covering of thick clear lac, with which the box is easily kept clean. Furthermore, the tank containing the ice is of galvanized iron plates, the ice being likewise placed upon a grating, the escaping water however here being carried away through a pipe at the back of the box leading to an iron receiver below, the air valves on the doors or the sides of these refrigerators to be kept open when in use.

This latter system is now regarded here as the most suitable and as such is now accepted by and is in use at all the hospitals.

Both of the above-named systems of refrigerators are almost entirely supplied by home manufacturers, only a very small number of a somewhat similar construction to system No. 1 being imported from Germany, but these are considered as being very inferior in design and workmanship to those of home make and have met with no success in the trade.

REFRIGERATORS IN FOREIGN COUNTRIES.

The dimensions and retail prices calculated in dollars and cents for the two kinds of refrigerators are as follows:

[Outside measurements.]

	Height.	Breadth.	Depth.	Price.
	Inches.	Inches.	Inches.	
No. 1	29	26	21	$8.57
No. 2	32	31	22	13.40
No. 3	39	29	23	17.42
No. 4	51	26	23	21.44
No. 5	53	33	26	29.48
No. 6	65	31	21	26.80
No. 7	39	42	25	26.80
No. 8	44	46	26	32.16
No. 9	53	55	27	48.24
No. 10	49	45	26¾	29.48
No. 11	64	50	27	53.60
No. 12	67	25	27	24.12

Retail prices of boxes are as follows:

[Outside measurements.]

	Height.	Breadth.	Depth.	Price.
	Inches.	Inches.	Inches.	
No. 1	36	27	24	$12.06
No. 2	...	...	...	13.40
No. 3	48	48	24	17.42
No. 4	41	41	24	21.44
No. 5	54	39	27	26.80
No. 6	74	34	24	32.16
No. 7	54	53	26½	32.10

In both cases a discount varying from 15 to 20 per cent. is given to wholesale dealers.

Ice is usually secured between the months of December and March, and it is kept in ice cellars, as before mentioned.

In the principal towns some companies keep large quantities of ice in stock and retail it for daily use during the summer months, the price ruling generally at about 20 cents per 100 pounds. Even in exceptionally mild winters, like the present, sufficient stocks of ice can almost always be collected during the short intervals of frost to meet all the requirements of the country, ice 3 inches thick being all that is necessary for safe preservation. In years of ice failure, which is, however, of very rare occurrence, the necessary supplies have to be made good by imports from Norway, when an enhanced price of the article will naturally be entailed.

I am not in a position to say whether the above given prices, with the concurrent charges of freight, insurance, customs dues, etc., would allow our manufacturers at home to introduce their own works with prospects of success. If so, the object would doubtless be best attained through the aid of an active and respectable commission agent on the spot, and we have now direct steam communication with the United States, which must always facilitate such enterprises.

HENRY B. RYDER,
Consul.

UNITED STATES CONSULATE,
Copenhagen, April 3, 1890.

FRANCE.

MARSEILLES.

REPORT BY CONSUL TRAIL.

Refrigerators are not used in the Marseilles consular district, in private houses. I found one at the "American Bar," which was English make, imported by the proprietor. They are not for sale in Marseilles, the inhabitants of this city not as yet being educated up to that point where they are regarded a necessity. At the Grand Hotel Louvre et Paix, the best hotel here, probably, with accommodations for one hundred and fifty guests, the method of keeping meat and fish fresh is as follows: An ice-box of stone and cement, 3 feet high, 2 feet in width, and about 7 feet in length, is built onto the wall in the kitchen. The bottom of this box is V-shaped to carry off the melted ice; above this comes the ice in pieces no larger than a man's fist; on the ice is a cloth, and above this the meat is spread. This box consumes 100 pounds of ice per diem, costing from 1 to $1\frac{1}{4}$ cents per pound, according to the season. Switzerland supplies Marseilles with nearly all the natural ice it consumes.

Butchering is done once a day in winter and twice a day in summer, and families supply themselves with meat that often. The meat is cooked only a few hours after the killing, and, as a consequence, tender meat is an unknown luxury here.

Practically no effort whatever is made to preserve foods and liquids, the dealer furnishing a fresh supply once or twice each day, and the consumer taking only the quantity that he has immediate need of, and that must be used at once.

Ice is also manufactured to some extent, there being quite a business in caraffe frappé.

These are to be found in all the cafés and restaurants.

As to the best manner of introducing refrigerators into this district, I regret to state that there are only two articles of American manufacture successfully introduced here and carried on with success in establishments devoted solely to their exhibition and sale, the Singer sewing-machine and the Waterbury watch. How these companies succeeded when so many others either failed or abandoned the idea of introducing their goods here after corresponding with the consul and securing his services in the interest of their respective enterprises, I am not informed. Business is conducted on such different principles here from what it is in the United States that, in many cases, owing to the ignorance of the peculiarities of trade here on the part of American merchants, little more than general dissatisfaction has resulted to both the American shipper and the Marseilles consignee as the return for the consul's best efforts for extending his country's foreign trade.

Experience has proved that the better plan is for the manufacturer or exporter to come in person or by his representative. Through the consul he can then meet the merchants, and from his own observation, judgment, and business experience will be able to decide if the field is a good one for his goods and as to the manner of their introduction.

Marseilles is one of the most backward cities in all Europe, slow to take advantage of improvements, as the sanitary condition of the place proves only too well. But with perserverance and patience a good agent to sell refrigerators, speaking the language and having a knowledge of the business methods, would in a reasonable time open up an active refrigerator market here.

The city has a population of more than 375,000 inhabitants. As the summers are very long and hot and the winters generally very mild, there never being any ice formed in or near the city, some means of preserving meats and liquids would seem so necessary that the advantages of refrigerators once explained their use would soon follow as a necessary consequence.

I will be most happy to do anything in my power to assist the manufacturers in extending their trade to this quarter of the globe.

O. B. TRAIL,
Consul.

UNITED STATES CONSULATE,
  Marseilles, February 5, 1890.

LIMOGES.

REPORT BY COMMERCIAL AGENT GRIFFIN.

This subject is one that has never before been considered in this section, and the little information that answers the questions has been obtained with difficulty.

Refrigerators are almost entirely unknown throughout this section of France. The only methods employed to preserve meat, milk, etc., are placing them in cellars, wells, or cool places. As a household article the refrigerator needs to be brought to the notice of the people, and after careful conversation with many, it is thought that such an article might be introduced, the chief difficulty being the lack of ice.

It would be advisable to have the smaller sizes introduced here, as the apartments are usually quite small and room must be economized in the average household. The construction should be such as to require little or no ice; could chemicals be employed in the place of ice it would be a great advantage in introducing the refrigerator.

The sizes that could be possibly introduced are the smaller ones and so constructed as to take the place of a closet or buffet; with a place specially adapted to keep the wine cool, the arrangement should be such that the bottles can lie upon the side. The price should be moderate; but there might some be introduced of fancy wood and ornamental form that would suit the dining-room better than the kitchen or cellar, as the kitchen is always small.

Ice is manufactured, and is very scarce and very dear. I know of no families who employ it as a household article; it is used in the markets to preserve fish, and among a few pâtissiers who make ice-cream, and a few of the better restaurants. The price is from $1 to $3 per 100 pounds.

The best way to introduce refrigerators in this district would be to show their practicability in the markets where there is a great loss occasioned by the spoiling of meats and vegetables, and where it would be easy to demonstrate their utility. I would strongly recommend that only Americans be intrusted with the work of introducing these goods, for it too often happens that superior articles of American manufacture are superseded by inferior foreign goods, simply because of a lack of proper American representation in placing them upon the market.

WALTER T. GRIFFIN,
Commercial Agent.

UNITED STATES COMMERCIAL AGENCY,
Limoges, January 16, 1890.

BORDEAUX.

REPORT BY CONSUL KNOWLES.

Refrigerators are comparatively unknown in this part of France, and yet there is perhaps no part of Europe where they could be used to greater advantage. Bordeaux has the reputation of being the "best fed city" in the world, and judging from what I have already seen and tasted I am of the opinion that its fame in this respect is not undeserved.

I find in the mind of many Bordeaux people a doubt or question as to the advantage and general utility of refrigerators. By many is held the idea that the present excellence of all our markets would be decreased by the introduction and use of refrigerators.

The few refrigerators I have been able to find in this city are seemingly very imperfect and open to many great objections. They are badly constructed and are really nothing more than a crude kind of ice-box. Take a large box and line it with zinc and you will have what goes for a refrigerator here. Of the five or six I examined, only one was provided with a lid or cover. The dimensions are about 7 feet long, $3\frac{1}{2}$ feet wide by 3 feet in depth. There is no separate compartment for the ice, and this defective arrangement is evidently the cause of the meats placed in the boxes becoming wet and soggy, a condition that annoys the butcher and which is the principal objection on the part of the marketmen to the system of artificial preservation of meats.

From the appearance of the boxes I should say they are "home-made," yet I have been informed that they are manufactured and sold by a firm in Paris, which has, so far as I can learn, the monopoly of manufacturing refrigerators (?) for the European trade.

There are several artificial ice manufactories in this city, and excepting the small amount of natural ice imported from Norway, the demand is supplied by them. The average price of ice in this city is about 75 cents per 100 pounds.

I am convinced that the non-use of refrigerators in this district is due more to a lack of acquaintance with the system of artificial preservation than to any existing prejudice against it. I am positive that the general use of the American refrigerators in this city would result in economizing living expenses and would ultimately reduce the price of food products. This happy advantage and benefit need only to be demonstrated, for then it would at once surmount any and all objections urged against the system, and the refrigerator that refrigerates would speedily become not only a necessity but a blessing to every home.

There is but one successful way to introduce the American refrigerators here, and that is to place a few of them with some of our reliable people, and let them be thoroughly tried and tested. If they are productive of good results the indorsements and testimonials would give them a recommendation and standing in the market here that they would not otherwise have and without which it would be very difficult if not impossible to sell at a profit. The French will not buy a new thing before they try it. They demand first a trial and if it proves satisfactory the article is purchased, but this, however, is a condition of purchase the fairness of which too few American firms recognize.

HORACE G. KNOWLES,
Consul.

UNITED STATES CONSULATE,
Bordeaux, March 6, 1890.

LYONS.

REPORT BY CONSUL FAIRFIELD.

Refrigerators are used somewhat, but by no means as extensively as in the Northern States of our own country. As far as I have been able to find out, their use here is almost entirely confined to those keeping restaurants and to butchers.

It is the general habit of the people here to buy only what they want for the day, and at night nothing remains to be kept over.

It has seemed to me, however, that if the conveniences of a first-class refrigerator were better understood they would be much more in demand, especially if they could be furnished at a lower price than that at which they are now sold.

My impression is that it would soon be as it is now with American base-burners, which this winter are for sale everywhere, so thoroughly have they proved themselves to be a convenience and an economy.

There are no peculiar features required in the construction of refrigerators for this district. Judging from my six months' experience in housekeeping here, I think that the refrigerator which we used in our Michigan home would meet our needs as fully here as there.

The refrigerators in use in this district are manufactured in Lyons; but yet I presume that they are probably made in two or three other of the larger towns. There are three establishments in this city where they are made, but in no large quantity. They are not kept in stock, as with us in America, but each one is made to order.

The sizes are various, and somewhat irregular, each, as before stated, being made to order. The formation is decidedly inferior to those that are made with us, and less convenient in arrangement. The prices are much higher, growing out of the fact, I think, that those who make them make but few, comparatively. The establishment in this city which does the largest business sells less than one hundred a year. A small refrigerator, about a yard wide, 40 inches high, and 20 inches deep, sells at $14. I found one 8 feet high, 7 feet wide, 2½ feet deep, for which the purchaser paid $75.

Some of the ice is manufactured artificially, but more of it is brought from the Jura Mountains. It sells in Lyons at 37½ cents per 100 pounds, or 80 cents 100 kilograms.

I am also requested to report upon the best manner of introducing the American refrigerators into this district.

This is a mere matter of " business judgment."

At present refrigerators are not kept in stock by any class of merchants or manufacturers.

I think if a few dozen refrigerators of assorted sizes were put into the hands of some of the more enterprising merchants, who would have them on hand, advertise them, and exhibit them, in the same way in which American base-burners have been brought to the attention of the people of this city, that they would soon come to be regarded as a necessary article of furniture, that no well-regulated family could do without. It would not then be a necessity, as it is now, that a housekeeper should buy simply for the day.

Ed'd B. Fairfield,
Consul.

United States Consulate,
Lyons, February 25, 1890.

NICE.

REPORT BY CONSUL BRADLEY.

Referring to circular of November 25, regarding use and introduction of refrigerators in my district I beg to offer the following answers to the questions:

Very few used. None for sale.
No peculiar features required.
Manufactured by the carpenters.
Ice is brought from the mountains near Nice and sells for 5 cents per kilo (2⅕ pounds).
The resident population are very conservative—not inclined to adopt new ideas which must be paid for.
They use no iced drinks. During the winter food which is bought in small quantities is readily preserved without ice. In summer perishable food is distributed several times each day. Meat enough for the day is butchered in the morning of each day.
A number of moderate-priced refrigerators placed where they could be seen in operation would be the best means of introducing them to the people.

WM. HARRISON BRADLEY,
Consul.

UNITED STATES CONSULATE,
Nice, January 7, 1890.

NORMANDY.

REPORT BY CONSUL WILLIAMS OF ROUEN.

The request for information on the subject of refrigerators arrived at a very inopportune moment. The influenza which generally pervaded this region left its victims in no humor to discuss the merits of refrigerators, for which articles they have very little interest, as they have existed for ages without them and seem inclined to spend their money for some more ornamental piece of furniture. The climate, mode of living, and habits of the Normans do not incline them to the use of ice.

The heat is not intense, and a cellar for storage of wine or cider is attached to every domicile. The fresh sea breezes of the northern and western coast render ice useless in these ports.

The people are accustomed to buy their supplies for daily use, and their purchases of fish, flesh, fowls, and vegetables and fruits are gauged so closely to their daily necessities that a refrigerator would be considered an incumbrance in their small apartments. They consider ice as detrimental to their beverages, of which water usually forms a small constituent.

Ice is used principally at the sea ports of this consulate for packing fresh fish for transportation to Paris and other inland cities, and breweries and distillers, who, however, resort to other means for cooling. They use a number of refrigerating machines which are manufactured by Lawrence & Co. at London and at Lille and resemble very closely the De La Vergne manufactured at New York. Replying to the interrogatories:

In Boulogne-sur-Mer there are few, if any, in use. The same may be said to apply to Lille, Dunkirk, Roubaix, Dieppe, and Amiens. At one restaurant at Rouen a refrigerator was formed in the construction of the building; the most diligent research could not unearth another.

In the city of Calais only two were discoverable, one at the lunch counter of the railway station (seldom employed), the other in possession of the consular agent of the United States at his country residence, used for preserving meat and fish.

Refrigerators adapted to the use of restaurants and country residences would be most apt to meet with sales and must be of the cheapest order.

Both of those at Calais were manufactured by Kent, the English manufacturer.

ICE.

It is brought chiefly from Sweden and Norway. At Rouen the quantity imported varies from 900 to 1,200 tons; price per 100 pounds varies from 5 francs to 10 francs, according to season and quantity. At Dunkirk it costs about 40 francs per 1,000 kilograms (a gross ton) and sells at 4 francs to 6 francs per hundred-weight. At Dieppe in 1888, 189 tons were brought from Norway. In 1889, 1,838 tons were imported, all used for packing fish. At Boulogne-sur-Mer an ice-factory can produce more than enough to supply the wants of the population; there were imported, however, 634,800 pounds of ice in 1889, some of which was forwarded to other destinations and the rest used in preserving fresh fish to supply the markets of Paris and other inland towns. Very little ice is sold by the small quantity, but generally by the ton at from 25 francs to 30 francs for both the manufactured and imported.

Ice-dealers in the cities of Lille, Amiens, Boulogne-sur-Mer, Roubaix, Rouen, and other large towns would be more apt and better fitted to urge sales of refrigerators. The ice-dealer and the leading confectioner of this city state that they believe fifty refrigerators could be placed at Rouen, and if supplied with circulars and price-lists I would place them in the hands of such persons, believing thereby that I could best carry out the desire of the Department to assist the manufacturers of refrigerators in their efforts to effect sales in this consular district.

CHARLES P. WILLIAMS,
Consul.

UNITED STATES CONSULATE,
Rouen, March 10, 1890.

PARIS.

REPORT BY CONSUL-GENERAL RATHBONE.

Refrigerators are much less extensively used in France, especially in private houses, than they are in the United States. Summer heat is not so great in France, and French people are not obliged to keep a large store of provisions, having every facility to buy them when necessary, at any time, from provision dealers. These are generally provided with refrigerators, as are also coffee and eating houses, which are very numerous in Paris. Special refrigerators for cooling wines and liquors are, to a large extent, used in most of the Paris public drinking-houses, which number about 30,000.

The only difference between refrigerators used in Paris and those used in the United States is that some have a receptacle for water and that their dimensions are generally smaller, as there is not much room in French houses or apartments to locate them.

The greater number of refrigerators used in France are manufactured in this country, especially in Paris, and most of them are manufactured by the firms that sell them.

The following drawings represent refrigerators constructed by Messrs. Williams & Co., of Paris, who obtained the first prize on their account at the Paris Universal Exhibitions of 1878 and 1882. Their several dimensions and prices are also given:

No. 1.—REFRIGERATORS OF LARGE DIMENSIONS FOR THE USE OF HOTELS, RESTAURANTS, BUTCHERS POULTERERS, ETC.

Exterior dimensions.			No. of doors.	Prices.
Height.	Width.	Depth.		
Inches.	Inches.	Inches.		
82.7	49.2	27.6	2	$91.68
84.6	59.0	27.6	4	115.80
88.6	78.7	27.6	4	134.40

Thickness of sides, 3.9 inches.

No. 2.—REFRIGERATORS OF ORDINARY DIMENSIONS FOR HOTELS, RESTAURANTS, BUTCHERS, POULTERERS, PRIVATE HOUSES, ETC.

Height.	Width.	Depth.	Prices.
Inches.	*Inches.*	*Inches.*	
88, 6	39. 4	29, 5	$77 20
78 7	39. 4	24. 0	67, 55
76. 8	30. 3	24. 0	53, 08
59, 0	27. 6	21. 7	42. 46

Thickness of sides, 3 inches.

No. 3.—REFRIGERATORS SPECIALLY USED BY PORK BUTCHERS AND POULTERERS.

Height.	Width.	Depth.	Prices.
Inches.	Inches.	Inches.	
37.4	39.4	25.6	$46.32
39.4	49.2	27.6	53.08

Thickness of sides, 3 inches.

No. 4.—REFRIGERATORS FOR THE SPECIAL USE OF PASTRY COOKS.

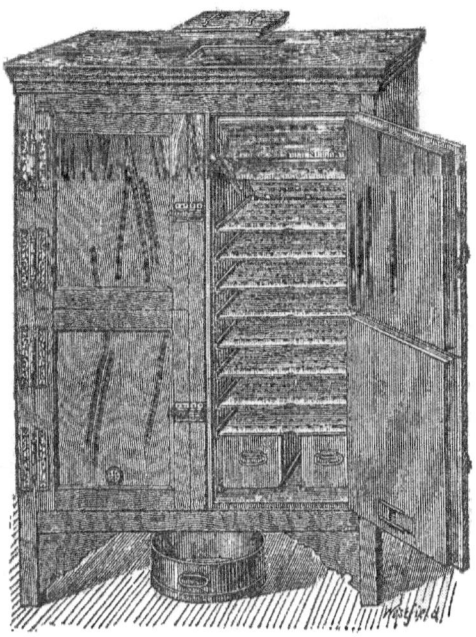

[Model with four doors and two distinct compartments.]

Description.	Height.	Width.	Depth.	Price.
	Inches.	Inches.	Inches.	
Decorated pine wood	70.9	43.8	23.6	$111.00
Varnished oak	70.9	43.8	23.6	125.45

[Model with two doors.]

Description.	Height.	Width.	Depth.	Price.
	Inches.	Inches.	Inches.	
Decorated pine wood	70.9	25.6	23.6	$57.90
Painted oak	70.9	25.6	23.6	67.55

No. 5.—REFRIGERATORS FOR THE USE OF FAMILIES.

Height, 39.4 inches; width, 23.6 inches; depth, 18.5 inches; thickness of sides, 23.6 inches; price, $26.

At the top of these above-mentioned refrigerators there is an opening under which ice is suspended in a basket. The air passing through meets the ice, and becoming much cooler and more dense goes down to the bottom of the refrigerator and escapes through an under opening, bringing out the exhalations and gases produced by the provisions stored in the interior. The warm air which penetrates into the refrigerator when the doors are open has its humidity condensed by the ice, and that humidity runs down with the water produced by the melted ice.

No. 6.—REFRIGERATOR.

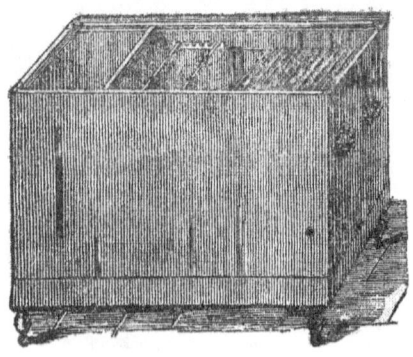

REFRIGERATORS IN FOREIGN COUNTRIES.

[New model.]

	Width.	Depth.	Height.	Price.
	Inches.	Inches.	Inches.	
No. 1	21.7	19.7	26.4	$14.50
No. 2	27.6	21.8	27.2	19.30
No. 3	33.5	22.0	28.0	24.10
No. 4	39.4	22.8	28.7	28.95
No. 5	45.3	24.0	29.5	33.80
No. 6	51.2	25.2	30.3	38.60

These refrigerators contain a support furnished with hooks to hang up provisions. In the Models Nos. 1 and 2 there are two movable gratings, and three, four, five, or six of them in Nos. 3, 4, 5, and 6.

NOS. 7 AND 8.—REFRIGERATORS FOR LIQUIDS.

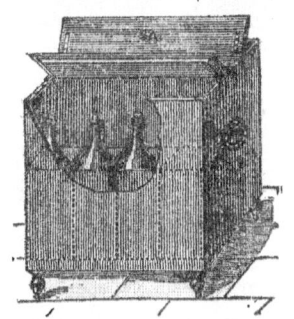

Length.	Width.	Height.	Capacity.	Price.
Inches.	Inches.	Inches.	Bottles.	
27.6	20.5	34.6	16	$19.30
30.7	16.5	34.6	18	23.15
47.2	16.5	34.6	21	29.00
53.9	20.5	34.	40	33.80

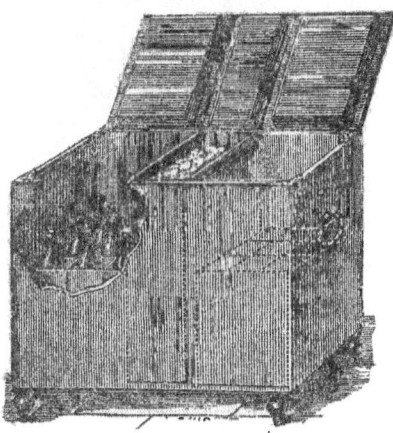

Height, 34.6 inches; length, 21.9 inches; width, 21.9 inches; price, $19.30. The ice is placed in the middle compartment.

No. 9.—REFRIGERATOR FOR MILK AND CREAM.

Price, $34.75.

No. 10.—REFRIGERATOR FOR CAFÉS, RESTAURANTS, AND DINING ROOMS.

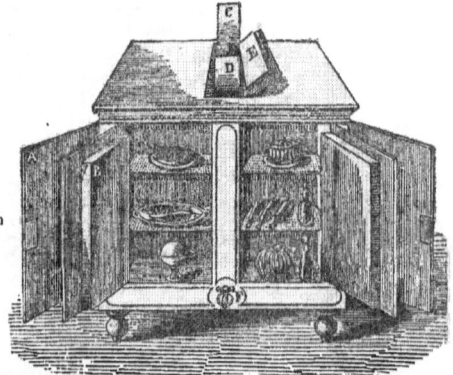

A. Exterior door.
B. Interior door.
C. Opening for the water.
D. Opening for the ice.
E. Marble cover.
F. Cock for the drawing of fresh water.

Depth, 39.4 inches; width, 20.1 inches; height, 37.8 inches; price, $72.40. (The top of the refrigerator is made of white marble.)

No. 11.—REFRIGERATOR FOR RESTAURANTS, CAFÉS, HOTELS, PASTRY COOKS, AND CONFECTIONERS, BUTCHERS, AND POULTERERS.

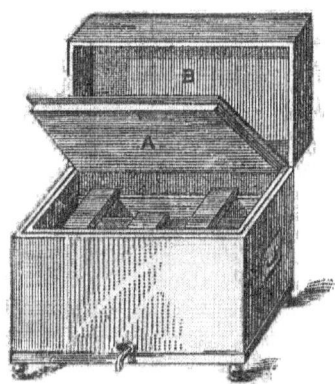

Number.	Length.	Price.
	Inches.	
No. 0	17.7	$13.50
No. 1	23.6	21.23
No. 2	27.6	25.10
No. 3	31.5	28.95
No. 4	35.4	33.78
No. 5	39.4	40.63
No. 6	43.3	50.20

These refrigerators are made like ordinary ice-boxes, lined inside with zinc, with a space of about 2½ inches between the wood and the lining, which is filled with a preparation of coke and sawdust; the ice is plac d on the bottom and on the shelves above.

There are three kinds of ice used in France: First. Natural ice, secured when possible in winter time from lakes and rivers. This ice is from 4 to 6 inches thick, and sells for 65 cents per 100 pounds. Second. Mountain ice, from Switzerland. This ice is very pure and clear and from 10 to 20 inches thick, and sells for 75 cents per 100 pounds. Third. Artificial ice, which is the most in use in France, and is made from filtered water congelated by mechanical process into blocks 6 to 10 inches thick and 4 to 5 feet in length; it is a very good ice, but does not last so long as the natural ice. The price is about 45 cents per 100 pounds.

As to the best manner of introducing refrigerators in my district, I should suggest that catalogues and price lists be sent to the following firms: Messrs. Plassard, Morin, Fillot & Cie. (Bon Marché), Rue du Bal; Messr. Directeur des Magasins du Louvre, Rue de Rivoli; Messrs. Jaluzot & Cie. (Au Printemps), Boulevard Haussman; Messrs. Druge (ménagère), 20 Boulevard Bonne Nouvelle; Messrs. Venière frères (special furnishers for drinking-houses), 2 Boulevard Richard Lenoir.

The duty on refrigerators is $1.22 per 100 pounds.

J. L. RATHBONE,
Consul-General.

UNITED STATES CONSULATE-GENERAL,
Paris, February 12, 1890.

ST. ETIENNE.

REPORT BY COMMERCIAL AGENT MALMROS.

In the town of St. Etienne (140,000 inhabitants) about one hundred refrigerators are used. From inquiries made in the towns of Roanne, 20,000, Grenoble, 45,000, Firminy, 15,000, Montbrison, 6,000, Millau, 14,000, and Le Puy, 20,000 inhabitants, the proportion of refrigerators to the number of inhabitants in each town is almost the same as in St. Etienne. In the farming districts more are used. Nearly all of the refrigerators used are by butchers, hotels, restaurants, and places where beer is sold by the glass. In St. Etienne, after much research, I have been able to hear of only four private families using refrigerators, and all of these had repeatedly and for longer periods of time sojourned in Paris, where they had become accustomed to the use of them. Refrigerators may, of course, be found in one or two families unknown to me, but I do not believe this to be the case. With the exception of thirteen, all the refrigerators used here in St. Etienne are common wooden ice-boxes, with double walls filled with sawdust, occasionally zinc lined with a hole in the bottom to let the melted ice run off. These boxes are made either by men servants employed in the houes or by carpenters. The thirteen refrigerators before mentioned as exceptions are patented by the French Government and manufactured and bought in Lyons. The most expensive of these thirteen is about 8½ feet high, 6 feet wide, and 4 feet deep, made of hard wood and the four walls lined inside with white marble slabs. In the center it has a hollow vertical partition wall, zinc lined, which at a point about two-thirds of its height is furnished on each side with six venetian blind-like slits. The top of this refrigerator can be raised and the partition wall is filled with ice from above. The front wall is divided lengthwise into halves, each of which hangs on hinges and serve as doors. The space on each side of the partition wall is again divided once by a horizontal wall. The upper compartments so produced are closed only by the two general outside doors while the two lower compartments are each, besides, provided with a separate thick inside door. This refrigerator costs 550 francs and gives satisfaction to its owner. The other twelve refrigerators are made by another manufacturer and under another patent, but none of these twelve are constructed under a different plan from the other eleven, and vary but little even as to size.

The ordinary size of these refrigerators is 7 feet high, 4 feet wide, and 26 inches deep. They are made of wood, zinc lined, and the interior constitutes but one compartment, furnished with movable shelves, and hooks on the upper portion of the walls to hang meat upon. The ice chamber, about a foot high, is immediately under the top lid, the latter constituting the upper covering of this chamber, which is drained by a zinc pipe, of about one-half inch in diameter, running down one of the inside walls of the refrigerator. These refrigerators are considered by those who use them as considerably superior to the one first described. The size mentioned is sold at 400 francs; smaller sizes are sold at 350 francs. None of the thirteen refrigerators are used by others than butchers. No refrigerators are manufactured within the limits of this consular district except the common home-made ice-boxes before referred to.

So far as is apparent from the foregoing statement, there is hardly any market in this district for refrigerators. Whether a market for them may be created depends to the greater extent upon the circumstance whether private families can be induced to use them. Hitherto these have been quite content with the comparative coolness of their cellars for the preservation of their food. It must be remembered also that the French people are a very conservative one in regard to their habits, and especially in regard to everything concerning their food. Notwithstanding this, however, as the advantages of having refrigerators are great, and as they are already much used in Paris, the example of which city the provinces are greatly inclined to follow, I believe that a considerable demand for them may be developed. But this will require much time and work, and the growth of the trade will at best not be rapid unless refrigerators can be placed in the market at prices lower than the current ones. The best way to introduce the article will be to expose it for sale in the principal towns of the district, which at present is not done by any firm; to advertise in the local newspapers, and to intrust the sale to persons who will take an active interest in pushing its sale.

No peculiar features are likely to be required in the construction of refrigerators for this district.

Full price lists will no doubt be forwarded by consuls in France in whose districts refrigerators are manufactured. In case the Department should desire it I can, however, procure them.

Ice is secured by farmers, who overflow their meadows in winter with water from the springs and brooks in which this region abounds. The ice is cut when from 4 to 5 inches thick and from four to five times during the season. The farmers sell ice delivered at St. Etienne at an average price of 5 cents per 100 pounds.

OSCAR MALMROS,
Commercial Agent.

UNITED STATES COMMERCIAL AGENCY,
St. Etienne, February 18, 1890.

GERMANY.

AIX-LA-CHAPELLE.

REPORT BY CONSUL PARSONS.

Refrigerators are used in this consular district by keepers of hotels and restaurants, by butchers and fish merchants, by vegetable and fruit dealers, and others who handle perishable goods; also in private families of the wealthier classes.

The following price list of Robert Schreiber & Co., the only important refrigerator-manufacturers in this district, will serve to show the sizes, formation, and prices of the refrigerators of a modern type in use here. The factory of Robert Schreiber & Co. is situated at Nos. 120-122 Adalbertstrasse, Aix-la-Chapelle.

PRICE LIST AND DESCRIPTIONS.

Refrigerators of solid, tasteful form, in fine polished oak. The sides of the ice-box are provided with lattices, through which the ice cools the refrigerator directly, preventing almost entirely the gathering of sweat-water, and securing a very low temperature. The ice-box is in this way better calculated to resist the pressure of the ice from within. For convenience in cleaning, the ice-box can be taken out. Upon the outer side of the refrigerator is a nickled faucet to carry off the ice-water.

	Doors.	Gratings.	Height.	Breadth.	Depth.	Weight.	Price.
			Centimeters.	*Centimeters.*	*Centimeters.*	*Kilograms.*	*Marks.*
No. 1	1	1	74	61	49	40	33
No. 2	1	1	80	77	58	62	44
No. 3	1	2	86	80	60	70	55
No. 4	1	2	103	82	64	83	66
No. 5	2	2	80	106	60	82	77
No. 6	2	4	86	108	62	90	95
No. 7	2	4	103	120	65	140	105
No. 8	2	6	121	123	67	175	120
No. 9	2	8	150	132	70	215	165
No. 10	2	8	173	143	76	285	195
No. 11	2	8	189	187	88	415	280
No. 12	2	10	200	200	88	520	420

7a. One door with 2 gratings upon the right side, the ice-box occupying the left side. Fish can be placed directly upon or between the ice. Practical for fish, vegetable-dealers, etc.

103 cm. height; 120 cm. breadth; 65 cm depth; 150 kilos.

Nos. 10, 11, and 12 have three bolts by means of which the door is tightly closed above, below, and in the middle.

Beer refrigerators, with and without place for articles of food, are delivered in every size and form; also refrigerators for *restaurateurs*, etc.

Refrigerators of fine polished oak, specially adapted for butchers, three gratings upon the left side and one upon the right side. On both sides, above, heavy rods with meat hooks, and on the right side of the ice-box, rods with smaller hooks for smaller pieces of meat.

REFRIGERATORS IN FOREIGN COUNTRIES.

	Doors.	Gratings.	Height.	Breadth.	Depth.	Weight.	Price.
			Centimeters.	Centimeters.	Centimeters.	Kilograms.	Marks.
No. 9	2	4	150	132	70	215	165
No. 10	2	4	173	143	76	285	195
No. 11	2	4	189	187	88	415	280
No. 12	2	4	200	200	88	520	420

Refrigerators in solid form, which may be conveniently taken apart. On the left, two large gratings; above, on both sides, heavy rods provided partly with ordinary meat-hooks and partly with movable hooks. On the right side of the ice-box, rods with small hooks. In these refrigerators there is room for the largest pieces of meat. The dimensions are those of the body of refrigerators, not actual measurements as above, inasmuch as a cornice 11 centimeters wide projects on both sides and in front and this cornice is not included in the given dimensions. The entire form and finish of this refrigerator are ornamental.

	Doors.	Height.	Breadth.	Depth.	Weight.	Price.
		Centimeters.	Centimeters.	Centimeters.	Kilograms.	Marks.
No. 13	2	230	200	100	850	500
No. 14	2	230	220	120	1,000	600

Refrigerators Nos. 10–14 are provided with bolts, by means of which the door is tightly closed above, below, and in the middle.

We deliver on command all refrigerators with ice-box above, provided with a new patent drop-contrivance, by which, through lattices, the cooling process follows directly, preventing the gathering and falling of sweat-water, which in the case of ice-boxes above, tightly closed, takes place to a great extent.

The prices of these refrigerators, in accordance with size, is greater by 3-20 marks.

It will be seen from this report that the refrigerator industry in this district is still in its infancy. I have spoken with several well informed men touching the matter. All had seen our American refrigerators and thought them much superior to the German in form and construction. In general, however, these American refrigerators are not known here and can only be introduced through judicious advertising, either through the press indirectly or directly through representatives of American houses. All are ready to admit the superiority of many American manufactures, and yet all have the idea that these articles are much more expensive than those of home production. Lack of definiteness in advertising is largely responsible for the misunderstanding which prevails so extensively in this respect.

It is the fact that in this district, except in wealthy families and large hotels and markets, refrigerators are generally of the most primitive form. Even in large hotels I have found ice-boxes consisting simply of a wooden box lined with zinc. This is the form of refrigerator usually found in shops of small dealers in perishable goods.

Up to within a few years ago very little attention was paid to the form or construction of refrigerators. Every carpenter and tinman was considered qualified to manufacture them, and even to-day most of the ice-boxes are ordered in this way.

Ice for the most part is manufactured in this district, the ratio between natural and artificial ice varying of course with the severeness of the winter. There are three ice factories in Aix-la-Chapelle, and ice can also be obtained from some of the largest breweries and also from dealers in natural ice. It is seldom, however, that natural ice attains a thickness of 6 inches here at Aix-la-Chapelle. It is often harvested when but 2 inches thick. Lack of means of transportation prevents the importation of natural ice from the mountainous portions of the district.

The price of ice varies greatly, as in America, from 50 pfennige to 3 marks per 100 pounds. Prices depend, as with us, upon contracts, upon quantity bought, upon season of the year, upon winter, whether mild or cold.

JAMES RUSSELL PARSONS, JR.,
Consul.

UNITED STATES CONSULATE,
Aix-la-Chapelle, February 1, 1890.

ANNABERG.

REPORT BY CONSUL HUBBARD.

The consular district of Annaberg, by reason of its elevation and latitude, is practically one immense refrigerator during almost the entire year. Lying wholly in the Ertzgebirge or Ore Mountains, on the northern border of Bohemia, at an average elevation of 2,000 feet, and in the same latitude as Labrador, in British America, the inhabitants rarely, if ever, experience an uncomfortably warm day, and *never* an uncomfortably warm night. On this great plateau, extending from the Elbe to Voigtland and embracing some of the wildest scenery in Europe, there are no natural ponds and the mountain streams are exceedingly variable, with steep and rocky beds, sometimes filled with wild, roaring torrents and again as dry and dusty as the highway in summer.

Ice is only obtained here from artificial ponds, but fortunately, and in obedience to the law of compensation, the demand for it is very limited and it is regarded as an article of luxury, not of necessity.

As before remarked the elevation and latitude are quite sufficient to insure refrigeration of both liquids and solids.

Other means than the use of ice, however, are sometimes employed here to secure the preservation of food in a condition which will not be prejudicial to the health of the inhabitants. It is a well known fact that no article of diet suffers so quickly by exposure to heat as fish, but artificial refrigeration is not required for the preservation of fish in the Ertzgebirge, as the sale of dead fresh fish is here forbidden by law. It was to me a most interesting sight to be shown the other day an enormous carp swimming contentedly about in a tub in my own kitchen. I had ordered fish for dinner the next day and the *Dienstmädchen* wished me to examine this sample, or *Muster*, as she called it and inform her whether it was satisfactory or not. The servant lifted the scaly visitor out of the water, opened and carefully examined its mouth, scrutinized its fins and scales, and explained to me that all appearances indicated the fish was in a normal state of health and entirely fit for a consul's table; to all of which this dull, phlegmatic carp submitted with the most touching resignation. It was pronounced in every respect satisfactory and again returned to its native element in the tub.

I will also remark that, with regard to hares, partridges, pheasants, and similar game, it is quite a common custom to hang them out of an attic window for three or four weeks, for the purpose it is said, of improving the flavor and it is claimed that exposure to the pure, dry, mountain air, always rich in ozone, is better than placing them in a close refrigerator.

From the foregoing statement of climatological facts it is readily seen that a good cellar in the Ertzgebirge fully meets the exigencies of the people in the preservation of food and drink and that this consular district does not offer a very brilliant prospect for the introduction and sale of American refrigerators.

I will now answer, categorically the questions proposed by the Department.

Refrigerators are used in this consular district to a limited extent, but their use is generally confined to the wealthy residents of cities.

Refrigerators which I have examined in Annaberg do not differ materially from, and are equal in all respects to, those which I have seen and used in America.

No refrigerators are manufactured in this district. I am informed that those used here are all made in Dresden.

The following tabulated statement of sizes and prices is taken from a price-list given me by Mr. G. Kirchhof, jr., a merchant of the city of Annaberg and sole agent for refrigerators in this district, so far as I know.

Height.	Width.	Depth.	Price.	Height.	Width.	Depth.	Price.
Inches.	Inches.	Inches.		Inches.	Inches.	Inches.	
31½	26	21	$7.25	44	34½	28	$15.50
34	32	25½	8.50	36½	46	26½	18.00
36½	33½	27	10.50	44	52	28	19.00
21½	40	21	10.60	64	56½	29½	34.00
34	32	25½	11.00	80	80	38	70.50
34	46	25½	13.50	93	93	40	100.00

Ice is secured in this district from small artificial ponds, and is delivered for about 20 cents per 100 pounds. The demand for it is very limited.

I would advise any American manufacturer, who desires to introduce his refrigerators into this district, to communicate with Mr. G. Kirchhof, jr., of Annaberg, a merchant of the highest honor and integrity.

I will add that the German Government imposes an import duty of about $1 per 100 pounds weight on refrigerators.

DANIEL B. HUBBARD,
Consul.

UNITED STATES CONSULATE,
Annaberg, January 28, 1890.

BERLIN.

REPORT BY CONSUL-GENERAL EDWARDS.

I have the honor to report that upon the receipt of the refrigerator circular of November 25 last, I addressed thirty-two separate inquiries to the manufacturers of and dealers in refrigerators in Berlin with regard to their prices, etc.

The sizes, formations, and prices of the refrigerators in use in this district may be seen from an examination of the price lists which accompany this report.

Ice is secured in the ordinary way from the river here which flows through the city, and is stored as with us in an ice-house built for the purpose. The price of the ice ranges from 50 pfennig to 70 pfennig per centner.

It occasionally happens that on account of an open winter the Berliners are compelled to send to Sweden for their ice, in which case the price is much dearer.

By an examination of the following illustrations the American manufacturers can readily see what chances they have in this market.

W. H. EDWARDS,
Consul-General.

UNITED STATES CONSULATE-GENERAL,
Berlin.

CHEMNITZ.

REPORT BY CONSUL MERRITT.

Refrigerators are used quite extensively in this consular district, being found in all restaurants, saloons, meat-shops, etc., and in the houses of most well-to-do private families.

Refrigerators are built here on the same principles and in the same style as in the United States, there being a number of manufacturing establishments engaged exclusively in this line.

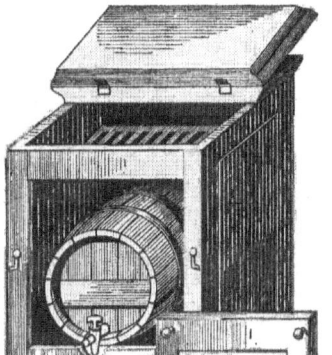

REFRIGERATORS IN GENERAL USE IN BERLIN.

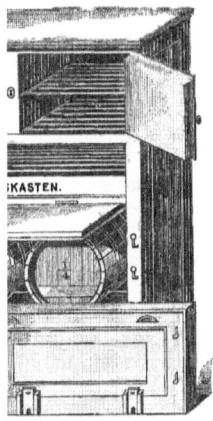
; width, 116 centimeters; depth, 76 centimeters; price, $33.32.

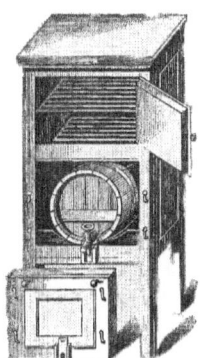
No. 11.—Height, 170 centimeters; width, 98 centimeters; depth, 79 centimeters; price, $15.47.

No. 10.—Height, 105 centimeters; depth,

; width, 13½ centimeters; depth, 66 ; price, $25.08.

No. 8.—Height, 105 centimeters; width, 107 centimeters; depth, 61 centimeters; price, $15.70.
No. 8a.—Height, 113 centimeters; width, 119 centimeters; depth, 61 centimeters; price, $17.14.

No. 7.—Height, 112 centimeters; width, 79 centimeters; depth, 60 centimeters; price, $12.88.

No. 6.—Height, 105 centimeters; depth, 58 centimeters;

width, 84 centimeters; price, $10.

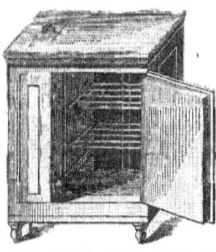
No. 4a.—Height, 89 centimeters; width, 84 centimeters; depth, 56 centimeters; price, $9.42.
No. 4.—Height, 80 centimeters; width, 75 centimeters; depth, 51 centimeters; price, $8.57.

No. 3.—Height, 80 centimeters; width, 78 centimeters; depth, 54 centimeters; price, $7.85.

No. 2a.—Height, 74 centimeters; width, 72 centimeters; depth, 51 centimeters; price, $6.43.
No. 2.—Height, 74 centimeters; width, 66 centimeters; depth, 50 centimeters; price, $5.95.

No. 1.—Height, 47 centimeters; price

REFRIGERATORS IN FOREIGN COUNTRIES.

In size the refrigerators here used run all the way from the large ones used by butchers and restaurant keepers down to the small boxes used in private families for keeping small quantities of butter, milk, etc., fresh.

As in the United States refrigerators are here made of various kinds of wood, are usually finished in oil, and are lined with plate zinc. The prices may be stated as follows:

Weight.	Height.	Width.	Depth.	Doors.	Compartments.	Price.	
						In oil.	Varnished.
Pounds.	*Inches.*	*Inches.*	*Inches.*				
80	28	30	24	1	2	$8.50	$9.25
90	36	30	24	1	2	11.50	12.50
125	44	30	24	1	4	15.50	16.75
100	52	30	24	2	4	20.25	21.50
185	44	44	24	2	6	23.75	25.75
210	60	46	24	2	8	28.50	31.00

The above prices are for retail with 4 per cent. off for cash. They are also sold on the installment plan on easy terms, at about the rates given above. The prices on larger sizes are proportionately greater.

For medicinal purposes artificial ice is used, and is sold all the year round at 1.30 marks per 100 pounds (German) equal to about 27 cents per 100 English pounds. For purposes other than medicinal, natural ice is used. This is very cheap, though only of medium quality, being delivered in winter at 15 to 20 pfennig (3½ to 4¾ cents) per 100 pounds. In the summer the price of ice is higher, but never passes above 50 pfennig, or 12 cents per 100 pounds.

The principal use to which ice is put is to keep beer and meat cold. All breweries furnish the necessary ice to their customers free of charge, and the same rule applies between the large butchers and the retail meat dealers.

For the manufacture of artificial ice, machinery of the most improved and scientific nature is employed. But ice-cutting and harvesting machinery is practically unknown, and ice on rivers and ponds is cut and harvested by hand in the old-fashioned process.

After consideration of the whole subject, I can hardly view the introduction of American refrigerators into this consular district as practicable. Refrigerators are sold here at quite as low prices as in the United States, and the freight on such bulky articles, together with the German import duty (10 marks per 100 kilograms—$1.10 per 100 pounds), would seem to shut out American competition completely.

HENRY F. MERRITT,
Consul.

UNITED STATES CONSULATE,
Chemnitz, March 8, 1890.

COLOGNE.

REPORT BY CONSUL WAMER.

Refrigerators are extensively used in this district, and almost every well-situated family is provided with one.

There are different styles. The oldest and best known refrigerator is constructed in such a manner that the space for the ice is on the side; this is, however, only for the smaller-sized ones. In the larger refrigerators the space for the ice is in the middle. A new style, by some considered the best one, has been patented by Mr. Alex. Heberer, of Mannheim. His refrigerator is constructed in such a manner that the space for the ice is on the top. The inclosed designs, "Refrigerators in general use in Cologne," show the different styles referred to.

Most of the refrigerators used in this district are manufactured in Dresden, Düsseldorf, and Gaggenau in Baden.

Ice is manufactured in all the larger towns in this district. There are three manufactories in this city. The price varies according to quantity ordered. For small amounts the price is 24 cents and for large amounts 17 cents per centner (centner equal to about 100 pounds).

W. D. WAMER,
Consul.

UNITED STATES CONSULATE,
Cologne, February 13, 1890.

CREFELD.

REPORT BY CONSUL BLAKE.

Refrigerators are in general use, not only in private families, but in hotels, wine and "restauration" dining-rooms.

All refrigerators are constructed with the ice reservoir either in the center or on the side of the zinc or porcelain lining, which will be explained more fully in answer to question 4.

Those in use in this district are manufactured in the local towns, and are largely manufactured in the city of Crefeld and shipped to the smaller towns of this district. They are made in all sizes, ranging from 3 to 10 feet square. The material used for the outside is fir wood. The lining is generally zinc, but occasionally porcelain is used about one-half an inch thick and 6 to 8 inches square. The smaller sizes have only one door, and are only in use by private families. The ice reservoir in this size is on the side and extends from the top of the refrigerator to the bottom of the zinc lining, and has a faucet at the bottom for drinking-water. Some have drainage only under the refrigerator. The larger sizes have two doors in front, with ice reservoir in the center, extending also from the top of the refrigerators to

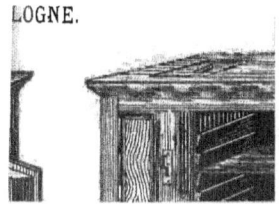

REFRIGERATORS IN GENERAL USE IN COLOGNE.

width, 81 centimeters.
No. 2a.—Height, 60 centimeters; width, 81 centimeters; depth, 56 centimeters.
No. 3.—Height, 81 centimeters; width, 81 centimeters; depth, 57 centimeters.
No. 4.—Height, 97 centimeters; width, 94 centimeters; depth, 60 centimeters.

No. 12.—Height, 188 centimeters; width, 185 centimeters; depth, 88 centimeters.
No. 7.—Height, 133 centimeters; width, 115 centimeters; depth, 68 centimeters.

No. 9.—Height, 170 centimeters; width, 72 centimeters; depth, 72 centimeters.
No. 10.—Height, 184 centimeters; width, 140 centimeters; depth, 84 centimeters.

No. 4.—Length, 150 centimeters; height, 84 centimeters; width, 60 centimeters.
No. 3.—Length, 115 centimeters; height, 82 centimeters; width, 56

the bottom of the lining, and have faucets at the bottom for drinking-water. The ice reservoir is usually made of zinc, occasionally of porcelain, and made water-tight nearly to the top, and then perforated with holes. All sizes of refrigerators have a dead air space between the wood and zinc or porcelain lining, and have an opening at the top, with a movable zinc-lined cover, through which the ice is put into the reservoir.

Refrigerators in use in meat markets have iron rods inside, near the top, provided with movable iron hooks.

Wine and dining "restaurations" have a peculiar refrigerator, usually made of carved and polished walnut, placed upon the counter in the dining room. This refrigerator is lined with zinc and has a dead-air space of about 2 inches. In the inside of this reservoir there are three or four separate coils of lead-pipe with a faucet attached to each from the outside. Beer and other kinds of liquor are forced through these pipes by means of an air-force pump.

The prices of refrigerators range from $10.47 to $95.20 and upwards, as the following table will show:

	Sizes.	Price.
	Feet.	
One door	3 by 3	$10.47
Do	3½ by 3	12.61
Two doors	4 by 3	18.08
Do	6 by 6	59.97
Do	7 by 8	84.25
Do	7½ by 8	95.20

The refrigerators lined with porcelain and furnished with ice reservoirs cost about 25 per cent more than those lined with zinc.

The weather in this locality is so mild that ice can not be obtained in sufficient quantities to supply the demands and needs of this city and locality; therefore ice-factories have been established, to supply this demand. There are now three ice-factories in active operation. Ice is furnished in large quantities for 28½ cents per 100 pounds and in small quantities for family use as follows:

	Weight.	Price per month.
	Pounds.	
One-half block	10	$1.78
One block	20	2.38
Two blocks	40	3.57

Evans Blake,
Consul.

United States Consulate,
Crefeld, February 25, 1890.

DRESDEN.
REPORT BY CONSUL PALMER.

Refrigerators are used to a very large extent in this consular district and there is hardly a hotel, restaurant, or household of any extent without one.

They are constructed in different sizes to suit various purposes. It is the general feature of these refrigerators to have one ice compartment and a second compartment for the food and liquid to be preserved. The refrigerator is generally divided by a vertical partition, the one compartment being in its lower part provided with a grating for the ice to rest on and to keep clear of the melting water, the other compartment being divided by horizontal boards to receive the articles to be preserved. In larger refrigerators the ice compartment is arranged in the middle of the furniture, the two sides forming the two compartments for receiving the articles to be preserved, the walls of the refrigerators being made double and filled with a non-conductor of heat, all the inner walls, grating, and boards in the refrigerator being covered with zinc.

The sizes, formations, and prices are varying. The refrigerators of this establishment are of oak, varnished, lined with strong zinc, and with all latest improvements. Nos. 1 to 4, one door; Nos. 5 to 8, two doors.

The measures are in centimeters for the height, width, and depth, and the prices in marks. These refrigerators are, of course, of the smaller kind and for household purposes.

Ice is stored here in cellars or in so-called "Americans," that is, overground, in light houses with double walls. The price for storing ice varies according to the character of the winter. It costs from 10 to 25 pfennig, all included, breaking, loading, carriage, and storage, per 100 pounds.

It is sold, according to variations of first costs, at subscription by the owner of the storage cellars to hotels, restaurants, and households. It is very often made a point by the restaurants that the brewery delivering the beer shall supply the ice gratis.

Formerly the refrigerators were especially constructed to receive casks with beer. This system is generally abandoned on account of the system for raising the beer in pipes by air pressure, the beer passing through a refrigerator consisting of a closed vessel filled with ice, through which the beer-pipe passes as a coiled serpentine.

In regard to the best manner of introducing refrigerators into this consular district, I can only say that the ordinary trade way of having them properly exhibited by a competent agent would be most likely to succeed.

AULICK PALMER,
Consul.

UNITED STATES CONSULATE,
Dresden, March 12, 1890.

REFRIGERATORS IN GENERAL USE IN DUSSELDORF.

Height, 103 centimeters; width, 84 centimeters; depth, 66 centimeters; price, $15.83.

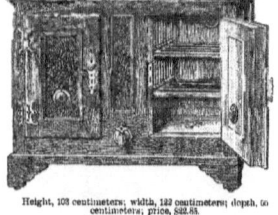

Height, 103 centimeters; width, 122 centimeters; depth, 60 centimeters; price, $22.63.

Height, 80 centimeters; width, 70 centimeters; depth, 60 centimeters; price, $10.

Height, 80 centimeters; width, 108 centimeters; depth, 60 centimeters; price, $13.09.

Height, 80 centimeters; width, 79 centimeters; depth, 65 centimeters; price, $13.09.

Height, 89 centimeters; width, 108 centimeters; depth, 63 centimeters; price, $17.85.

Height, 30 inches; width, 24 inches; depth, 19½ inches; price, $7.14.

Height, 31½ inches; width, 42 inches; depth, 24 inches; price, $10.71.

RF.

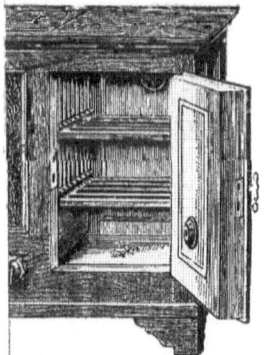

; width, 122 centimeters; depth, 66
ters; price, $22.85.

rs; width, 108 centimeters; depth,
meters; price, $13.09.

DÜSSELDORF.

REPORT BY CONSUL PARTELLO.

Refrigerators are used in this consular district, but only within the last few years to any extent. On account of the location of the district in a northern latitude, the absence of great heat during the summer months, and the fact that most of the houses have good cellars, the necessity for their use seemed not to be felt until of late, except in the case of large ones constructed as a part of the business place of butchers, dairymen, etc.

The improvement that seems to be gradually making its way in the building of houses and in other comforts and conveniences in the domestic life of the Germans has among the better classes brought into general use refrigerators.

The peculiar features of refrigerators for this market are shown by the inclosure, "Refrigerators in general use in Düsseldorf," which shows the general plan of their construction.

The refrigerators used in this district are manufactured in the several cities within the district, the principal establishments being Düsseldorf and Cologne.

Ice is secured in this district from small lakes and ponds, a number of which are kept expressly for the purpose. They are carefully watched, kept clean, and specially cared for. The cutting and hauling is about the same in manner as is customary in the States, and ice-houses are built on the same general plan.

The price of ice per 100 pounds will average about 24 cents to hotels and restaurants; the rate to private consumers about 30 cents.

GENERAL REMARKS.

Refrigerators for use of hotels, butchers, and dairy stores are constructed as a part of the establishment. The plan is mostly of wood, with stone floors, hollow sides filled with sawdust; though numbers are built of stone, sometimes marble, laid in cement, and others neatly tiled on the outside. In regard to the American system of preserving food and liquids, it is believed with the knowledge the Germans have in this respect and the general use of refrigerators it would be a difficult matter to induce them to make any change.

The general plan of the new refrigerators manufactured here is fairly good, many ideas having been copied from the American goods, and on account of the duties, that would have to be paid, added to freight, and considering the reasonable price of those manufactured in Germany, it is my opinion that it would be a difficult matter to introduce with any profit the refrigerators of American manufacture within this consular district.

D. J. PARTELLO,
UNITED STATES CONSULATE, *Consul.*
Düsseldorf April 19, 1890.

FRANKFORT-ON-THE-MAIN.

REPORT BY CONSUL-GENERAL MASON.

Refrigerators are very generally used in this district, particularly in Frankfort, where the average of wealth is high and the prevalent style of living luxurious and liberal. The use of ice for domestic purposes, which was considered a luxury a generation ago, is now regarded a necessity of daily life during the summer season. The use of ice in winter is far less general here than in the United States, for the reason that ice-water is rarely or never drank. Brewers and butchers use ice in this country precisely as they do in the United States. When winters are cold enough to furnish natural ice they gather it from ponds and overflowed meadows; when the natural supply fails they manufacture it, most of the large breweries being equipped with ice-making machinery of their own.

The refrigerators used in this vicinity are manufactured mainly by two large factories, one of which is located in Frankfort, the other in the neighboring village of Bockenheim. They are nearly all more or less literal copies of American or English ice-chests, and therefore can hardly be said to embody any important original features to distinguish them from the models from which they have been adopted. In answer to the queries concerning the sizes, formations, and prices of the refrigerators manufactured and used here, there is appended to this report a page from the illustrated circular of one of the local establishments already alluded to, which not only manufactures refrigerators at its factory in Bockenheim, a mile beyond the city limits of Frankfort, but has natural ice ponds and store-houses at Hanau, about 12 miles distant, and an artificial ice manufactory in this city from both of which ice is supplied and delivered to customers throughout the season the same as in American cities. As will be seen from the illustrations, the ice-chests offered do not differ essentially in form or construction from those in ordinary use at home. They are made of light wood, painted and grained to resemble oak or walnut, and are lined with zinc. In large chests the walls are double and filled with charcoal. The prices given in the circular are those of 1889. On account of the advance in the cost of coal and iron, mainly by reason of strikes among miners and iron workmen, the price-list of the coming season will be 10 per cent. higher than those printed in the circular, the equivalents of which are added in American currency. It will be seen that the prices given are low. This is true of all German copies of American machinery or appliances that I have examined. The quality is also more or less inferior to the original, particularly in respect to exterior finish and nicety of adjustment, but they are all good enough for every-day use, and their cheapness is an argument which, to the German purchaser, is decisive in favor of the home-made article.

No. 6 and No. 6b.—Price, $10.71 to

Nos. 1-4.—Price, $4.28 to $9.52.

REFRIGERATORS IN GENERAL USE AT FRANKFORT ON THE MAIN.

No. 0 and No. 0b.—Price, $10.71 to $18.00.

No. 10.—Price, $29.71 to $41.00.

Nos. 1-4.—Price, $4.28 to $9.54.

No. 9.—Price, $16.66 to $20.23.

No. 8.—Price, $16.66.

No. 6a.—Price, $15.47.

No. 5 and No. 5a.—Price, $8.56 to $13.00.

No. 7.—Price, $13.00 to $17.85.

Ice is secured in this district, as already intimated, both from natural and artificial sources. There are no large lakes in this region and the Main is too swift a stream to make thick ice except during the occasional severe winters, which are too rare and uncertain to be depended upon. But there are a number of small artificial ponds made by damming small streams, from which a fair supply is obtained in ordinary seasons.

From an illustrated catalogue before me it is apparent that the Germans have horse-plows, steam traction, and all the essential modern improvements in ice gathering. Their store-houses are of wood with the exterior walls filled with tan-bark, and in respect to convenience of equipment are in no respect inferior to the great establishments along the Hudson River. Prices vary according to the success which attends the harvest of natural ice and consequently the proportion of artificial ice which has to be made to meet the deficit in the natural supply. The schedule for 1890 has not yet been announced, but thus far little or no ice has been gathered, and as it is now probably too late to expect more than a limited harvest of thin and poor quality, it is probable that prices during the coming summer will be considerably higher than during the warm months of last year, which was a fair average season. The prices which ruled then may be accepted as the average for ordinary seasons and were as follows:

For daily delivery from April 12 until September 30. Per day for the season, 5 pounds, $4.28; 10 pounds, $5.99; 15 pounds, $8.33; 20 pounds, $10.

Monthly subscription for not less than thirty consecutive days, per day, 5 pounds, 3½ cents; 10 pounds, 4¾ cents; 15 pounds, 6 cents; 20 pounds, 7½ cents.

Persons living near the depots of the company in this city can save 10 to 15 per cent. from these prices by taking their ice from the depot instead of the delivery-wagons.

Coming finally to the main question whether there is in this district any practical field for the introduction and sale of American refrigerators, it would seem to follow from what has been already stated that the prospect is not highly encouraging. Some years ago refrigerators of the Brainard (American) pattern were introduced here by means of originals or copies, but they did not please and the effort was abandoned. If there is an American refrigerator capable of being made in suitable sizes and patterns for the varied uses of families, cafés, and hotels, and which, besides being superior to those in ordinary use, is so original and distinctive in construction that it can be protected by patent from indiscriminate imitation, there might be an opportunity here for its successful introduction. The duty on fixtures of that class imported from foreign countries is $1.19 per 220 pounds, but the bulkiness of such merchandise in proportion to its value would make the question of ocean freights of vital importance.

In the manufacture of artificial ice, or almost any industrial application of chemistry or other kindred science, the Germans are masters, and have little to learn from any other people. Their machinery, implements, and many forms of manufacture lack originality and the perfection of finish and fitting which characterizes American goods, but they manage even in these departments to make something that will answer the purpose, and to make it cheap. In respect to a fixture so simple and easy to imitate as a refrigerator they would probably be very difficult people to compete with on their own ground.

FRANK H. MASON,
Consul-General.

UNITED STATES CONSULATE-GENERAL,
Frankfort-on-the-Main, January 31, 1890.

HAMBURG.

REPORT BY CONSUL JOHNSON.

On receipt of the Department's circular of November 25, 1889, I applied to the proper Hamburg authorities for the information called for in the same; but, owing to the dilatoriness of these authorities, I was only furnished with a very unsatisfactory reply under date of March 10, 1890. This report being non-responsive to the interrogatories propounded in the Department's circular, I have endeavored to collect the information myself and submit the result below.

Refrigerators are used in almost every household in the towns and cities of this district; their use is, however, confined to the summer season alone, the cellars in most houses being sufficiently cool to preserve articles of food, etc., during the winter months. The restaurants and beer taverns, however, make an exception, using ice in their refrigerators almost throughout the year.

There are hardly any peculiar features required in the construction of the refrigerators. They vary in size only and consist of wooden cases lined with zinc, a space of a few inches between the wood and the metal being filled with thoroughly dried sawdust. Those in use in this district are mostly manufactured in Hamburg or Altona. As the simplest means of illustrating the sizes, formations, and prices of the refrigerators in use in this district, I annex an illustrated price-list of the Actien-Gesellschaft-Eiswerke, Hamburg, which is about the most important concern of the kind in Hamburg. Only these seven sizes are constantly manufactured and kept in stock, but orders for larger ones are executed to suit the purchasers. There are only three or four firms in this city who store and deal in ice. The ice is cut in canals and small lakes near the city and stored in ice-houses very similar to those in use in the United States. The quality, however, is poor, owing to the filthiness of the water; the ice is consequently fit only for cooling purposes. The price per 100 pounds varies from 12 to 15 cents; after mild winters, however, it has commanded as high as 18 cents.

REFRIGERATORS IN GENERAL USE IN HAMBURG.
PRICE-CURRENT.

No. 1.—Price, $3.67.

No. 2.—Price, $8.93.

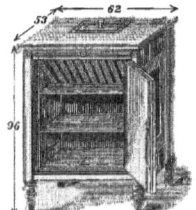

No. 3.—Price, $10.71.

No. 4.—Price, $11.90.

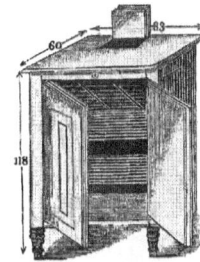

No. 5.—Price, $15.47.

No. 6.—Price, $22.51.

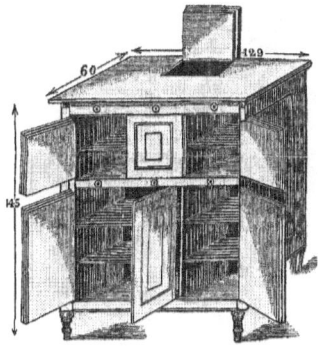

No. 8.—Price, $32.13.

The consumption of ice in the city of Hamburg alone, exclusive of the breweries, slaughter-houses, etc., is about 100,000 tons per annum.

As the best means of introducing refrigerators into this district I should suggest a direct communication with the dealers through the aid of our consular officers.

CHAS. F. JOHNSON,
Consul.

UNITED STATES CONSULATE,
Hamburg, February 28, 1890.

[Translation.]

HAMBURG CHAMBER OF INDUSTRY,
Hamburg, February 24, 1890.

His Honor Senator Dr. BURCHARD, etc.,
Present:

The Chamber of Industry has the honor to comply with the request of January 17, received January 20, 1890.

There can be no doubt that ice-boxes, and not other cooling-apparatus, are meant by the term "refrigerators," as it appears defined in the two passages following interrogatories 1-5 of the inclosure which is returned.

Refrigerators are extensively used here; they are of various sizes and construction, and the prices also vary greatly according to quality.

As far as we know there are no manufactories in Hamburg which build refrigerators on a large scale. Some few are manufactured at Ottensen (near Hamburg), but otherwise they are imported from districts with cheaper lumber and labor-prices.

Respectfully,

THE CHAMBER OF INDUSTRY,
BAUR, *President.*

MAYENCE.

REPORT BY COMMERCIAL AGENT SMITH.

Refrigerators are used to a considerable extent in this consular district by people of the upper and middle classes, and they are coming more and more into general use all the time. They will soon be found in every family of fair standing.

So far as I have been able to ascertain, no peculiar features of construction are called for by the public. The chief requirement is that they should be cheap, and they are sold at remarkably low figures—prices with which, I think, the Americans could not possibly compete with any satisfaction. Price always plays a very important rôle with the German, and is, to a large extent, the determining factor with him in the purchase of many articles. The manner of construction of the different kinds of refrigerators chiefly in the German market will be shown by the descriptive catalogues herewith transmitted. Slight improvements of various kinds in construction are constantly taking place.

The refrigerators sold by the leading firms here at Mayence and at Wiesbaden, a city near by of some 55,000 inhabitants, are all of German make, and are manufactured in Dresden, Gaggenau, near Rastatt, in Baden, at Düsseldorf, at Aschaffenburg, and at Cassel. These are said to be the leading places of manufacture in Germany. There are no others of any account, I have been told, except, may be, at Chemnitz, where handsome and expensive articles, not much purchased by the general public, are manufactured.

The best refrigerators now made in Germany, a large dealer informs me, are probably those manufactured at Gaggenau, in Baden. They are constructed upon a new principle and have been in the market only two or three years. Being the best, they are also the dearest, but not much dearer than other makes.

The Eschebach & Hausner refrigerator (Dresden) are lined with zinc and the spaces between the sides are filled in with wheat chaff, I am told. All of their refrigerators, except the catalogue numbers 1701, 1702, 1703, 1704, 1705, 1706, and 1735 are made of oak, with the inlaid parts varnished to resemble maple, while these numbers are of old oak, with the inlaid pieces painted to look like English walnut; that is, like light walnut. The refrigerators Nos. 1711 to 1714 have a good lock, with a nicely nickel-plated brass escutcheon and key, while all the others have a double lock with a handle, the key, escutcheon, and handle being of brass, nicely nickel-plated. The refrigerators 1701 to 1719 and 1735 have each a divisible grate, so that but half of it need be taken out whenever desired. All the sizes 1701 to 1722 and 1735 are provided with removable ice chests or boxes, to make the cleaning of them easy. The stop-cocks for letting the water off are all of nicely nickel-plated brass. The tops of the refrigerators present a smooth surface when the lids, by which the ice is let into the refrigerators, are down, as the handles to them are made to fit into them so as to make a flat surface. The upper outer surface of the lids is of iron plate. Provision is made for the carriage of the sweat-water that forms on the ice-boxes into a receptacle therefor, and thus prevent it from collecting on the bottom of the compartment for food. The refrigerators 1701 to 1722 and 1735 are sold with pinked ice-boxes, to accelerate the refrigerating. An enameled ice-water cooler can be had with all the refrigerators for a dollar or two extra, and a filter also to go with it. The ice is put into the refrigerators at the top into a compartment that reaches from the top to the bottom of the refrigerator. The cooling is effected from the sides of these compartments.

On Eschebach & Haussner's refrigerators the trade are given 20 per cent. discount on the catalogue prices. The packing and freight are borne by the trade.

One dealer selling Eschebach & Haussner's refrigerators informed me that he sells most of No. 1713 on the catalogue, which is sold at $8.56 retail, without ice-water cooler. The wholesale price is $7.14.

The refrigerators of the Eisenwerke Gaggenau, in Baden, are constructed upon what is known as the jalousie system; that is, ventilated by means of slats or bars, upon the principle of the Venetian blind. In this refrigerator the cooling is done from the top, which is its leading characteristic and a departure from the established method, I understand. The inventor of it claims that thereby more room is obtained in the refrigerator with the least waste of ice and lowest degree of temperature with proper circulation of air. The ice-chest or box hangs freely in the upper part of the refrigerator. It is made with slats. The cold air streams out between the slats and naturally passes down into the refrigerator, while the arising warm air becomes commingled with the cold streams coming from above and brings about a regular circulation of air. The water, as it condenses in the ice-box, drops from slat to slat, collects at the bottom, and runs through a pipe into a reservoir, where it can be used to cool liquids, etc. The ventilation is claimed to be superior to that in other refrigerators. Hitherto it has been effected through the door in front and the back, which the inventor of the Gaggenau refrigerators claims has been only to bring in warm air without actually airing the refrigerator. The bad air he gets out by means of a pipe through which it ascends. Through this arrangement the refrigerator is freed of unpleasant odors and the melting of the ice materially retarded by the exclusion of all warm air. The filling is of slag-hair.

Of Schmidt & Keerl's refrigerators I have only a descriptive sheet, with cuts of the refrigerators and their sizes upon it. Their wholesale prices have been given me by a dealer. On these prices they allow 10 per cent. off, but the packing and freight equalizes this. Three months' time is granted, with a discount of 1½ per cent. for cash payments made within two weeks. The refrigerator that sells best is No. 3, sold at about $9.50 retail. Their refrigerators are constructed on the jalousie system, are lined with strong zinc, and the spaces between the sides are filled in with slag-hair. They all have removable ice-boxes, permitting easy cleansing. Waste water is carried off by a pipe into a basin that goes under the refrigerator, when there is a superfluity of water through neglect to let it off by the regular stop-cock. Their refrigerators can all be had either plainly painted or nicely varnished. The refrigerating is done from the sides of the compartments or boxes containing the ice.

 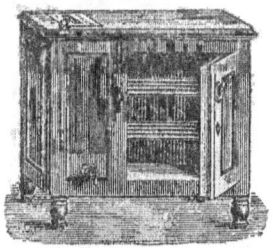

No. 2.—Height, 30⁷⁄₁₀ inches; length, 26⁷⁄₁₀ inches; depth, 19 inches; weight, 79 pounds; price, *$6.50.

No. 3.—Height, 31½ inches; length, 31½ inches; depth, 19⁸⁄₁₀ inches; weight, 90 pounds; price, $8.50.
  a This lid raises and the ice goes in here, from top to bottom.

* The prices are all for varnished refrigerators.

No. 5.—Height, 35½ inches; length, 32$\frac{2}{10}$ inches; depth, 20⅔ inches; weight, 116 pounds; price, $10.25.

No. 6.—Height, 30$\frac{7}{10}$ inches; length, 34$\frac{7}{10}$ inches; depth, 22$\frac{3}{10}$ inches; weight, 154 pounds; price, $12.

No. 7 a.—Height, 39$\frac{3}{10}$ inches; length, 45$\frac{3}{10}$ inches; depth, 23$\frac{1}{10}$ inches; weight, 215 pounds; price, $16.66.

No. 7 b.—Height, 50 inches; length, 45$\frac{1}{10}$ inches; depth, 26½ inches; weight, 286 pounds; price, $22.

a Ice receiver extending from top to bottom of refrigerator.

REFRIGERATORS IN FOREIGN COUNTRIES. 135

No. 17. (For a store).—Height 50 inches; length, 55 inches; depth, 31½ inches; weight, 484 pounds; price, $29.75.

No. 16. To hold food and wine for a store.—Height, 51/₆ inches; length, 55 inches; depth, 31½ inches; weight, 455 pounds; price, $25.

No. 27.—Height, 59 inches; length, 55 inches; depth, 31½ inches; weight, 484 pounds; price, $32.13.

No. 19.—Height, 62₁⁰₀ inches; length, 35½ inches; depth, 26½ inches; weight, 286 pounds; price, $20.25.

REFRIGERATORS IN FOREIGN COUNTRIES. 137

No. 36 (for butchers and hotels).—Height, 62 1/10 inches; length, 49 inches; depth, 27½ inches; weight, 528 pounds; price, $38.

No. 9.—Height, 43 3/10 inches; length, 34 6/10 inches; depth, 22 8/10 inches; weight, 176 pounds; price, $15.23.

There are two or three more cuts of refrigerators for large butchers and hotels, which I do not think it necessary to give.

In conclusion, I have to say that the catalogues and prices furnished by me have been given me by dealers, and that the trade expect to make a profit of 20 to 30 per cent. on refrigerators sold by them.

JAMES H. SMITH,
Commercial Agent.

UNITED STATES COMMERCIAL AGENCY,
Mayence, March 3, 1890.

MUNICH.

REPORT BY CONSUL MEALEY.

Refrigerators are used, but very few; outside of the city of Munich you may say not at all. The hotels and restaurants use them, but not all of them, and very few private families make use of them. The business in perishable articles of food is done by small stores or shops, of which an immense number are located in every quarter of the city, and it is the universal custom for people to buy from day to day such articles as they need. In fact very many buy twice a day; that is, for each meal.

The only thing, or the main thing, asked for by would-be purchasers of refrigerators here is that they be cheap, and the endeavor of the maker is to supply a very cheap article. There is only one peculiar feature to be noted: the ice-box is made to receive a rectangular block of artificial ice about two feet long and about five inches square, the ice being first placed in a sort of a wire cage which just fits and has handles to facilitate its being lowered and raised from the ice box in the refrigerator.

I can learn of none that are sold here which are manufactured anywhere except here in Munich, and by the persons who sell them. I can only learn of those people who sell them here in Munich.

Both natural ice and artificial ice are used, the former by butchers, beer breweries, and large consumers, the latter mostly by private consumers, the artificial ice being cleaner. But compared with the use of ice in the United States there is very little ice used here. It is a rare thing for a private family to use ice in any manner, and when they do it is a very small quantity. There are several reasons for this. Suffice it to say that the weather in summer is so much cooler than in the United States that there is not the same demand for the use of ice; then the custom of buying in very small quantities everything needed in the house, and the cellars of the houses are made use of by house-keepers for the keeping of all articles that may be perishable. The price for artificial ice, delivered in the refrigerator, is about 75 cents per 100 pounds; the price of natural ice about 70 cents per 100 pounds. The ice is delivered to private families twice a week in summer and about once a week in spring and fall. Some restaurants and cafés have refrigerators for keeping the barrel of beer they are drawing from, but they are few as the beer is considered to be somewhat spoiled by being kept too cold by means of ice. I very much doubt if the sale of refrigerators could by any possible means be much increased here, as there is very little demand for them, and, as I have stated above, the climate does not make their use very pressing or necessary.

EDWARD W. MEALEY,
Consul.

UNITED STATES CONSULATE,
Munich, February 4, 1890.

STETTIN.

REPORT BY CONSUL FAY.

The common house ice-chest is extensively in use and is sold at a very low price in Stettin.

One may purchase an ice-chest sufficiently large for family use for $5. They are very conveniently arranged and well made.

As the duty on refrigerators of any sort is very high, about $1.25 per 100 pounds, I imagine it would be hard to compete with the German manufacturers in this branch at the prices at which they are sold in Stettin.

The larger class of refrigerators, such as are in use by provision dealers and butchers in America, are not to be seen here.

Ice being so very plentiful and cheap, such dealers fill their cellars therewith in winter and preserve the meats, etc., therein during the hot season. Ice is retailed at one-eighth to one-quarter cent per pound during the summer season.

ANDREW F. FAY,
Consul.

UNITED STATES CONSULATE,
Stettin, February 9, 1890.

HOLLAND.

AMSTERDAM.

REPORT BY CONSUL ECKSTEIN.

Refrigerators are used in Holland in nearly all hotels, restaurants, cafés, butcher-shops, hospitals, and in other public institutions, but only to a limited extent in private families or boarding-houses.

By the general public, refrigerators are regarded more in the light of an article of luxury than of necessity so far as their use is concerned in private houses.

A variety of circumstances obviate the necessity of their use, chief amongst which are that intensely hot weather rarely prevails many days together during any summer, whilst there always exists more or less humidity or moisture in the atmosphere, which keeps articles of food, such as meat, fish, vegetables, etc., in a sound condition for such time as such supplies are ordinarily provided for.

Besides there exist in this country, in the large cities, smaller towns, and even in the country, great facilities for procuring all sorts of perishable articles conveniently for daily use.

I am assured no particular or special features are required in the construction of refrigerators for use in this country for either preserving food or liquids. In answer to this point, more detailed information is conveyed in reply to the fourth question.

Most of the refrigerators used in Holland are imported from Aschaffenburg, Bavaria, and other places in Germany, and some are imported from England and France.

Formerly they were an article of domestic production to a certain extent, but their manufacture in this country has stopped, from all I can learn.

The greater part of the ice used in this country consists of sweet-water or artificial ice. It is manufactured by the principal breweries for their own consumption as well as for sale.

There are also two large ice companies, one operating in natural ice and the other manufacturing the artificial article.

Natural ice is secured here by being cut out of the river Amstel, in ever varying quantities and qualities from year to year, according as the season is mild or severe. It is also imported in large quantities from Norway.

The price per 100 pounds is about 0.50 florin (20 cents), and in large quantities, by the ton of 2,200 pounds, it can now be contracted for and delivered at 8 to 9 florins ($3.20 to $3.60) per ton.

As is represented to me, it would be advisable for American manufacturers of refrigerators who desire to introduce into this country successfully the product of their manufacture, and with a prospect of finding a permanent market for it here, to consign to some trustworthy person or persons, as agents in this city and in a few of the other large cities in this country, small assortments of refrigerators of different styles and sizes and varying prices.

Having secured energetic and pushing agents for the introduction and sale of the article the demand for them may spring up if the prices of our manufacturers can compete with those at which the product of other countries is selling here.

As such an agent I can unhesitatingly mention and recommend the firm of Fred Stieltjes & Co., at Amsterdam.

I would also mention here the firm names of the principal retail dealers in refrigerators at Amsterdam, with whom some of our manufacturers of refrigerators may find it to their advantage or desirable to correspond or make offers to.

They are: E. B. Vieth, F. L. A. de Gruyter, L. Dake & Son, Widow Kirchmann & Co., J. Peignat & Co., L. A. C. Victor, Becht & Dyserinck, and J. B. Gorris.

D. ECKSTEIN,
Consul.

UNITED STATES CONSULATE,
Amsterdam, March 28, 1890.

ITALY.

CATANIA.

REPORT BY CONSUL LAMANTIA.

There are no manufactories of any such articles, and the American refrigerator is entirely unknown in this section of country.

I have also made inquiries of the several hotels and restaurant proprietors on the subject, who told me that they use no refrigerators in their establishments, as they have no use for them, for the reason that during the summer season they buy sufficient provisions to do for the daily consumption.

Mr. M. Patriarca, however, an importer and wholesale and retail dealer in national and foreign goods, of this city, informs me that he imports small refrigerators from Germany, the size being 20 inches wide by 24 long and 30 high, which he sells for 45 lires each, but says that there is a very little sale of them, on account of such a high price; consequently it is a hard matter in this section of country to dispose of such articles at more that 30 lires ($8.68) each. If, however, he adds, small American refrigerators of said size, economically constructed, could be laid in this market for 20 or 25 lires ($3.86 to $4.83) each, he thinks at such a price their introduction, extension, and sale could be easily secured.

As far as ice is concerned, there are two ice factories in this city, supplying the wants of the people, and the same is sold at 9 lires per 100 kilos.

VINCENT LAMANTIA,
Consul.

UNITED STATES CONSULATE,
Catania, February 15, 1890.

FLORENCE.

REPORT BY CONSUL DILLER.

Refrigerators are used in this district by the leading hotels, pensions, coffee, and beer houses, and by a few of the prominent residents and clubs.

No peculiar features are required in their construction. Many of them are of the most primitive construction, being merely an ordinary box, with a compartment for ice, not lined, with perforated bottom. The better kinds used are generally poor imitations of the American or

English styles, and are manufactured in Milan and Germany. The sizes and formation are similar to the above, with the exception that, instead of wood, zinc or tin is used as the outside covering, and the non-conducting space between the outside and inside lining is greatly contracted, thus deteriorating from their value as preservatives. The imitation American refrigerators, in three sizes, are sold at $9, $17, and $27 respectively, and the English, in the form of benches, in two sizes, at $25 and $30.

The ice used in refrigerators in this district comes from the Appenines, is of poor and porous quality, and is sold at about 20 cents per 100 pounds. Pure clear ice for drinking purposes comes from Poretta, on the boundary between Florence and Bologna, and costs about 25 cents per 100 pounds.

The usual way of preserving food and liquids at the present time is by keeping perishable articles in cool cellars or by suspending them in wells.

I am of the opinion that if a cheap form of refrigerator, made of wood, was introduced it might in time be quite generally adopted, but in order to sell it at a low price, the adjuncts, such as lock, knob, hinges, zinc, wire fittings, and castors should be unattached to the wooden case, accompanying the same, however, in a separate package, to be fitted after arrival.

According to the Italian tariff the duty on manufactures of wood averages about $9 per 100 kilos (220.46 pounds), while the duty upon the fittings, such as I have mentioned, would be at least $14 per 100 kilos; and according to the manner of estimating duties in Italy the duty would be levied on the complete machine, as a whole, at the higher rate, while on the contrary, if the fittings were not attached, the duty would be levied on each article separately, according to weight and kind of material. This is an important item to be considered in exporting refrigerators to Italy. It is not the component material of which an article is composed which regulates the duty charged on the article as a whole, but upon any other material which forms a part of it, however small, upon which the duty is greater than that of the component part, if attached to it.

ISAAC R. DILLER,
UNITED STATES CONSULATE, *Consul.*
Florence, January 17, 1890.

GENOA.

REPORT BY CONSUL FLETCHER.

Introductory.—It is no exaggeration to state that more refrigerators can be found in any city of 10,000 inhabitants in the United States than in this entire consular district of over 900,000 souls. Further, it is safe to say that no more ice is consumed in the city of Genoa with its 180,000 inhabitants than in any city of the United States whose population contains not more than 10,000 or 12,000 people. All this, too, in a country with mild winters, warm spring-time and fall, and very hot summers.

Several reasons can be given for this limited demand for refrigerators and ice, a few of which are as follows:

The Italian people do not consider ice necessary at any season in order to enjoy good health or a good appetite; many of them believe ice injures rather than soothes the palate and stomach.

Economy is practiced here to such an extent that fully ninety-seven families out of every one hundred purchase only sufficient food for daily wants. Nothing remains over for the morrow—not even bread or vegetables. Such being the case, the question, "Why are not refrigerators used in the homes of the Genoese more?" is easily answered.

The use of refrigerators in this consular district is very limited.

There is nothing peculiar in the construction of those in use here.

Those now in use were either brought from Germany or England. Of late the Italians have commenced the manufacture of these articles, but on a limited scale.

The sizes, formation, and prices of refrigerators offered for sale here are as follows:

Portable refrigerators.
[All finely polished in varnish and lined with zinc.]

Fig. A.

WITH ONE DOOR.

	Height.		Width.		Depth.		Price.	
							Improved quality.	Common quality.
	Feet.	Inches.	Feet.	Inches.	Feet.	Inches.		
FIG. A.—No. 1	2	5.13454	2	0.01631	1	7.20179	$6.95	$5.60
No. 2	2	6.70938	2	3.55970	1	9.65405	7.70	
No. 3	2	7.49680	2	5.13454	1	11.62260	8.90	6.75
No. 4	2	9.85906	2	6.70938	2	0.41002	10.60	8.70

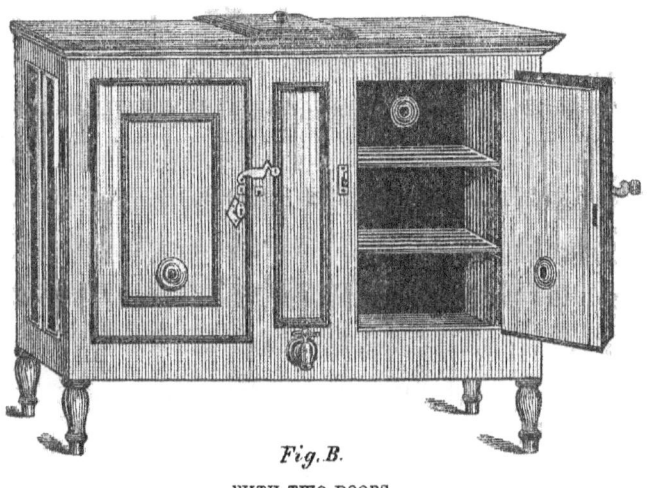

Fig. B.
WITH TWO DOORS.

	Height.	Width.	Depth.	Price of Improved quality.
	Feet. Inches.	Feet. Inches.	Feet. Inches.	
Fig. B.—No. 5	2 5.18454	3 1.40245	1 7.6855	$12.55
No. 6	2 7.49680	3 6.52068	1 11.62200	15.45
No. 7	3 3.37100	3 3.37100	2 0.41002	17.40
No. 8	3 7.30810	3 7.30810	2 1.19744	19.30

Ice fit for table use is taken from the little ponds and streamlets along the mountain sides (along the maritime Alps and Appenines). It is packed in small caves especially prepared for the purpose in the hill sides, near the place where it is harvested. When these caves are nearly filled a covering of leaves from chestnut trees, about two feet in thickness, is placed on top of the ice—nothing more.

Ice is brought into Genoa both by wagons and by rail. A city tax of about 39 cents per 100 pounds is imposed on all ice conveyed within the gates of Genoa. But, notwithstanding this tax, cartage, etc., the article is sold and delivered where ordered at $1 per 100 pounds.

* * * * * * *

Conclusions.—As already stated, the people here purchase day by day the requirements for the day—no more. This habit is also practiced as much as possible at hotels and restaurants, and the consequence is that very few refrigerators can be found even in those places. Some of them have common boxes, in which is placed the ice, and over which are thrown woolen cloths or blankets.

Some of the liquor shops have boxes also, with ice covered as above. But in the 2,000 or more wine shops and liquor stores in this city, it is no strain of imagination to say that you can not find a particle of ice in more than 150, no matter how hot the summers may be.

Fig. C.—Beer Refrigerator, from $23.30 to $48.55.

As far as personal observation goes the people of this district prefer wine, liquor, and even water, each in its normal temperature, much more than when cooled by ice or by any artificial process.

Foreigners, chiefly Americans and English, are the great patrons of ice in this part of the country; but even those people, after a lengthened stay here, adopt the habits of the natives and abstain from the use of this cooling substance.

Managers of hotels, owners of provision stores, of restaurants, liquor shops, and meat markets, might be pursuaded to invest in American refrigerators providing parties interested in the sale of such wares were here personally to point out the merits of the goods.

The establishment of agencies under foreigners, unless said foreigners have money invested in the manufacture of the wares, will not pay in Genoa.

JĀMES FLETCHER,
Consul.

UNITED STATES CONSULATE,
Genoa, February 1, 1890.

PALERMO.

REPORT BY CONSUL CARROLL.

Refrigerators were introduced into Palermo about one year ago, since which, it is understood, about forty have been sold.

To suit the requirements of this district, refrigerators should be of medium size, gorgeous in finish, and moderate in price, the maximum not to exceed 100 lire, or about $20 each. Walnut, or imitations thereof, embellished by various decorative designs, would take well, so would also pitch-pine, similarly finished. All articles, in order to find favor or a market here, must be of a gaudy nature, as a rule.

The refrigerators in use here are of German manufacture, but are generally represented to have been manufactured in the United States.

Refrigerators should be of various sizes and forms, showy or attractive in appearance, with brass or nickel knobs or other showy material. The most expensive refrigerator in Palermo is understood to be offered for 250 lire, or about $50, but few, if any, at this price can be sold. The refrigerator which is understood to have met with the most favor here thus far, costs 60 lire, or about $12. Refrigerators whose forms are somewhat similar to book-cases or ladies' dressing-cases, containing a mirror, would, it is said, meet with great favor here.

Ice is manufactured in Palermo, and costs, at retail, from 4 to 6 cents per kilogram, depending on the season and the weather; the wholesale price thereof varying in like manner, but never being less than 2 cents per kilogram, and often 3 or 4, or more. Snow is also used, and costs from 3 to 5 cents per kilogram retail and about 2 or 3 wholesale, the price, however, varying as in the case of ice.

Unquestionably not only refrigerators but all other articles of American manufacture are more popular here than those of any other country, and the best proof of this is the fact that nearly every dealer or merchant advertises American articles for sale, while the great majority have not a single article of American manufacture in stock; but as a good business appears to be transacted in thus misleading the public, dealers are happy and content.

The best manner of introducing refrigerators here is for dealers therein to send samples of each variety to some reliable person, in order that those desiring them may see by comparison the difference between the spurious and genuine American article. They should be offered for sale on the same conditions accorded dealers here by the Germans, English, etc., which is from three to six months' credit. Few, if any, houses in Palermo can be induced to pay upon delivery.

There is no method of preserving foods or liquids save leaving the doors and windows of butcher-shops open during the night, in order to let in the cool air, the reverse being done during the day. In private houses liquids, and such meats, etc., if any, as may be in the house, are placed on the balconies with a view of preserving them.

Living is so expensive here, and the people generally so poor, that the purchase of meats and certain other articles of food has become somewhat of a science, so that when the meal is completed there is nothing left, as a rule, to preserve. Hence the necessity for refrigerators is not great.

PHILIP CARROLL,
Consul.

UNITED STATES CONSULATE,
Palermo, January 29, 1890.

SOUTHERN ITALY.

REPORT BY CONSUL CAMPHAUSEN, OF NAPLES.

In answer to questions 1, 2, 3, and 4 of the circular, I respectfully report that the use of the refrigerator is at present almost as unknown in this district as in the time of the old Romans.

The Neapolitan keeps no private stores on hand, nor is provision made for more than a single day. Thus, after the hour of dining, even in houses of the wealthy, little else than bread and macaroni will be found.

Most Neapolitan families employ male cooks, who purchase all provisions, and it is not considered advisable to allow them more than the limited sum of money necessary for each day's supply. Every morning the cook provides a stock for the day of meat, fish, vegetables, fruit, and milk. Butter is brought to customers in pails of fresh water. Since the spring of 1885 Naples obtains an immense quantity of the purest water from the Apennines, which is always quite cold, even during the hottest part of the summer.

As Italians prefer olive-oil in cookery to butter, the latter is only bought for table use, and not kept on hand in any quantities.

Butchers, restaurants, wine merchants, fish venders, and dealers in petroleum have grottoes in which to preserve their wares. Tufa rocks extend along the entire north and west of the city of Naples at an elevation of from four to seven hundred feet. Innumerable grottoes have been cut into these rocks, for the double purpose of obtaining the tufa stone for building purposes and of using the grottoes for cellars and store-rooms. The best of these are reached through long tunnels or passages, ending frequently in immense caverns.

The object of the long passage is to exclude outside air. The annual rent of such a grotto or cave is from 150 to 200 francs.

During the summer months comparatively little meat is consumed in this climate, the poorer classes living exclusively on bread, vegetables, macaroni, and fruit. Butcher-shops during that part of the year are only open in the forenoon. The meat remaining unsold at noon is returned to the grotto until next day. Meat inspectors daily visit the butcher-shops and confiscate all tainted meat.

It is extremely difficult to introduce new inventions among a people who use tools and farming utensils which are fac similes of those excavated at Pompeii and Herculaneum, exhibited in the museum at Naples.

The municipal authorities of the city of Naples for the consideration of 200,000 lire per annum have granted to the "Societa delle Neviere" the monopoly or exclusive right to sell snow or ice in the city of Naples.

This society manufactures ice to a very limited extent, but sells large quantities of snow collected on the Apennines, which is preferred by the people here. The *modus operandi* of procuring snow is as follows: During the coldest part of the winter holes are dug on the mountains at an elevation of about 2,500 or 3,000 feet above the level of the sea. These holes are filled with snow, packed down as solid as possible and covered with the leaves of the chestnut tree to a sufficient height to protect the snow against rain, etc. From these holes the snow is packed in straw mats or baskets, transported on mules or donkeys to the nearest railroad station, and thence to the cities. The supply for Naples is brought from Monte San Angelo, about 16 miles from Naples.

The Societa delle Neviere had to enter into a bond in the amount of 100,000 lire for the true performance of their agreement. They are obliged to have at all times a sufficient quantity of ice and snow on hand in their warehouse or cellar at Naples, and supply purchasers at the rate of lire 4.55 per 100 pounds (lire 10 per 100 kilo). Retailers are allowed to sell snow or ice obtained from the society at the rate of 9 centimes per pound.

EDWARD CAMPHAUSEN,
Consul.

UNITED STATES CONSULATE,
Naples, January 21, 1890.

VENICE.

REPORT BY CONSUL JOHNSON.

The refrigerator as a piece of household furniture has been, until very recently, almost unheard of in this consular district, and is at present far from being in general use. Where foods and liquids have been preserved for any length of time, such as in most of the hotels, butcher shops, and breweries, the most primitive methods of preservation by packing directly in ice have been practiced, and no attempt has been made to economize in the use of ice in such cases.

The people in general use very little ice, and rarely keep perishable foods and liquids in their houses in sufficient quantities to necessitate their preservation for any length of time.

I am informed that in many of the towns of this consular district ice-houses exist, belonging to the communal authorities, or in some cases to private companies, and in these the butchers of the town can keep their meats, each one by the payment of a small tax, reserving a space in the ice-house for his exclusive use.

In the construction of refrigerators for this consular district no peculiar features are required.

The only manufactory of refrigerators to be found in this district is in the city of Venice, having been started about a year ago by a firm of Germans, the Herion Brothers, who are engaged in various commercial enterprises in this city and who are going into the manufacture of refrigerators as an experimental operation. The specimens I have examined are of simple construction, the wood used being American pitch pine, and the makers claiming that they are made after the latest system in use in Germany.

Ice is secured in the winter from ice-ponds, streams, and bodies of fresh water on the mainland (in the case of Venice) near Mestre, stored in ice-houses, and brought to Venice during the summer in boats, the price of ice per 100 pounds being on an average 45 cents.

Outside of those refrigerators made by Herion Brothers there are to be found in Venice a very limited number of refrigerators of German make and these sell at prices slightly higher than those of domestic make, but as the sale of refrigerators generally speaking is so restricted, the greater part of the merchants here do not care to risk importing them.

The best manner of introducing the American refrigerator would be to have samples at the shops of the principal dealers in the important towns of this district, as Venice, Verona, Treviso, etc., bearing in mind that the chief requisite for a ready sale and general popularity is a diminutive price, as high-priced goods would be absolutely unsalable here no matter what superior qualities the article might possess.

H. ABERT JOHNSON,
Consul.

UNITED STATES CONSULATE,
Venice, July 12, 1890.

RUSSIA.

REPORT BY CONSUL-GENERAL CRAWFORD, OF ST PETERSBURG.

Refrigerators are little known here; they are exclusively used at restaurants and shops as yet. Many houses in this city have ice-cellars in which is stored the ice necessary for the season. Artificial ice is unknown here.

On inquiry I have learned that refrigerators are considerably used in the western and southern provinces; but these refrigerators in no way compare in excellence with those of American manufacture.

In my opinion there is a large and lucrative field in Russia for this industry, and American firms would do well to open it up and work it.

J. M. CRAWFORD,
Consul-General.

UNITED STATES CONSULATE GENERAL.
St. Petersburg, January 25, 1890.

FINLAND.

REPORT BY VICE-CONSUL DONNER, OF HELSINGFORS.

There are no refrigerators in use in this country.

The railway carriages used for the transport of butter, etc., are kept cool in summer by putting ice in an iron cylinder, about 2 feet in diameter, which is placed horizontally across the carriage inside. Steamers use small ice-safes for the purpose of preserving the food during the voyage.

Any one who chooses may take ice from the sea or the lakes in Finland, so that the cost is only that of the labor employed.

As there is at the present time increasing attention given to the export of butter, etc., from this country, I think if I could be furnished with specifications of smaller and larger refrigerators, together with the prices delivered here, there might be a good opening for their introduction into Finland. If the manufacturers would like to send samples of the machine they should be forwarded by the Wilson line from New York, via Hull, to Helsingfors.

HERMAN DONNER,
Vice and Acting Consul.

UNITED STATES CONSULATE,
Helsingfors, January 14, 1890.

POLAND.

REPORT BY CONSUL RAWICZ, OF WARSAW.

Refrigerators for the preservation of foods and liquids are extensively used in this consular district. The refrigerators are constructed in such sizes and shapes as suit the house furnitures of different classes of the population of this country. As I was informed, it is a fact that all refrigerators now in use in Poland are exclusively manufactured in the city of Warsaw, from whence they are also exported to the Russian western governments.

The ice is usually secured in the winter season, during which both ice dealers and brewers supply themselves with the necessary quantity of ice drawn either from the Vistula River or from the neighboring ponds. Its price depends on the season and ranges from 10 to 15 cents per 100 pounds.

The American system of refrigerators can be introduced here and compete with the local one if it will prove cheaper and more convenient.

JOSEPH RAWICZ,
Consul.

UNITED STATES CONSULATE,
 Warsaw, January 21, 1890.

No. 1, with three gallipots of 10 pints each, costs 100 rubles.

Fig. 28.—Ice conservators with four gallipots. No. 1, with four gallipots of 8 pints each, costs 110 rubles; No. 2, with four gallipots of 10 pints each, costs 120 rubles; No. 3, with four gallipots of 12 pints each, costs 135 rubles.

Fig. 34.—Refrigerator for one beer barrel without Price, 80 rubles.

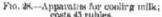

Fig. 28.—Apparatus for cooling milk; costs 45 rubles.

Fig. 29.—Refrigerator for milk with eight pots; costs 85 rubles.

Fig. 30.—Refri

tor for preserving victuals and meat, with two doors; No. 2, costs 15 rubles.

Fig. 39.—Refrigerator for preserving victuals, with one door and a pantry. Price, 50 rubles.

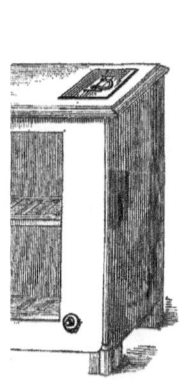
rator, with one pantry and one side
—No. 1, 25 rubles; No. 2, 30 rubles;

Fig. 45.—Refrigerator with two pantries and six grates; costs—No. 4, 80 rubles; No. 5, 90 rubles; No. 6, 100 rubles; No. 7, 120 rubles.

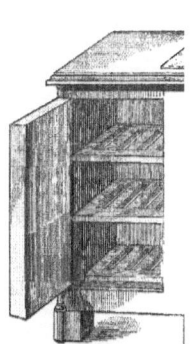
Fig. 46.—Room refrigerator with one pa costs—No. 4, 40 rubles; No. 5, 45 ruble

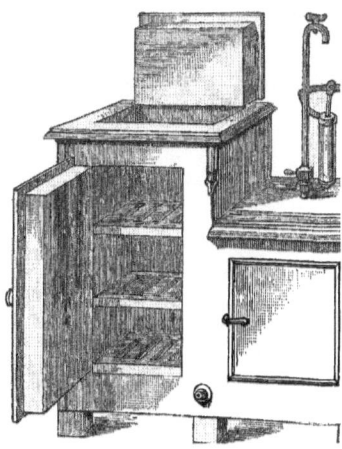

SPAIN.

BARCELONA.

REPORT BY CONSUL SCHEUCH.

Refrigerators are virtually not in use in Barcelona, Catalonia, or the Balearic Islands, and as all food and necessaries of life are strictly bought fresh from day to day, I think refrigerators will not be appreciated for many years as they are in other European countries. Private families never use ice at home, excepting the few English and German families. I remember Mess. Ros y Ca of this city, then dealers in American goods, imported some five years ago six refrigerators, and after two years' unsuccessful efforts sold them to several foreign families at ruinous prices, losing duty, freight, insurance, etc.

The restaurants, coffee-houses, saloons, and hotels receive daily during the summer quantities of ice-snow gathered in the neighboring hills, placing it in their cellars. This sort of ice is cheap, often dirty, but suits all their purposes, selling at $1.50 per 100 pounds. Some years ago a Norwegian house here brought a cargo of fine ice from Norway and lost heavily. The snow-ice gathered in the hills is placed in deep ice-wells, and brought in summer daily in carts to the city. Two years ago an artificial ice factory was started, but, as already stated, the Catalonians using no ice at home, this factory depends entirely on hotels, restaurants, etc., doing little business on account of the cheapness of the snow ice, the city tax on manufactured ice being high.

My opinion is the introduction of refrigerators will be very difficult in this district, as it will take years to convince the people at large of their great utility.

FREDK. H. SCHEUCH,
Consul.
UNITED STATES CONSULATE,
Barcelona, January 26, 1890.

CARTHAGENA.

REPORT BY CONSUL MOLINA.

There are no refrigerators used in my consular district. The people are not accustomed to preserving food.

We use artificial ice, and this is simply used in summer drinks. The price of ice is about $2 per 100 pounds.

C. MOLINA,
Consul.
UNITED STATES CONSULATE,
Carthagena, January 31, 1890.

GRAO OF VALENCIA.

REPORT BY CONSULAR AGENT MERTENS.

American refrigerators are not known here. A few years ago a German house sent here a few refrigerators, which were sold after some time at half their cost price. They did not please the buyers, because there was no economy of ice in their use.

The ice used here is artificial, and its manufacture is not of a superior kind, the ice being too soft. Besides this, the snow which falls during winter time on the surrounding mountains is gathered in and stored in rice husks.

There is not such a general use of ice here for preserving foods and liquids as in the United States, and the little which is used for refreshing the beverage at dinner time is generally sent after to the manufacturers.

Restaurants and hotels keep their daily need of ice preserved in a heap of rice husks in the cellar or a cool place of the house.

My opinion is that even a very plain and economical kind of refrigerator would find difficulty in selling here, as there is little desire amongst the natives of this place to spend money for household improvements, and the number of foreigners is very small. The latter, however, possess this article, imported mostly from Germany.

THEODOR MERTENS,
Consular Agent.

UNITED STATES CONSULAR AGENCY,
Grao of Valencia, January 8, 1890.

CADIZ.

REPORT BY CONSUL TURNER.

Replying to Department circular regarding refrigerators, I have the honor to inclose herewith replies to same from the consular agents at Jeres de la Frontera, Seville, and Port St. Mary's. I can add but little to what these inclosures contain. Ice sells here at 5 cents per pound to small consumers, and is used in sparing quantities, except in the manufacture of iced drinks, etc.

Fresh meat during the summer is obtainable only in the morning. It is prepared for market during the night, and every butcher expects to dispose of his entire stock before the following noon.

The first and only cargo of ice ever landed here from abroad came from Boston in 1856. It arrived in June, and was not discharged for several weeks on account of the stupidity of the custom officers, who insisted that it must be landed on the docks in a burning sun and weighed as other cargo. This was prevented by the governor of the province, who interfered in behalf of the shippers. It was the first ice ever seen by many people and attracted large crowds.

Regarding the introduction of American methods of preserving fruits, vegetables, meats, etc., I must differ from Mr. Hall, for living must always be high here so long as the hand to mouth process to which he refers continues. The abundance of prosperous years is wasted for lack of methods of preservation. The distress following partial or total failure of crops is always doubly great because the excess of fruitful years has not been preserved. In this land of fruit peaches sell for 20 cents per pound, the dried article for 35 cents. Green apples and pears sell for 15 cents per pound. Preserved fruits are hardly known.

It is difficult to tell how our goods and methods can be introduced when there is no such thing as an American doing business here. All these things would naturally and rapidly introduce themselves were this country traversed by salesmen representing American merchants and American goods. In the absence of such a force, and in the absence also of a direct trade in breadstuffs, canned meats, vegetables, fruits, etc., between this country and the United States, I see no method of bringing about the desired results, if it is not done by private enterprise. I believe it would pay our farmers if the Department of Agriculture would demonstrate the cheapness and purity of our canned goods and the uses of Indian maize at Spanish fairs. In closing I might add that the expressed observations of all American travelers that I have had the pleasure of meeting since coming to Cadiz are in harmony with everything that has been written in favor of trade with this country.

The high prices of all kinds of food supplies surprise all.

I am informed by the captain of the American bark *Kennard*, which trades regularly between Boston and Fayal, that Cadiz is a much better point than Fayal for trade, and he proposes changing accordingly. He has posted himself on prices while here for future use.

R. W. TURNER,
Consul.

UNITED STATES CONSULATE,
 Cadiz, January 29, 1890.

JEREZ DE LA FRONTERA.

REPORT BY CONSULAR AGENT HALL.

[Inclosure 1 in Consul Turner's Report.]

Refrigerators.—In this district I consider myself as authorized in saying that refrigerators are not only unknown but that they are unnecessary, owing to the simplicity of the Spanish cuisine.

Spanish families, high and low, make their market purchase daily, and only in such quantities as shall be necessary for the consumption or use of the day.

It is doubtful whether in any family, no matter what its social standing is, such a thing as a roast of veal, leg of mutton or pork, or a fowl would be found from one day to another. Pies, cakes, custards, etc., are unknown culinary luxuries.

I am confident there is no opening for the introduction of refrigerators in this district.

Preserving foods and liquids.—This is completely unknown in all senses. A long residence in this country warrants me in affirming that preserving fruits, fowls, meats, fish, etc., is only done by the use of spirits of wine for fruit, and oil and lard for the other articles mentioned.

Ice.—This article, manufactured in Seville, is only used during the summer, when it is used for making ice creams, etc. It wholesales in this city at $2 per hundred weight, and retails at from 3 to 5 cents per pound.

SEVILLE.

REPORT BY CONSULAR AGENT CALDWELL.

[Inclosure 2 in Consul Turner's Report.]

Refrigerators are not used here. Ice is manufactured here, and sells in summer for 7½ pesetas per 100 pounds and in winter for 14 pesetas per cwt. Food is bought from day to day. I think there is no opening for American refrigerators.

PORT ST. MARY'S.

REPORT BY CONSULAR AGENT DANIELS.

[Inclosure 3 in Consul Turner's Report.]

Referring to the refrigerator circular you sent me a few days ago, I regret to say that, after making all possible inquiries, I am unable to give answers to its questions, for I find that refrigerators are not used, or even known, here. The very small consumption of ice is provided for by supplies from Seville, the price of which I am unable to give, for it is only used during the summer months. It is used only for iced drinks, and the price varies.

MALAGA.

REPORT BY CONSUL MARSTON.

Refrigerators are not used in this part of Spain.

The ice used in Malaga is artificial, and only to be had from May until October, and very little is used, except in cases of illness. Spaniards never drink ice water as in the United States. There are two ice factories in the city of Malaga. A single kilo costs 1½ reais (about 7½ cents), or you can purchase a package of ice tickets of 30 tickets each at the following prices, viz: 30 tickets of 1 kilo each, $1.64; 30 tickets of 2 kilos each, $3.08; 30 tickets of 3 kilos each, $4.53; 30 tickets of 6 kilos each, $8.88; 30 tickets of 10 kilos each, $14.47. The above is delivered at your door at any regular hour you may state. The manner of living here does not require the use of either ice or refrigerators. There are no milk cans, consequently no butter is made in this part of Spain. All butter is imported in cans, mostly from Ireland or Copenhagen. The milk used is goat's milk, these goats being driven from door to door in the early hours of the morning, the servants purchasing what each family requires. The cook goes to market every morning and makes her purchases for the day. Meat is but little used, even by the well-to-do, hardly ever by the middle classes, and it is a rare occasion when the poor ever taste it, bread, fish, and vegetables being the principal diet. In Malaga the fish is the very best, and it can be bought at any hour of the day, passing your door, fresh from the Mediterranean, at a very small cost, and is never purchased until required for cooking. This state of things dispenses with the necessity of all classes of refrigerators, for none could be sold here.

H. C. MARSTON,
Consul.

UNITED STATES CONSULATE,
    Malaga, January 20, 1890.

GIBRALTAR.

REPORT BY CONSUL SPRAGUE.

Refrigerators are very little used in this city.

The very few in use possess no peculiar features, either in construction or application.

Those in use are generally of English manufacture.

Ice is manufactured at the north front, outside the gates of this garrison, from rain-water, and is sold at about $3 per 112 pounds, but can be obtained much cheaper if regularly taken in larger quantities.

Provisions and liquids are generally kept in underground cellars and stores during the summer months, so that refrigerators are not in any demand.

HORATIO J. SPRAGUE,
Consul.

UNITED STATES CONSULATE,
Gibraltar, January 14, 1890.

SWEDEN.

GOTHENBURG.

REPORT BY CONSUL MAN.

Refrigerators are not nearly so extensively used here as in the United States but are nevertheless quite generally found in the city and country houses of the middle and upper classes.

There are no peculiar features required in the construction of refrigerators for this district.

They are manufactured at so called "mechanical workshops" which are extensive concerns, engaged in the manufacture of a large line of articles composed more or less of metal, and embracing all varieties of kitchen utensils, stoves, farming implements, plumbers' materials, tools, machinery, etc., even constructing steam-ships and armored war vessels.

The general dimensions of the refrigerators in use here are confined to three sizes, the smallest being $2\frac{1}{2}$ feet square; the middle and most used $2\frac{1}{2}$ feet front width, $2\frac{1}{2}$ feet side width, and 3 feet in height; the largest $2\frac{1}{2}$ feet front width, $2\frac{1}{2}$ feet side width, and 4 feet in height.

These consist simply of a zinc-lined wooden box protected by an intermediate non-conductor furnished with a door in front, a lid on top, and several galvanized wire racks, the ice being nearly at the bottom of the chest, while the racks are above it.

The prices for these three sizes at retail are, respectively, $8.58, $9.38, and $12.06.

Ice is cut from the lakes and rivers by the brewers, and supplied by them to the public at an average price of 37 cents a hundred pounds.

As to the best method of introducing them into this country I am of the opinion that the only advisable way would be through energetic agents, who, by convincing the people of the superior qualities of the American refrigerator, could find a market for them here, notwithstanding the low prices of the Swedish article, and the fact of the strong disinclination of the people to adopt new methods at a greater outlay.

ERNEST A. MAN,
Consul.

UNITED STATES CONSULATE,
Gothenburg, February 14, 1890.

STOCKHOLM.

REPORT BY CONSUL ELFWING.

I have not been able to find the use of any refrigerators anywhere in Sweden, nor do I believe that the introduction of them there could meet with success. Ice in this cold climate is a very cheap and hardy article; it is sold at retail here in Stockholm, delivered in the houses, at about 40 cents per 100 pounds. Breweries and like establishments which use much take up their own quantities and pay, of course, much less. There is never any warm or hot weather; perhaps for a couple of weeks in July or August it is hot, and nothing is therefore done for the preservation of food and liquids.

NERE A. ELFWING,
Consul.

UNITED STATES CONSULATE,
    Stockholm, January 28, 1890.

SWITZERLAND.

HORGEN.

REPORT BY CONSUL ADAMS.

In the forest and mountain cantons, which occupy nearly the whole of this district, the refrigerator is an article hardly needed or known. The altitude of the region and the vicinity of perpetual ice and snow keep the temperature down, except in midsummer during the day-time, while for the leading industries of the country, lumbering and cattle-raising, temperature is almost a matter of indifference. So far as I can learn it is only in the large dairies (butter and cheese factories) that artificial refrigeration is employed. In these the chamber for storing milk, as it is delivered by the neighboring herdsmen, is converted into a refrigerator by cementing the floor and the walls for a foot or more above the floor, and introducing flowing water from the nearest brook. The milk, placed in shallow wooden (usually ash) vessels, is surrounded by the water. As water is supplied in abundance by the melting snows and ice, at the cost of a little ditching and piping, the system is not likely to be superseded. It is only in the valleys and lowlands, where the conditions are different, that the questions of the circular apply.

In this lower region, refrigerators are in common use, especially in the towns where they are to be found in nearly all the larger hotels, boarding-houses, restaurants, and hospitals, in the shops of butchers, poulterers, fishmongers, and pastry cooks, in many public institutions and private families. In the country the large dairies use them in place of the mountain system, but not the farmers, who now deliver all their milk to the dairies.

The butchers use a refrigerator of large dimensions, with an outer case of stone or cement, and an inner one of wood lined with zinc. In others in use there seem to be no peculiar features of construction.

Most of the refrigerators in this district are of local manufacture. Perhaps 10 per cent. come from Germany or Holland.

The sizes vary from 1 by 1 by 1 meter to 5 by $1\frac{1}{2}$ by $1\frac{1}{2}$ meters. They usually consist of an inner case, zinc-lined, separated by a packing of sawdust or pulverized charcoal from the outer case. The ice-box is filled from the top, and fitted with drain-pipe and tap. The following table gives details:

Refrigerators used by—	Dimensions in meters.	Prices.
Dairies	1 to 1½ by 1 by 1	$14 to $23
Butchers	5 by 1 by 1	75 100
Poulterers		15 80
Hotels	3½ to 5 by 1½ by 1 to 1½	96 150
Pensions	1 to 2 by 1 by 1	15 96
Pastry cooks	1 to 2 by 1 by 1	15 40

The dairies use 2, or more; the butcher 1; poulterers 1 to 3; hotels 3 to 5; other establishments usually 1.

Ice, supplied by the lakes and ponds, usually not of the best quality, is abundant in summer at 40 cents per 100 pounds retail, and $1.93 per wagon-load wholesale.

Finally, as to the readiness of the people to adopt the American system of preserving foods and liquids, as much would depend on the economy as on the superiority of the system. A market might be found, at least in the larger Swiss towns, for the American article if it could be shown by actual trial to be more efficient than the local article at the same cost, or equally efficient at a less cost. It would be well, perhaps, for manufacturers to communicate with the leading hotels of the country, whose managers are more attentive to matters of this sort than any other class interested. None of the dealers in American goods here import direct. The general importers at Basle or Geneva might be induced to do so.

LYELL T. ADAMS,
Consul.

UNITED STATES CONSULATE,
Horgen, January 30, 1890.

ZURICH.

REPORT BY CONSUL CATLIN.

Refrigerators are extensively used in this consular district. Their sizes and formations are extremely varied in character. So far as I have been able to learn, none of them possess any peculiar features not known to manufacturers elsewhere. A large number of those in use are manufactured in Switzerland—there are two factories here in Zurich, and many are made by individual joiners—but in this, as in everything else, German competition is overwhelmingly strong, and the Swiss makers have all they can do to stem the tide and keep up their prices to paying rates. I have heard of an English refrigerator having been imported hither, but it does not seem to have elicited further orders of the same kind. The Swiss and German articles control the market.

Owing to the number of beer saloons, both large and small, and the necessity of keeping and serving the beer cool during warm weather, the number of refrigerators of a medium size in actual use is much larger than it would be in a non-beer-drinking community of the same population. Refrigerators are also used by the hotels, great and small, boarding-houses, restaurants, butchers, confectioners, apothecaries, hospitals, and to a limited extent in private families.

In size and formation, as above stated, they greatly vary. I give herewith a description of a number of those here offered for sale :

No. 1.—Ice chamber on top. Refrigerator divided into three compartments, viz, (1) with room for two kegs of beer of 100 liters each, one being on draught while the other is cooling; (2, middle) for keeping raw meats in large pieces, game, poultry, and fish ; (3) for cooling food, bottles, and glasses; outer measurements, side compartments (1 and 3) 1.65 meters long, .85 wide, 1.75 high; middle compartment (2) 1.53 meters long, .90 wide, 2.40 high; price only obtainable by purchase.

No. 2.—Ice chamber on top. Refrigerator has room for 10 kegs of beer of 80 liters each, 2 of them on draft while the rest are cooling; also room for food, bottles, and glasses. Takes 2,000 pounds ice. Length 4.50, width 1.29, height 2.25 meters.

No. 3.—Ice chamber on top and sides. Has room for 4 wine jugs of 18 liters each, and 2 kegs of beer of 50 liters each on draft; also 3 spaces for glasses, bottles, and food. Takes 600 pounds ice. Length 3.21, width .87, height 1.59 meters.

No. 4.—Desk form. Cushioned doors, if desired. Ice chamber on top. Has two compartments, for keeping raw meat, game, poultry, and fish cool. Takes 640 pounds ice. Length 1.85, width .92, height 1.61 meters.

No. 5.—Secretary form. Ice in center, for cooling all kinds of food and bottled liquids. Made in five sizes.

	Length.	Width.	Height.	Ice.		Length.	Width.	Height.	Ice.
	Meters.	Meters.	Meters.	Pounds.		Meters.	Meters.	Meters.	Pounds.
A	0.96	0.63	1.08	90	D	1.80	0.78	1.80	280
B	1.29	0.69	1.38	160	E	1.90	0.85	1.98	340
C	1.47	0.78	1.68	240					

No. 6.—Sideboard form. Ice chamber above; contains four separate compartments for preserving cooked food and liquids of all kinds on marble slabs; is finished in oak, is similarly decorated on both sides, and can be placed in the center of a dining-room. Takes 300 pounds ice. Length 2.71, width .76, height 1.04 meters. Marble slabs extra.

No. 7.—Sideboard form for smaller hotels, restaurants, boarding-houses, and large families. Ice-chamber above. Takes 130 pounds ice. Length 1.03, width .88 (below), .63 (above), height 2.16 meters.

No. 8.—Ice chamber above. Contains two separate compartments. Length 1.28, width .68, height 1.69 meters. Takes 140 pounds ice.

No. 9.—Bureau form. Ice-chamber in upper center. Length 1.32, width .68, height 1.32 meters. Takes 100 pounds ice.

No. 10.—For small families. Ice-chamber at side.

	Length.	Width.	Height.	Ice.		Length.	Width.	Height.	Ice.
	Meters.	Meters.	Meters.	Pounds.		Meters.	Meters.	Meters.	Pounds.
A	1.02	0.65	0.84	60	B	1.21	0.76	1.00	110

No. 11.—For small families. Ice chamber below.

	Length.	Width.	Height.	Ice.		Length.	Width.	Height.	Ice.
	Meters.	*Meters.*	*Meters.*	*Pounds.*		*Meters.*	*Meters.*	*Meters.*	*Pounds.*
A	0.70	0.52	0.65	30	C	1.40	0.76	0.94	110
B	0.98	0.65	0.84	60					

No. 12.—For same. Ice chamber above. One compartment. Length .87, width .71, height 1.52 meters. Takes 110 pounds ice.

No. 13.—For apothecaries, doctors, and hospitals. Bureau form. Ice chamber at side. Length 1, width .60, height 1 meter. Takes 150 pounds ice.

No. 14.—For cooling bottles or preserving victuals. Ice chamber above. Finished as a piece of furniture with double front. Length 1.15, width .75, height 1.15 meters. Takes 140 pounds of ice.

No. 15.—Ice chamber in center. Has four separate compartments for preserving foods and liquids. Length 1.38, width .67, height 1.01 meters. Takes 80 pounds ice.

No. 16.—Desk form. For butchers and sausage-makers. Ice chamber below. Has two separate compartments. Length 1.85, width .76, height 1.05 meters. Takes 200 pounds ice.

No. 17.—Desk form. For same. Ice chamber below. Length 1.36, width .72, height 1.05 meters. Takes 160 pounds ice.

No. 18.—For cooling beer. Ice chamber above. Holds four kegs of beer, two on draught while the others are cooling. In three sizes, according to size of kegs, viz:

	Kegs.	Length.	Width.	Height.	Ice.		Kegs.	Length.	Width.	Height.	Ice.
	Liters	*Meters*	*Meters.*	*Meters.*	*Pounds.*		*Liters.*	*Meters.*	*Meters.*	*Meters.*	*Pounds.*
A	60-70	1.60	0.93	2.30	700	C	20-30	1.00	0.70	1.08	280
B	40-50	1.30	0.80	2.00	400						

No. 19.—For cooling beer. Ice chamber on side.

	Kegs.	Length.	Width.	Height.	Ice.		Kegs.	Length.	Width.	Height.	Ice.
	Liters	*Meters.*	*Meters.*	*Meters.*	*Pounds.*		*Liters.*	*Meters.*	*Meters.*	*Meters.*	*Pounds.*
A	60-70	1.96	0.93	1.93	600	C	20-30	1.30	0.70	1.50	220
B	40-50	1.60	0.80	1.70	500						

No. 20.—For cooling beer. Ice chamber above. Holds two kegs of beer on draught.

	Kegs.	Length.	Width.	Height.	Ice.		Kegs.	Length.	Width.	Height.	Ice.
	Liters.	*Meters.*	*Meters.*	*Meters.*	*Pounds.*		*Liters.*	*Meters.*	*Meters.*	*Meters.*	*Pounds.*
A	60-70	1.45	0.93	1.70	400	C	20-30	1.30	0.70	1.40	300
B	40-50	1.45	0.80	1.55	320						

REFRIGERATORS IN FOREIGN COUNTRIES.

No. 21.—For cooling beer. Ice chamber above. Holds one keg on draught, with space for keeping food, bottles, etc.

	Kegs.	Length.	Width.	Height.	Ice.		Kegs.	Length.	Width.	Height.	Ice.
	Liters.	*Meters.*	*Meters.*	*Meters.*	*Pounds.*		*Liters.*	*Meters.*	*Meters.*	*Meters.*	*Pounds.*
A	60–70	1.45	0.93	1.70	300	C	20–30	1.05	0.70	1.45	160
B	40–50	1.30	0.80	1.55	220						

No. 22.—For cooling beer. Ice chamber on side. Holds one keg beer with low pressure.

	Kegs.	Length.	Width.	Height.	Ice.		Kegs.	Length.	Width.	Height.	Ice.
	Liters.	*Meters.*	*Meters.*	*Meters.*	*Pounds.*		*Liters.*	*Meters.*	*Meters.*	*Meters.*	*Pounds.*
A	60–70	1.25	0.78	1.05	200	C	20–30	1.04	0.55	0.75	1.30
B	40–50	1.10	0.65	1.90	160						

No. 23.—For cooling beer. Ice chamber on side. Holds one keg beer with low pressure.

	Kegs.	Length.	Width.	Height.	Ice.		Kegs.	Length.	Width.	Height.	Ice.
	Liters.	*Meters.*	*Meters.*	*Meters.*	*Pounds.*		*Liters.*	*Meters.*	*Meters.*	*Meters.*	*Pounds.*
A	60–70	1.30	0.93	1.45	220	C	20–30	1.00	0.70	1.20	90
B	40–50	1.15	0.80	1.30	150						

No. 24.—Washstand form, with faucets. Ice chamber on side. For keeping four different kinds of beer on draught and cooling drinking water. Length, 0.80; width, 0.70; height, 0.75 meters. Takes 260 pounds ice.

No. 25.—For confectioners and pastry cooks. Ice chamber in center. Has two compartments for preserving and cooling unbaked dough, eggs, butter, cream, etc. Length, 1.50; width, 0.81; height, 0.87 meters. Takes 140 pounds ice.

Ice boxes for keeping raw ice are made in various sizes, viz:

	Length.	Width.	Height.	Ice.		Length.	Width.	Height.	Ice.
	Meters.	*Meters.*	*Meters.*	*Pounds.*		*Meters.*	*Meters.*	*Meters.*	*Pounds.*
A	0.84	0.84	0.96	200	G	1.29	1.29	1.41	1,400
B	0.96	0.96	1.04	400	H	1.33	1.33	1.45	1,600
C	1.05	1.05	1.17	600	I	1.38	1.38	1.50	1,800
D	1.14	1.14	1.26	800	K	1.41	1.41	1.53	2,000
E	1.20	1.20	1.32	1,000	L	1.44	1.44	1.56	2,200
F	1.24	1.24	1.36	1,200	M	1.47	1.47	1.59	2,400

The various sizes and formations here described—it is impossible to obtain the prices in any case without actually purchasing—will enable our American manufacturers to form a fair idea of the demands of the trade in this section.

Ice sells at from 18 to 24 cents per 100 pounds when delivered in large quantities and at from from 30 to 40 cents in smaller lots. It is obtained from the neighboring lakes—the Greifensee, the Katzensee, and other smaller bodies of water. The Klönthalersee, in the neighboring canton of Glarus, freezes over every winter. The glaciers are also made, in Canton Wallis, tributary to the demand which, of late years, owing to the growth of the Swiss beer-brewing industry, has become enormous. The four hundred breweries in Switzerland alone consume 100,000 tons annually, at an expense, including freight and labor, of 500,000 francs. The manufacture of artificial ice has consequently greatly developed, there being two firms in this city and one at Geneva engaged in the business.

For the introduction of American refrigerators into this district a sharp, pushing agent, provided with a full line of samples and speaking the German language thoroughly, would be the first requisite. The appointment of a local agent here would hardly suffice; he must be a man thoroughly conversant with the American trade and manufacture, and should be sent out for that purpose. Even then his success would depend entirely on whether he could compete in prices with the local and German manufacturers. The former have no freight or entry duties to pay; the latter, too, are near by, and, spite of the duties, can, it seems, deliver their goods here at competing prices. But when the freight from New York to Zurich, plus the entry duties, come to be added to the original price of an American refrigerator, be its merits what they may, it will require a sharp and tireless salesman here to overcome the local competition and make the sale of the American article a paying one in this remote inland market.

GEORGE L. CATLIN,
Consul.

UNITED STATES CONSULATE,
Zurich, January 23, 1890.

TURKEY.

REPORT BY CONSUL-GENERAL SWEENEY, OF CONSTANTINOPLE.

Refrigerators are not used in this consular district, except in a very few houses or hotels. The refrigerators in use are of European or local make; and should any American refrigerators be introduced into this district they should cost very little. People in this country, however, as a general rule, have a very primitive way of preserving foods and liquids by keeping them in subterranean caves or cellars. The best manner of introducing refrigerators in this district is by continued advertisement on a very extended scale, both in all the newspapers published in this city and in all conspicuous places, such as hotels, beer establishments, clubs, etc.

Ice is secured in this district by manufacture by a company which obtained an imperial concession for the exclusive manufacture of this useful article. The factory is situated at Stenia, one of the villages on the European side of the Bosphorus. The use of ice is rather limited in this country, as heretofore it was secured only from its natural sources; but it is increasing gradually. The price per 100 pounds of ice is $1.

In conclusion I beg to remark that this district may adopt the American refrigerators if they can be manufactured in such a way as to sell very cheaply.

Z. T. SWEENEY,
Consul-General.

UNITED STATES CONSULATE,
Constantinople, January 14, 1890.

THE UNITED KINGDOM.

ENGLAND.

BIRMINGHAM.

REPORT BY CONSUL JARRETT.

Refrigerators are used in this consular district chiefly by butchers and fishmongers and at hotels and large restaurants. By private families, so far as I can find, they are used to a very limited extent only.

There are no peculiar features required in the construction of refrigerators so as to adapt them for use in this country. Those now in use in large establishments are very similar in construction to American refrigerators, but though the general features of smaller refrigerators adapted for family use are similar to those of American make, there is a marked difference in their construction, the American being better in design and utility. I may add that the price of American refrigerators is lower than the price of similar ones of English make.

The large fixed refrigerators for preserving perishable food are manufactured in this consular district. Those for the brewery purposes are manufactured in Burton-on-Trent. Small refrigerators for family use are not manufactured here. The principal of this class of refrigerators in this country are of Manchester make.

The ice used in this consular district is all manufactured, being the product of the Linde British Refrigeration Company, a concern that not only manufactures ice for consumption in England, but also on the Continent. Natural ice is imported into this country at London and Hull, from Norway. Last year it was about 200,000 tons at London and about 75,000 tons at Hull. The price of ice a short time ago was very low, being about $1.93 per ton. A consolidation of the different concerns then existing was effected, when the price of ice was considerably advanced. Mr. G. H. Jackson, of the Linde British Refrigeration Company, limited, has kindly furnished me with the following present selling price of ice:

	Per ton.*
Birmingham	$7.29
London	4.38 to 7.29
Grimsby and Hull	4.86¼
Cardiff	6.08
Liverpool	4.38 to 7.29

The concern that does the largest business in the sale of refrigerators in this city is that of Evans & Matthews. Their sales amount to

---

*2,240 pounds.

about two hundred and sixty in each year. The manager informs me that the sales of Mr. Kent, of London, will not exceed sixty per week during the summer season.

Should the American manufacturers conclude to introduce their refrigerators into this district, I can not suggest any better means than that they do so through Evans & Matthews, as I know it to be the most reliable house doing business in that line in the Midlands. I may say, in conclusion, that the climate of this country is not the most favorable to insure the general use of refrigerators. The temperature rarely exceeds 85° Fahrenheit. Warm periods of long duration seldom take place. This probably accounts for the fact that refrigerators have not been adopted into general family use, even by persons of fair means.

JOHN JARRETT,
Consul.

UNITED STATES CONSULATE,
Birmingham, January 28, 1890.

BRADFORD.

REPORT BY CONSUL TIBBITS.

Refrigerators are used in this consular district, but only to a comparatively limited extent. Their use is mainly confined to hotels, and the better class restaurants, eating-houses, and fish and game markets. They are found in but few private residences, and only in those of the wealthy class. Regarded as household necessities in the United States, they are here considered articles of luxury. In the town of Bradford, with a population of nearly 250,000, there are but two firms that deal in refrigerators, and inquiries made of them disclose the fact that their combined annual sales will not average more than 6 dozen.

No particular features are required in the construction of refrigerators adapted for use in this district.

The refrigerators in use in this district are manufactured in the United States and by a single firm in London. The American refrigerator principally in use is that known as the "Alaska."

The sizes of refrigerators kept in stock by local dealers are as follows:

	Width.	Depth.	Height.	Price.		Width.	Depth.	Height.	Price.
	Inches.	*Inches.*	*Inches.*	£ s.		*Inches.*	*Inches.*	*Inches.*	£ s.
No. 2....	27	21	30	4 4	No. 4..	39	24	32	6 6
No. 3 ..	33	22	31	5 5	No. 6...	50	27	34	8 8

The ice here in use is imported from Norway. The price per 100 pounds varies from 3 to 5 shillings, the former rate being charged when delivery is at the place of sale, and the latter when it is at the premises of the purchaser. The retail price is 3 pence per pound.

Where refrigerators are not in use, foods and liquids are preserved in cellars, and the temperature is rarely high enough to cause any difficulty to be experienced.

The American refrigerators, as at present constructed, met all local requirements in this district and are, according to the statements of the local dealers, considered superior to those of home manufacture.

Taking into consideration the climatic conditions that here prevail, and the high price which ice must always command owing to the lack of any home product, there is but little room for any substantial extension of trade by American manufacturers of refrigerators in this consular district.

JOHN A. TIBBITS,
Consul.

UNITED STATES CONSULATE,
Bradford, January 21, 1890.

BRISTOL.

REPORT BY CONSUL DELILLE.

The use of refrigerators is extending in Bristol. To begin with the Bristol Dock Company, it is noteworthy that their refrigerating plant at Avonmouth is now extensive. There are, however, no peculiar features in the construction of these refrigerators. They were supplied by Messrs. Pontifex & Wood, Shoe Lane, London, England, and are on the ammonia principle, with brine circulation in the cold stores, the contract amount of heat to be eliminated per hour being 267,000 British thermal units; and the cost, inclusive of buildings and steam boilers, £2,288 ($11,134.55). In my opinion, an excellent opening is now offered for the introduction and sale of refrigerators of American manufacture throughout the Bristol and West of England district. One recent and noteworthy event confirms this view. The large firm of Messrs. Nelson & Son, meat importers, of London and Liverpool, have lately opened a branch establishment of their business in this port, and are now having constructed spacious buildings for the storage of meat. The refrigerators which they will use are of American manufacture, being named the "Hercules," and are supplied by a Chicago firm.

In Messrs. Nelson & Son's new Bristol meat-houses there will be five storage chambers of considerable dimensions. Eventually, the firm hope to receive their dead meat from South America by fast steamers plying direct to Bristol instead of London. Bristol would thus become the distributing center for the whole of the West of England, and indeed, thanks to the economy of time and money by this transit, this port may perhaps attain to the position of supplying London with frozen meat, instead of being supplied therefrom as at present. It will thus be seen that American refrigerator manufacturers might do well to turn their attention to this part of the United Kingdom, especially as their machinery has been so favorably brought under public notice by Messrs. Nelson & Son's selection, as noted above, of the "Hercules" patent.

From special inquiries on the subject, I have reason to believe that soon there will be a large demand among the local butchers, fish-mongers, and Bristol trades-people generally, for the smaller sized refrigerators so extensively used in the United States. Up to now very inadequate methods of preserving foods and fluids have prevailed here among this class of people.

As to ice, the local supply is fairly abundant, being almost entirely in the hands of Messrs. Bigwood, fish and ice merchants, who import nearly all their ice from Norway. Very little is manufactured on the spot. The wholesale price is 30 shillings ($7.29) per ton.

JOHN D. DELILLE,
Consul.

UNITED STATES CONSULATE,
Bristol, February 14, 1890.

FALMOUTH.

REPORT BY CONSUL FOX.

The temperature here is very mild, and refrigerators are not required. Butchers' meat, etc., which is not disposed of when fresh, is salted for use of ships.

The best way of introducing refrigerators in the west of England would be to exhibit them in the north and west of England and royal Cornwall agricultural shows.

HOWARD FOX,
Consul.

UNITED STATES CONSULATE,
Falmouth, February 17, 1890.

LEEDS.

REPORT BY CONSUL WIGFALL.

Inquiry addressed to house-furnishing firms in Leeds has elicited replies to the following effect.

One says:

The trade you refer to is a very limited one with us, and appears to be very well met by the freezers we buy from the United States through factors.

The freezers referred to by this firm are presumably ice-cream freezers, and not refrigerators.

Another answer, concerning the extent to which refrigerators are used in this district gives for hotels and restaurants universally; public houses very little; private residences in town moderately; in country very little.

The leading confectioner and caterer in Leeds, who is constantly employed for private entertainments, and who would therefore naturally be conversant with such details among the well-to-do classes of the community, thinks, as a rule, in the houses which he knows, that refrigerators are not in use.

The impression derived by the writer himself from personal observation is quite in accord with this last-expressed opinion. The mere fact of the use of a refrigerator in a private house would indicate a style of living more than simply comfortable. It would be the exception rather than the rule to find them where incomes were less than £1,000 ($4,866.50), and doubtless even at a higher range of expenditure their employment is not universal.

It can not be said that there are any peculiar features required in the construction of refrigerators for use here. The chest-shaped refrigerator is said to be the shape usually sold, and my informant states that an effort to introduce the cabinet or upright shape was not successful, as he thinks.

The bulk of the refrigerators used here come from London and Birmingham, according to my advices. No importations from the United States have come to my knowledge.

Sizes of refrigerators in use and likely to meet with sale are given by one firm as ranging from 18 inches high, 24 inches wide (front), 18 inches deep (front to back), for the smallest size, to 24 inches high, 36 inches wide (front), 24 inches deep (front to back), for the largest size. Range of prices, according to quality and finish: Small size, $14.60 to $19.47; large size, $29.20 to $48.67.

The 24 by 36 by 24 inches is quoted by this firm as the most convenient and best suited to ordinary use, selling at retail at from $29.20 to $34.07.

Another estimate of size makes them vary from 22 by 20 by 29 inches to 7 feet 6 inches by 10 feet by 2 feet 6 inches, with prices rising from $12.17 to $243.33.

They mention a size of about 27 by 21 by 30 inches as most convenient and best suited to ordinary use, and quote a price therefor of $21.90 to $24.33.

A third firm names the dimensions as here:

Smallest size, 30 inches high, 22 inches wide (front), 20 inches deep (front to back). Range of price for such a size, according to quality and finish, $17.88 to $23.60.

Largest size, 36 inches high, 50 inches wide (front), 27 inches deep (front to back). Range of price for such a size, according to quality and finish, $38.32 to $45.99.

Average size most convenient and best suited to ordinary use 33 inches high, 26 inches wide, 24 inches deep (back to front). Such a refrigerator would be sold at retail for $24.33.

The conditions of climate are not such in this district as to necessitate the employment of artificial temperatures for the preservation of perishable articles. Many years go by without bringing weather, beyond a few days perhaps, when a refrigerator would be of use; and it may be said that it never is warm enough to require such appliances beyond a few weeks during the twelve months, and even that at broken intervals. Every house occupied by persons whose circumstances would warrant the outlay necessary to obtain a refrigerator is provided with cellarage, where meat, vegetables, and so forth are kept before being used. These cellars, while below the exterior level of the ground, are generally well ventilated, and, being furnished with stone tables, they serve the purpose of a cold-air chamber, with the great advantage of abundant space and conveniences of storage.

If United States manufacturers were prepared to place sample stocks at central points and advertise and solicit, it is quite probable an increase in the demand for refrigerators could be brought about, and possibly a remunerative trade established. The progress at first would in all likelihood be slow. The tendency here, however, is continuously in the direction of luxury, and the ability to buy, once granting the existence of the wish, is beyond any peradventure. Trade of all kinds is flourishing, and there could hardly be a more propitious time than the present for the introduction into general use of anything designed to add to the comfort of living.

Ice at retail is only to be had from fishmongers, who, in connection with their regular business, are in the habit of supplying ice to those who require it. There are no regular ice dealers making that their sole business in Leeds. This fact alone would seem to show how far from general is the use of ice in the community.

Two of the largest fishmongers in Leeds report sales of ice; one at the rate of 2 to 3 tons per week, the other at 4 tons per week in winter and 12 to 15 tons in summer. A ton a week is 320 pounds a day, which would give thirty-two families 10 pounds a day. There are probably seventy-two thousand families averaging five persons each in Leeds at the present time. The dealer last referred to sells about six refrigerators in a season, and says the principal demand for ice is for hotels and restaurants.

Retail prices of ice in Leeds are about as follows:

Less than 7 pounds at a time, 3 to 4 cents per pound.
Per 7 pounds, 18¼ to 24⅓ cents per 7 pounds.
Per 14 pounds, 18¼ to 36½ cents per stone.
Per 56 pounds, 48½ to 61 cents per half hundred-weight.
Per 112 pounds, 73 to 97⅕ cents per hundred-weight.

The last price, it will be observed, makes an average of about three-quarters of a cent a pound for 112-pound parcels.

F. H. WIGFALL,
Consul.

UNITED STATES CONSULATE,
Leeds, *February* 10, 1890.

LIVERPOOL.

REPORT BY CONSUL SHERMAN.

Refrigerators are used in this consular district, but only to a very limited extent, confined almost wholly to butchers.

There are no peculiar features required in the construction of refrigerators in this district.

The refrigerators in use in this district are manufactured in Liverpool.

Those used by butchers are of all sizes and a variety of forms. Those for the larger butchers are made on the principle of a steamer's ice-house, holding say 30 hundred-weight to 2 tons of ice, leaving room to hang joints from bars running through near the top. Few are used in families, and the style preferred seems to be that shown with prices in the annexed cut marked A.

It is a double box with two lids, the inner one being lined with zinc and fitted with shelves. The space between the two is filled with charcoal or sawdust.

The ice is placed in the bottom of the inner box.

Three-fourths of the ice used in Liverpool is brought from Norway, and the remaining one-fourth is manufactured here.

The retail prices are as follows:

	s.	d.
Under 12 pounds, per pound	0	1½
12 pounds	1	0
28 pounds	1	6
35 pounds	2	0
42 pounds	2	6
56 pounds	3	0
1 cwt	5	0

Much lower rates are charged to people contracting for stated quantities regularly.

The wholesale price is 25 to 40 shillings ($6.08 to $9.73) per ton.

There is and can be but very little demand for refrigerators for family use in this climate, where all ordinary food of the household can be kept sufficiently well in all seasons without them.

One dealer advertises "The American Refrigerator" for family use, but evidently very little effort is made to push it.

As to the best manner of introducing refrigerators into this district, I can only say that if some active and enterprising local agent were to take a well-made, serviceable, low-priced refrigerator for family use he might find many customers.

THOS. H. SHERMAN,
Consul.

UNITED STATES CONSULATE,
Liverpool, January 21, 1890.

REFRIGERATORS IN FOREIGN COUNTRIES. 175

Refrigerators, or portable ice-houses, to preserve the ice and furnish a provision safe under one lock.

[Inclosure in Consul Sherman's report.]

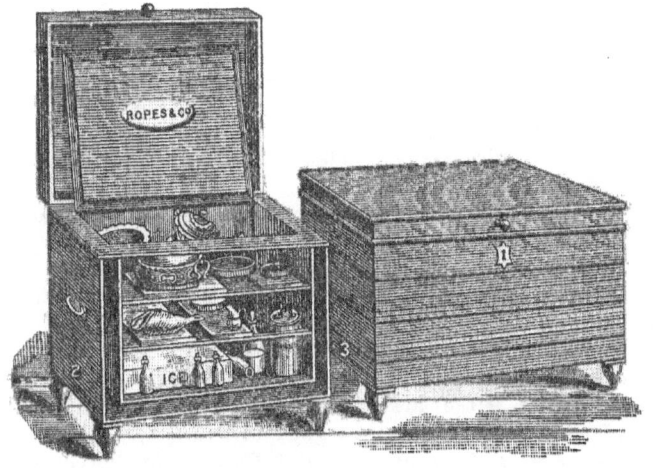

EXTERIOR DIMENSIONS.

	Length.	Width.	Height.	Price.		Length.	Width.	Height.	Price.
	Ft. In.	Ft. In.	Ft. In.	£ s.		Ft. In.	Ft. In.	Ft. In.	£ s.
No. 1	1 6	1 1	2 2	2 10	No. 4	3 6	2 4	2 11	6 0
No. 2	2 4	1 9	2 4	3 10	No. 5	4 0	2 8	3 2	8 0
No. 3	3 3	2 1	2 8	5 0					

LONDON.

REPORT BY CONSUL-GENERAL NEW.

I have personally visited or been in correspondence with all the extensive manufacturers and dealers in refrigerators of whom I have had or could obtain any knowledge, and will answer the interrogatories of the Department as best I can from the information thus obtained.

Refrigerators are used in this consular district quite extensively in the larger meat and vegetable warehouses and markets, but to a very limited extent for domestic or household purposes.

While no peculiar features in the construction of refrigerators exist in this district other than would be required for like purposes in the United States, yet as a matter of fact the refrigerators are here more generally permanent fixtures rather than movable furniture, as with us, when they are used for ordinary or household purposes.

They are mostly manufactured within this district, although there are a few houses dealing in American refrigerators.

They are of all sizes and prices; of those that are permanent fixtures, they being constructed by special contract because of convenience, location, and adaptation, it is not possible to give cost, being cost of days' labor and material used; but of those that are movable and made in numbered sizes I furnish herewith price lists from the leading dealers.

For very large and extensive uses, such as the larger breweries and meat-preserving stores, ice is extensively manufactured here, but for other uses ice is imported from Norway, there being several lines of steamers engaged in the trade to various parts of the United Kingdom. But it should be borne in mind that the use and consumption of ice in the United Kingdom is very limited and inconsiderable as compared to its use in the United States.

The price of ice per 112 pounds at warehouses is 28 cents; delivered within a radius of 3 miles from warehouse, from 49 to 73 cents.

The reason that refrigerators and ice are not more extensively used in the United Kingdom is because of the climatic conditions and the general comparatively uniform and moderate temperature.

The best manner of introducing refrigerators in this consular district would be, in my opinion, the establishment of large central agencies and show-rooms in the cities of the United Kingdom, with some competent person to explain their uses and convenience.

I inclose herewith a quantity of literature, viz, descriptive catalogues, price lists, etc., which I have picked up in making the inquiries necessary to furnish the information required by the circular of the Department. The inclosed documents furnished in detail a great amount of information and data that will be valuable to American manufacturers of refrigerators who desire to enter their goods in competition with those manufactured in this country and is largely descriptive of the methods now in use.*

JNO. C. NEW,
Consul-General.

UNITED STATES CONSULATE,
London, February 3, 1890.

THE PONTIFEX ICE MAKING AND REFRIGERATING MACHINES.

[Inclosure in Consul-General New's Report.]

These machines are now so well known and have been so extensively and successfully adopted that it would almost appear superfluous to enter into any detailed description of their merits and of their system of working. The subject of artificial refrigeration, however, is often not clearly understood. It is a comparatively new one, and has not yet received that attention which has been bestowed on other branches of mechanical science.

Pontifex & Wood, Limited, therefore take this opportunity to bring before their friends a description of their patent apparatus, and to make a comparison between it and other inventions intended to achieve similar results.

---

* Only one inclosure printed herewith; the whole being too voluminous for publication.

Ammonia and ether are the only two agents which produce cold sufficiently cheaply for ordinary commercial purposes, and which are not attended with other overwhelming difficulties. The comparison for all practical purposes may, therefore, be confined to them.

The boiling-point of ammonia is 120° lower than that of ether. Its latent heat is nearly six times as great. The tension of its vapor at an equal temperature is nearly thirteen times as great.

Apart from the advantages which ammonia affords in dispensing with the use of large and costly air-pumps, its above-named properties enable it, by the Pontifex process, to produce ice at one-fifth the cost for fuel of its production by ether.

Ammonia also posesses the advantage over ether that it is not inflammable, and the insurance companies therefore make no objection to its use. Neither does ammonia corrode the metal with which it comes in contact; on the contrary, it possesses the property of preserving the iron and steel of which the machine is made. It is also by far the least expensive in its first cost.

At the time the Pontifex ammonia machine was first placed commercially in the market, in 1875, the ether machines which were of earlier invention were already well established as being the only process then available; and in view of the comparatively large first cost and the little understood character of all descriptions of artificial refrigerating machines, it is easily to be understood that the prejudice against any new process was hard to overcome.

However, as time has gone on, the merits of ammonia machines have been realized, and ether machines have been gradually driven out of the market. At this present time scarcely any, if any, of them are being made. Nothing can more clearly show that the ether machines are practically extinct than the fact that the manufacturers of them finding their trade gone are endeavoring to place upon the market various forms of ammonia machines, modified in the hope of evading the patents held by Pontifex & Wood, Limited.

It is, therefore, unnecessary at this date to recapitulate the further advantages which the use of ammonia presents over that of ether, and the comparison rests between the various forms of ammonia machines. Before preceeding with it, however, some description of the Pontifex apparatus will be desirable.

DESCRIPTION OF THE PONTIFEX PATENT AMMONIA ABSORPTION REFRIGERATING MACHINE.

It is a well-known physical law that on the change of any liquid into the gaseous form, with a corresponding increase of bulk, a large amount of its contained heat is rendered latent; and on the reverse operation taking place the latent heat in the gas is rendered sensible, so that it can be readily removed. The Pontifex machine works on this principle. It consists of a number of very strong cast-iron cylindrical vessels connected together by pipes and cocks. The first of these is a large horizontal vessel called the generator, into which a charge of commercial liquor ammonia is placed. This vessel contains a coil of steam-pipes, heated by steam from the ordinary steam-boilers, so as to evaporate the ammonia, which rises up a vertical cylinder called the separator, placed on the top of the generator. This separator is so constructed that any watery vapor rising with the ammonia is condensed and returned to the generator. From the top of the separator a pipe conveys the gas to the condenser, consisting of a number of coils of pipes, contained in a wrought-iron vertical cylinder, which is kept full of water in circulation. In this condenser the evaporated ammonia gas is condensed into a liquid form by the pressure caused by its own accumulation. This liquid next passes to the cooler, which is a vertical cast-iron vessel containing coils of wrought-iron pipes. In the cooler the liquid ammonia, which leaves the condenser at a temperature of about 70° or 80° Fahr. is allowed to expand into gaseous form. In doing so its sensible heat is rendered latent, as above described, and its temperature is ordinarily reduced down to about 10° to 20° Fahr., or say 22° to 12° of frost; but it can be reduced to a much lower point if desired. A circulation of water or brine is run through the coils of pipes in the cooler, and the expanding ammonia gas cools this water or brine down to any desired temperature. After doing this the ammonia gas passes away through a pipe into another vertical cylinder called the absorber, in which it meets with and is absorbed by the water from which it was first evaporated in the generator. From the absorber the liquid ammonia is drawn by pumps which force it back through an economizer or heater (thereby raising its temperature by means of the water which is running from the generator into the absorber) into the generator. From this generator it is evaporated again, and the operation is continuous, the same ammonia and water being used indefinitely.

The method of work is as follows: After all the connections are made, the machine is started by filling the generator with the ordinary ammoniacal liquor of commerce, and a little steam is admitted into the coil of pipes inside the generator, so as to raise just sufficient pressure of gas to expel all the air in the machine through a valve provided for the purpose on the absorber.

When all the air is thus expelled, the full pressure of steam is turned into the generator coil. The ammonia in the solution being very volatile is immediately driven off in the form of gas, and passes through the separator into the top of the condenser, the water of the solution being left behind in the generator.

The condensing water is admitted at the bottom of the condenser and run off at the top, the ammoniacal gas passing down through a coil of pipe contained in the condenser.

The upper part of this coil is called the rectifier, and is fitted at intervals with traps or pockets. The gas, passing down the coil, is cooled by the condensing water, and parts with any watery particles that may have been carried over with the ammonia. This water is caught in the traps and is at once passed out of the coil and returns into the separator.

The ammoniacal gas, after passing the lowest trap, is quite dry or anhydrous, and, as explained elsewhere, the attainment of this perfectly dry ammoniacal gas is the principal cause of the great superiority of the Pontifex machine over all others.

The dry ammoniacal gas continues to pass on down the coil in the condenser until by its accumulation it reaches a pressure at which the gas becomes liquefiable, the liquefaction being greatly assisted by the reduction of temperature due to the condensing water used.

We have now obtained liquid anhydrous ammonia, and the apparatus is so arranged that, as the gas becomes liquefied, it passes into the cooler.

The ammonia in this vessel, being quite free from water, vaporizes, under the ordinary pressure of the atmosphere, at a temperature as low as 60° below freezing point. At any higher temperature it passes freely into a gaseous form, and at the moment of thus changing its form it absorbs and renders latent an immense amount of heat.

The only source from whence it can abstract this heat is from the contents of a coil of pipe provided for that purpose in the cooler cylinder.

In breweries the water to be cooled is passed direct through this coil; and for icemaking a strong solution of chloride of calcium, or brine, as it is called, is passed through it, which, after being cooled to a very low temperature, is pumped to the ice boxes, there to freeze the water and convert it into ice, returning again to the machine to be recooled for further use.

The ammonia, now again in the gaseous form, passes from the top of the cooler into the absorber. A pipe connects this vessel with the bottom of the generator, through which the pressure in the latter forces a constant stream of the water left in it at starting into the absorber. This water, containing little or no ammonia, greedily absorbs the gas coming from the cooler, and the two form a strong solution of ammoniacal liquor similar to that originally put into the generator. This solution is then drawn away by one of the pumps and forced through a coil of pipe in the economizer or heater G into the top of the separator. The solution, now rich in ammonia, then passes down the cylinder through a series of trays; these trays being heated by the hot vapor rising from the generator, the ammonia is again separated from the water in which it is dissolved, and the solution gradually becomes weaker until it falls into the generator almost entirely exhausted of ammonia.

The ammonia, now once more in the form of gas, passes into the condenser as before, to be again made dry and liquefied, thence to the cooler, where by its reconversion into vapor it again produces the cold, and passes once more back to the absorber and pumps.

Thus the whole process forms a continuous cycle, the same changes from liquid to gas and gas to liquid being constantly repeated, with no destruction of material whatever except of the little quantity of coal consumed under the boiler.

The economizer or heater utilizes the heat of the water as it passes from the generator on its way to the absorber, by heating up the ammoniacal solution before it enters the separator, and so saves steam; whilst at the same time the reduced temperature of the water enables it to re-absorb a larger proportion of ammoniacal gas.

We now proceed to a comparison between the Pontifex absorption and other forms of ammonia refrigerating machines.

First as to other forms of ammonia absorption machines:

English machines, number in use.—There are some two or three other forms of these besides the Pontifex offered for sale in this country. These have been patented within the last twelve months, but so far as is known not one of them has been made and worked. Thus, they have not yet even reached the experimental stage, and it is consequently impossible to make any practical comparison with them.

It will be observed, therefore, that in the United Kingdom the ammonia absorption machines have from the first maintained their pre-eminent position. On the Continent and in America they have only recently been introduced. The latter country is the great field for the use of artificial refrigeration, and the most recent advices from the United States remark that "there is no doubt that the absorption are going to supersede the compression machines."

Foreign machines.—In addition to the English machines above mentioned, there are one or two continental and American manufacturers who have attempted to make ammonia absorption machines. They have, however, lacked the perfect arrangement of analyzer or separator, which is the most important and distinguishing feature of the Pontifex machine, and, therefore, it has been found impossible to work them continuously. In addition to this, they have been so badly designed and constructed that their leakages of ammonia have been excessive, break-downs frequent, and costs of repairs very heavy, so that they have obtained a very bad reputation. None of these machines have been placed on the English markets.

Next as to ammonia compression machines. In these machines the ammonia gas, as it leaves the refrigerator or cooler of the apparatus, is drawn into a gas-pump worked by a steam-engine or other convenient motive power, and there compressed into a liquid by the direct application of the steam power. It is manifest that an enormous amount of steam-engine power is required to work this gas-pump and to compress such large volumes of gas into liquid by means of the heavy pressure which is required for the purpose.

STEAM-ENGINE POWER REQUIRED.

In the Pontifex machine, this is only about one-sixth part of that required by all ammonia compression machines. The following table shows this:

No. of machine	B.	C.	D.	D1.	E.	E1.	F.	G.
Size of machine in water cooled from 55° to 45° Fahr. per hour	450	1,200	2,200	2,750	3,250	4,350	5,500	8,000
Steam-engine power required by the Pontifex machine, about	1½	2	3	3½	4	4½	5	6
Steam-engine power required by ammonia compression machines, about, with condensing water at 50°	....	10	15	....	25	....	....	45
Steam-engine power required by ammonia compression machines, about, with condensing water at 85°	....	15	22	....	37	....	....	67

In all such cases the indicated horse-power required, which, of course, is much greater than the "nominal" or "effective," has been taken, including the power required for driving the brine and water circulating pumps.

STEAM-BOILER POWER REQUIRED.

In the Pontifex machine, besides the steam required to drive the small steam engine, some is required for heating the coil in the generator, but the quantity is still very much less than in the ammonia compression machine, as shown by the following comparison:

No. of machine	B.	C.	D.	D1.	E.	E1.	F.	G.
Size of machine in water cooled from 55° to 45° Fahr. per hour	450	1,200	2,200	2,750	3,250	4,250	5,500	8,000
Steam-boiler power required by the Pontifex machine, about	4	5	6	7	8	10	12	15
Steam-boiler power required by ammonia compression machines, about, with condensing water at 50°	....	10	15	....	25	....	....	45
Steam-boiler power required by ammonia compression machines, about, with condensing water at 85°	....	15	22	....	37	....	....	67

The amount of coal consumed is approximately proportionate to the amount of steam-boiler power required by the two systems.

These two points, i. e., relative sizes of steam-engine and boiler required, are of the utmost possible importance. With a small engine and boiler, the coal bill is kept small, the amount of lubricant for the engine is reduced, and one man can look after one or even two machines and can also stoke the boiler. With a large engine and boiler, in addition to heavy coal and oil bills, a separate engineer is required to run the machine, and a stoker to look after the boiler. The charges arising from these necessities are constant—recurring daily—and will very soon amount to the value of the machine.

AMOUNT OF CONDENSING WATER REQUIRED.

In consequence of the great height of the Pontifex condenser, the water entering at the bottom is enabled as it rises and gets warmer to continue to do work in cooling the hotter gases as they descend from the top of the coils, consequently much less condensing water is wanted by the Pontifex than by the ammonia compression machine, as shown by the following comparison:

No. of machine.	B.	C.	D.	D1.	E.	E1.	F.	G.
Size of machine in water cooled per hour from 55° to 45° Fahr.	450	1,200	2,200	2,750	3,250	4,350	5,500	8,000
Condensing water at 50° Fahr. required by the Pontifex machine, about, galls. per hour	200	400	800	1,050	1,250	1,700	2,100	3,000
Ditto required by ammonia compression machine, about, galls. per hour	....	750	1,500	....	2,500	....	....	5,000

This question of condensing water is often of the utmost possible importance; as, for instance, in breweries, where frequently the water has to be brought by measure from water companies, or pumped from great depths. In such cases, the smaller consumption of the Pontifex machine is an enormous advantage, and by making special arrangements the quantity can, if required, be reduced still further. It must, however, be clearly understood that the quantity of the water can only be reduced to its minimum when care is taken to keep the condenser coils clean, so that the surfaces may be fully effective; and that care is taken that water is not allowed to run to waste through the machine. If the initial temperature of the condensing water is higher than 50° Fahr. the quantity required is correspondingly increased.

The amounts of steam power and condensing water above given for the ammonia compression machines are taken from the latest issued catalogues of the makers of these machines. Although these quantities can be to some extent varied, it is impossible from the nature of the case that they can be materially altered, except by increasing them.

AMOUNT OF LUBRICANT REQUIRED.

In the Pontifex machine this is reduced to the infinitesimal amount of oil required to lubricate the eccentrics and pins of the ammonia pumps, their plungers or rods being lubricated by water. In addition to this, a little oil or tallow is wanted for the small engine which drives the pumps.

In the ammonia compression machine a very considerable amount of special lubricant is required for the large piston, piston rod, and cylinder of the gas pump, which has to pump a very hot dry gas against a heavy pressure. As ordinary oils are unsuitable for this purpose by reason of their liability to sapouification by the ammonia, glycerine, or other special lubricant has to be used and in such quantities that a special pump is generally required to force it into the gas pump cylinder. The glycerine is largely carried over mechanically from the gas pump into the condenser, and to prevent its clogging the machine it has to be drawn off through traps, and to be rectified in a special apparatus to enable it to be re-used. Nothing of this sort has to be done with the Pontifex machine.

DURABILITY AND NON-LIABILITY TO BREAK DOWN.

Wear and tear in all machines only occur in those parts which move or which are liable to corrosion.

In the Pontifex machine the only moving part is a small single or double acting pump with one or two suctions and one or two delivery valves. This pump is of the simplest design, can be repaired by any ordinary mechanic, and gives no more trouble in looking after than a common little boiler feed-pump. It has to pump a comparatively cool liquid solution of ammonia and water, and therefore no trouble is experienced in keeping tight its one stuffing box-joint or gland. It requires no lubrication. To prevent the possibility of breakdown, this, the only moving part of the machine, is generally made in duplicate, with cocks so arranged that if one pump gets out of order it can be shut off from the apparatus and the other started to work without one moment's stoppage, and repairs to the idle pump can be made while the machine is running. Thus the only moving part of the machine is duplicated so that those having one Pontifex machine are in practically as good a position as those having two of any other design.

In ammonia compression machines, on the other hand, the moving and most important parts consist of a very powerful steam-engine and large dry hot gas pump, with a large and ponderous fly-wheel often weighing several tons, pistons and rods, connecting rods, cranks, shafts, etc. The liability to and cost of repairs and breakdowns is therefore of course proportionately greater.

With regard to corrosion, ammonia either in its anhydrous state or combined with water has no injurious action on iron or steel surfaces with which alone it comes in contact in the Pontifex machine. On the contrary it has a directly preservative effect, coating the surfaces with a fine protective film or enamel, and doing nothing further. A competitor states that the hot solution of ammonia and water in the Pontifex machine has a corrosive effect on iron. This is absolutely incorrect and erroneous, as indisputably proved by the fact that after working the number of Pontifex machines for so many years no single case has ever been discovered of any corrosion whatever having taken place, and the whole of the Pontifex machines ever made are now at work and as fit for work as when first started. No machine has ever worn out, and, indeed, no limit can be placed upon the duration of these machines.

Safety.—The Pontifex machine consists chiefly of a number of wrought-iron lap-welded coils of pipes, capable of bearing a pressure of several thousand pounds per square inch, placed in very heavy and thick cast-iron vessels, which are designed to bear a strain of over ten times the usual working pressures, and very carefully cast from special brands of pig-iron. The whole apparatus is tested twice to more than three times the ordinary working pressures. It is, therefore, practically impossible for any accident to occur; in proof of which it may be stated that no accident whatever causing danger to or loss of life or limb, or damage to property, has ever occurred with any Pontifex machine.

Foundations.—The Pontifex machine having such very small moving parts requires simply a floor to stand it on which is capable of carrying the weight; the ammonia compression machine requires very large and extensive foundations to take the strain of the heavy moving parts.

In hot climates another advantage of the Pontifex machine comes in with special importance. Where the condensing water is hot the ammonia has to be evaporated and condensed under greater pressure and a higher temperature, and therefore a correspondingly higher steam pressure is required to work the machine. For example, a Pontifex machine working in this country with condensing water at 50° Fahr. would require steam at a pressure of 20 to 30 pounds per square inch; while in the tropics, with condensing water at 85° to 95° Fahr., the steam pressure required would be 40 to 50 pounds per square inch. This means a higher pressure of steam, but only about 10 to 20 per cent. more in quantity to do the work—meaning a coal bill increased by 10 to 20 per cent. But with an ammonia compression machine, as the same amount of gas has to be compressed into a liquid under all conditions of condensing water, and as an increase from 50° to 95° in the initial temperature of the condensing water causes the gas to require nearly double the pressure to condense it, it follows that in the tropics the amount of steam-engine power required to do the same useful work is nearly doubled, which means a coal bill increased nearly 100 per cent.

Chemicals.—A point of minor importance in favor of the Pontifex machine is this: The liquor ammonia used in it is an ordinary commercial article, which can be readily and commonly procured at a cost of 3d. to 4d. per pound. It is conveyed in ordinary light iron kegs, without trouble or danger. The anhydrous ammonia, used in the ammonia compression machine, is a special article, only obtainable in this country at one or two places, costing about 3s. per pound, and it can only be conveyed in special steel or welded iron tubes under heavy pressure, and can only be transferred from the tubes to the machines by coupling them up together with special pipes, and at some trouble and risk of loss.

The amount of ammonia required to be added after the first charge in the Pontifex machine depends upon the care taken in packing the ammonia pumps. It should not exceed, and in many cases has been found to be less, in value than £3 to £5 per annum.

TABLE OF RESULTS OBTAINED BY THE PONTIFEX MACHINES.

COOLING WATER.

Size of machine.	Ice, equivalent in tons, melted per twenty-four hours.	Gallons of water reduced in temperature 10° Fahr., per hour.	Floor space required.	Power of steam-engine.*	Power of steam-boiler.†	Size of machine.	Ice, equivalent in tons, melted per twenty-four hours.	Gallons of water reduced in temperature 10° Fahr., per hour.	Floor space required.	Power of steam-engine.*	Power of steam-boiler.†
			Ft. Ft.	H. P.	H. P.				Ft. Ft.	H. P.	H. P.
A	1½	225	10 by 5	1	2	E	20	3,250	20 by 12	4	8
B	3	450	12 6	1½	4	E1	28	4,350	22 13	4½	10
C	8	1,200	15 9	2	5	F	35	5,500	22 13	5	12
D	14	2,200	17 10	3	6	G	50	8,000	23 14	6	15
D1	17	2,750	20 12	3½	7						

* It is to be observed that in very many cases existing steam-engines can be made available for supplying the very small amount of engine-power required, the pumps being driven from existing shafting by pulleys and leather belts. In such cases o special steam-engine is not required.

† These figures denote the horse-power of boiler, which would be supplied with a machine, but much less power would be required if any can be spared from boilers already in use. In such cases all that is required is to run a small steam-pipe from the boilers to the generator of the machine.

The following reduces the above table of quantities of water cooled into the form in which it is most useful to brewers:

Barrels (thirty-six gallons each) of water cooled in twelve hours.

Size of machine	A.	B.	C.	D.	D1.	E.	E1.	F.	G.
Ice, equivalent in tons, melted per twenty-four hours	1½	3	8	14	17	20	28	35	50
Degrees Fahr.									
From 50 to 40	75	150	400	733	917	1083	1450	1833	2666
50 45	150	300	800	1466	1834	2166	2900	3666	5332
55 40	50	100	266	488	611	722	966	1222	1777
55 45	75	150	400	733	917	1083	1450	1833	2666
55 50	150	300	800	1466	1834	2166	2900	3666	5332
60 40	37	75	200	366	458	541	725	916	1333
60 45	50	100	266	488	611	722	966	1222	1777
60 50	75	150	400	733	917	1083	1450	1833	2666
60 55	150	300	800	1466	1834	2166	2900	3666	5332
65 40	30	60	160	293	366	433	580	733	1066
65 45	37	75	200	366	458	541	725	916	1333
65 50	50	100	266	488	611	722	966	1222	1777
65 55	75	150	400	733	917	1083	1450	1833	2666
70 40	25	50	133	244	305	361	483	611	888
70 45	30	60	160	293	366	433	580	733	1066
70 50	37	75	200	366	458	541	725	916	1333
70 55	50	100	266	488	611	722	966	1222	1777

COOLING AIR.

Size of machine.	Ice, equivalent in tons, melted per twenty-four hours.	Number of cubic feet of air reduced in temperature 10° Fahr., per hour.	Floor space required.	Power of steam engine.*	Power of steam boiler.†	Size of machine.	Ice, equivalent in tons, melted per twenty-four hours.	Number of cubic feet of air reduced in temperature 10° Fahr., per hour.	Floor space required.	Power of steam engine.*	Power of steam boiler.†
			Ft. Ft.	H.P.	H.P.				Ft. Ft.	H.P.	H.P.
A	1½	60,000	10 by 5	1	2	E	20	850,000	20 by 12	4	8
B	3	120,000	12 6	1½	4	E1	28	1,050,000	22 13	4½	10
C	8	250,000	15 9	2	5	F	35	1,250,000	22 18	5	12
D	14	550,000	17 10	3	6	G	50	1,900,000	23 14	6	15
D1	17	700,000	20 12	3½	7						

* It is to be observed that in very many cases existing steam-engines can be made available for supplying the very small amount of engine-power required, the pumps being driven from existing shafting by pulleys and leather belts. In such cases a special steam-engine is not required.

† Care must be taken not to confound the number of cubic feet of air with the cubical contents of the chambers to be cooled. In consequence of the air circulation and the radiation through the roof and walls, etc., the cubical contents of the air in a chamber usually require to be cooled from eight to fifteen times every hour, in order that the temperature of the chamber may assimilate to that of the air passing out from the machine. Circumstances, however, vary so much that no useful rules can be laid down, and in every case a special inspection of the building is desirable.

Only one man is required to work any of the above machines, including stoking the boiler, and for the four smaller sized machines he would have spare time for other work. A man can attend two or more machines if required.

The cooling machines consist of an ammonia machine complete with all the usual connections and fittings, with ammonia pumps fitted on a cast-iron bed-plate and supplied with rods and eccentrics and shaft; or crank-shaft mounted in cast-iron A frames, and provided with pulley ready to be driven by a belt from an existing shaft or engine.

PONTIFEX MACHINES FOR COOLING WATER FOR USE IN REFRIGERATING AND ATTEMPERATING IN BREWERIES.

The most important purpose for which the Pontifex machine can be used in breweries, and that to which it has been most largely applied, is the cooling of the water to be used for refrigerating and attemperating. Where an unlimited supply of well water at 50° to 54° Fahr. temperature can be obtained, a cooling machine becomes of minor importance; but where, as particularly in many large towns, the well water supplies run short or give out, and the brewer has to rely on the town supply as provided by the water company, or on river water, a cooling machine becomes indispensable for the summer production of sound beers, and in many cases for the production of any commercial beers at all.

During the five summer months the town's water usually rises to from 65° to 68° Fahr. or even higher, and it is of course impossible with this to cool the worts down to the usual pitching temperatures of 57° to 59° Fahr. It is also impossible to control the fermentations in the tuns or squares with water of such high temperatures in the attemperators, and, on completion of fermentations, equally impossible to cool the finished beers down to the temperature desirable for racking. Under these circumstances the cooling machine gets the brewer out of all his troubles due to the high temperature of his water supply. The water, at a temperature of 65° or more, as it comes from the company's main or from the brewery water-pump, is run direct through the coil in the cooler of the Pontifex machine, and leaving it reduced to 50°, 45°, or any desired lower temperature, is forced still under its original water company's pressure, and without pumping, to the upper part of the brewery, where, at a height commanding the refrigerators and attemperators, it is discharged into a tank (by preference made of wood, or of iron lagged with wood and sawdust) from which the water is drawn off as required for refrigerating and attemperating.

H is the water-service from the company's main or from well or river water pumps to the cooler of machine. A cock on this pipe is adjusted to pass more or less of the water so that the latter may leave at the desired temperature as shown by a thermometer on the pipe J at the outlet from cooler.

I is the cooled water pipe leading away from the cooler of machine up to—

J, the ice-water tank in which the cooled water is stored to be drawn off as required for refrigerating or attemperating.

The arrangement is simplicity itself. The machine is fixed by preference on the ground-floor near the brewery steam-boilers and placed under the charge of the stoker or engine driver, no special man being required to work it. No special steam-boiler is required, so little steam being wanted that it generally only means the stoker putting on the boiler fire an extra two or three shovelfuls of coals per hour.

In ordinary daily working the machine is started in the morning in time to fill up the ice-water tank by the time the beer refrigerators are started. The machine continues running till the refrigerating is done, and is kept on till the tank is filled up again, leaving a supply of ice-water for the use of the attemperators during the night and until the machine starts again next day. Doubts have been expressed by many brewers as to whether the ice-water would remain cold when left standing in tank during the night and longer. Pontifex and Wood, limited, have therefore made very careful inquiries on this point, and they find that in covered wood tanks, or ordinary iron tanks covered and lagged with wood and sawdust, the rise of temperature has been quite insignificant—not more than 1° Fahr. during from twelve to twenty-four hours.

The practical results in a brewery are, in addition to the improvement in the beer and the complete control obtained over the refrigeration and fermentations, that the beer refrigeration can be done in very much less time and the day's work completed much earlier; and a complete stoppage of the enormous waste of water caused by the necessity to rattle the greatest quantity of the comparatively hot company's water through the refrigerators and attemperators to keep any sort of control of the operations.

It has been found, in most cases, that a saving of more than half the water company's bill for refrigerating and attemperating water has been made.

In large breweries, where great quantities of ice water are required, the machines are generally run continuously day and night. Pontifex machines have been fitted up in the above manner and for the above purpose at sixteen large breweries, the names of and introductions to which will be given upon application.

PONTIFEX MACHINES FOR COOLING THE AIR IN THE FERMENTING AND YEAST ROOMS.

Another very important purpose to which the Pontifex machine has been extensively applied is cooling the air in the fermenting and yeast rooms. Even in those breweries where an unlimited supply of cold water is obtainable it should always be remembered that the water can only be applied—in the fermenting vessels—to cooling the beer itself, and not to the head of yeast above the beer. Therefore, in hot weather, it is not of unfrequent occurrence for the fermenting beers to be well under control by the use of the attemperators, while the yeast above is going wrong, because of the great temperature of the air in the room. Under these circumstances, the Pontifex machine is extremely valuable. It enables the brewer to obtain an October temperature (50° Fahr. or less) at will in the hottest fermenting room and the hottest summer weather.

A circulation of brine (a solution of chloride of calcium in water) is pumped by the brine pump through the coils of pipes in the cooler, and the ammonia gas cools this brine down to somewhere near its own temperature—say about 10° to 20° Fahr. or 22° to 12° of frost, or very much lower, if desired.

From this cooler cold brine flow and return mains are run through the brewery, and up to the top of the building.

In the fermenting rooms rows of cast-iron flanged pipes are fixed over the tuns and squares to be cooled, and through these pipes branch circulations of the cold brine are carried from the brine flow and return mains. This cold brine cools down the pipes to below freezing point, and the surfaces of the pipes cool the air in the rooms down to 45° or 50° Fahr., or any desired temperature. By means of cocks provided on the various branch mains the speed of flow of brine through the various circulations, and consequently the temperature of the rooms can be regulated and reduced or increased at pleasure.

The air in the yeast rooms is cooled in the same manner.

In the simplest arrangement of the brine mains, the whole of the area of the fermenting room is cooled. A separate brine circulation is run over each row of rounds or squares, and all are cooled at once.

In a more elaborate arrangement, where a number of very large squares have to be cooled, the sides and tops of the squares are boxed in with light boarding, and under this boarding the brine pipes are fixed, a separate circulation to each square. This plan enables the temperature of the air over each square to be regulated separately, and the brine to be shut off separately from empty squares; it also economizes the work the machine has to do, as only the air directly over each vessel has to be cooled; but it is most suitable for adoption where the fermenting vessels are very large.

In this case, also, the machine is by preference fixed on the ground floor near the brewery steam-boilers, so that it can be attended to by the existing stoker.

In ordinary working, the machine is run during the day time, and when it is shut off at night and the fermenting rooms are closed up, the large amount of cold stored up in the brine in the pipes over the fermenting vessels is generally found sufficient to keep the rooms down to the desired temperature during the night. In very hot weather, and in very large breweries, however, the machine is generally run at night as well as day.

PONTIFEX MACHINES USED FOR THE COMBINED PURPOSES OF COOLING WATER FOR USE IN REFRIGERATING AND ATTEMPERATING AND COOLING THE AIR IN THE FERMENTING AND YEAST ROOMS.

This is accomplished by one machine in the following manner:

The machine is fitted up with brine pipes in the same way as last described. The fermenting and yeast rooms are cooled by brine pipes in the same way as last described. To cool the water the following plan is adopted, as shown by the illustration on opposite page.

At the top of the brewery building at a height commanding the refrigerators and attemperators, the ice-water tank is fixed. Over this tank is fixed a brass pipe brine refrigerator, consisting of horizontal rows of brass pipes through which a branch circulation of the cold brine from the brine mains is run, while over them the water from the company's mains, at 60° to 65° Fahr. or any other temperature is allowed to trickle, and in so doing it is cooled by the brine inside the pipes, and after cooling runs into the cold-water tank from which it is drawn through the pipes and as required for refrigerating and attemperating. By this arrangement the water can be cooled down to 33° Fahr. or any desired temperature above that.

On this plan by simply opening, shutting or regulating cocks, the whole or any desired proportion of the power of the Pontifex machine can be applied to cooling air or to cooling water, or both at the same time, according to the requirements of the brewery; and with the apparatus so arranged brewing can be conducted in the hottest weather with the same facility, certainty, safety, and convenience as in the autumn or winter.

COOLING THE AIR IN LAGER BEER FERMENTING ROOMS AND STORE CELLARS.

The illustration on the opposite page shows the method of cooling lager beer fermenting rooms and store cellars. The plan here adopted is similar to that for cooling the air in fermenting and yeast rooms, with the differences that the temperature required being lower (about freezing point), larger quantities of brine pipes, and in some cases wrought-iron brine pipes of smaller diameter are provided.

APPLICATION OF THE MACHINES TO THE MANUFACTURE OF ICE IN ADDITION TO THEIR ORDINARY WORK.

It is frequently desired in breweries to make a small quantity of ice, either for use in keeping yeast cool, or to send out to public houses, or for private use.

When machines have a brine circulation this is very easily accomplished. If opaque ice will do, it is only necessary to place in the brine-tank galvanized iron pails or molds made of the shape of which the blocks of ice are required. These molds being filled with water and suspended in the brine-tank are, in a few hours, frozen by the brine outside into solid blocks of ice. The molds are then lifted out and turned upside down, when the ice-blocks drop out, the molds being made taper to allow of this.

When clear ice is required it is necessary to keep the water in motion while freezing, and then a more complete arrangement is required, called a patent pyramid ice-box. The illustration on the page opposite 16 shows this.

This shows a small special brine-tank made of wrought iron and lagged with wood and filled in with sawdust. A small branch brine-pipe with regulating cock—taken off the brine main from cooler—runs into one end of this brine-tank, and the warmed brine overflows from the other end of it running into the ordinary brine-tank. In this special brine-tank a number of ice-molds made of galvanized wrought iron and of pyramidal form are placed. Each of these molds is provided with a spiral agitator or endless screw, which being kept constantly revolving, keeps the water in process of freezing in motion. The agitators are kept revolving by means of a counter-shaft and pulleys driven by a gut band from the nearest convenient shafting. When freezing is finished the agitator is taken off and the mold lifted out and turned upside down, when a beautiful, clear, crystal pyramid of ice, as shown on illustration, appears. As the center of the mold freezes up last, freezing can be stopped at any point, and the hollow left in the block filled in with flowers, fruit, lobsters, etc., which can then be frozen up in the block.

When machines have no brine circulation, but are used for cooling water direct, the same pyramid ice-box is used. In this case, however, as there is no brine circulation, a coil of iron pipes is placed in the ice-box brine-tank, through which ammonia from the cooler is allowed to circulate, expanding in doing so into a gas, and so producing the necessary cold.

When larger quantities of ice are required, it is desirable that the refrigerating machine should be specially arranged accordingly and provided with either "cell," "wall," or "can" ice-boxes.

COST OF WORKING.

The cost of working a given size of refrigerating machine, whether used for cooling water or air or both, is approximately the same. It is about as follows per day of twelve hours.

	A	B	C	D	D1	E	E1	F	G
Quantity of coal used, about cwt............	2	3	4	5	5½	6	8	10	12
	s. d.	s. d.	s. d.	s. d.	s. d.	s. d.	s. d.	s. d.	s. d.
At 10s. per ton	1 0	1 6	2 0	2 6	2 9	3 0	4 0	5 0	6 0
Ammonia to replace loss, say............	0 3	0 3	0 3	0 6	0 6	0 6	0 6	0 9	0 9
Oil, say................................	0 3	0 3	0 3	0 6	0 6	0 6	0 6	0 6	0 9
Total	1 6	2 0	2 6	3 6	3 9	4 0	5 3	6 3	7 6
If coals cost 15s. per ton add to above totals..	0 6	0 9	1 0	1 3	1 5	1 6	2 0	2 6	3 0
If coals cost 20s. per ton add to above totals..	1 0	1 6	2 0	2 6	2 9	3 0	4 0	5 0	6 0

The above are practical working figures where ordinary care is taken. No doubt with good coal and skillful firing and care in working the coal consumption can be reduced, but these conditions seldom exist. When a machine runs continuously for a long time at much less than full power—as in cooling rooms—the coal consumption is proportionately reduced.

The existing engine driver or stoker is assumed to be taking charge of the machine. Of course if a special man is provided his wages, say 3s. 6d. to 4s. per day, be added.

Nothing is put down for condensing water, as the coal consumption is sufficient to include the steam power required to pump it from surface or a moderate depth, and it is assumed that the water itself is provided.

Depreciation and interest on capital—each usually taken at 5 per cent.—every purchaser will calculate on his usual system.

PONTIFEX MACHINES FOR ICE-MAKING.

Table of results obtained by the Pontifex machines.

Size of machine.	Ice made in 24 hours.	Ice equivalent in tons melted per 24 hours.	Coal consumed per hour.	Space required.	Power of steam-engine.	Power of boiler.	Size of machine.	Ice made in 24 hours.	Ice equivalent in tons melted per 24 hours.	Coal consumed per hour.	Space required.	Power of steam-engine.	Power of boiler.
	Tons.	Tons.	Pounds.	Feet.	H. P.	H. P.		Tons.	Tons.	Pounds.	Feet.	H. P.	H. P.
B	1½	3	27	25×20	2	5	E	9	20	80	55×35	5	10
C	4	8	48	35×25	3	6	E1	12	28	100	70×40	5½	12
D	6	14	65	46×30	4	8	F	15	35	120	70×40	6	15
D1	7½	17	72	55×35	4½	9	G	24	50	165	90×50	7	20

Ice-making machines are invariably required to run night and day, and the staff of men required to work them is usually about as follows:

Size of machine.	Engine driver or stoker, day.	Engine driver or stoker, night.	*Laborers to remove ice, day.	Total number of men required.	Size of machine.	Engine driver or stoker, day.	Engine driver or stoker, night.	*Laborers to remove ice, day.	Total number of men required.
A, B or C	1	1	1	3	E1 and F	1	1	3	5
D, D1, and E	1	1	2	4	G	1	1	4	6

The ice-making machines consist of an ammonia machine complete, with steam engine and boiler, patent ice-boxes, with agitators and fittings capable of making perfectly clear, transparent ice; ammonia, brine relieving, boiler feed and condensing water pumps with driving gear; hot and cold brine tanks, shafting, riggers, and belts, and all brine and steam pipes between the various parts of the apparatus.

The Pontifex machine when applied to ice-making is similar to that used in breweries.

In addition, however, to the machine itself, ice-boxes are required in which to freeze the water into ice. These are made on different plans, as follows:

ICE-MACHINES WITH CAN BOXES.

The can box consists of a wrought or cast iron tank of large size, lagged with wood filled in with sawdust. This tank is filled with brine. A circulation of brine (a so-

---

* The number of laborers varies according to the class of men available and the facilities for removing, storing, and loading the ice. In hot climates, where black labor has to be employed, many more men are required.

lution of chloride of calcium in water) is pumped by the brine-pump through the coils of pipes in the cooler, and the ammonia gas cools this brine down to somewhere near its own temperature, which varies according to the thickness of the ice being made from 15° Fah. (above zero) to minus 10° (below zero) Fah. or lower. From this cooler a cold brine-pipe is run into one end of the brine-tank. From the other end of the brine-tank a warm brine-pipe is run back to the brine-pump, which continually draws brine away from the brine-tank as fast as it delivers it into the cooler, and so keeps up a constant circulation.

In the brine-tank galvanized iron ice-molds are placed. These are filled with water, and provided with agitators. These agitators are wood blades mounted in frames above the ice-molds, and being continually reciprocated by means of the steam-engine they keep the water in the molds in motion, which causes it to freeze up into clear ice. When freezing is completed the agitators are removed, and the ice-molds, being lifted out by means of the traveler, are carried horizontally to the relieving-tank (which is filled with part of the warm water running waste from the absorber) and dipped therein for a few seconds. The molds are then drawn out and reversed, when the block of ice drops out; and the mold is then filled with water and returned into the brine-tank and commences refreezing.

On this system of making ice the cans are each made of such a size as to produce a rectangular block of ice of given weight. For example:

Blocks weighing 1 cwt. each are made in cans 2 feet $\times$ 2 feet $\times$ 6 inches thick. Blocks weighing 1½ cwt. each are made in cans 2 feet 6 inches $\times$ 2 feet 6 inches $\times$ 6 inches thick. Blocks weighing 2 cwt. each are made in cans 2 feet 6 inches $\times$ 2 feet 6 inches $\times$ 8 inches thick. Blocks weighing 3 cwt. each are made in cans 3 feet $\times$ 3 feet $\times$ 8 inches thick. Blocks weighing 4 cwt. each are made in cans 3 feet 6 inches $\times$ 3 feet 6 inches $\times$ 8 inches thick. Blocks weighing 6 cwt. each are made in cans 3 feet 6 inches $\times$ 3 feet 6 inches $\times$ 12 inches thick, or larger or of altered proportions as desired.

This is the oldest and simplest plan of making ice, and has many advantages:

(1) The first cost of an ice plant is considerably lessened.

(2) Where opaque ice is all that is required, it is not necessary to keep the water in motion, and agitators can be dispensed with.

(3) The blocks are produced of a uniform given size and weight, convenient to load and pack, and no weighing is necessary.

(4) If a can leaks it can be immediately placed on one side for repair, and a spare one takes its place without delay or any partial stoppage of the apparatus.

(5) The whole of the parts of the ice-box are very simple, and can be repaired or remade by any ordinary engineer without special knowledge of ice machinery.

On the other hand there are certain objections:

(1) The agitator blade occupies the middle of the can while the block is freezing, and as the ice freezes up it closes round this; to prevent it freezing in, the agitator has to be withdrawn and the space occupied by it in its traverse frozen up without agitation. Consequently each block has a narrow core of semi-transparent or almost opaque ice in the center. This, however, is only of slight disadvantage in appearance, and even this disadvantage disappears when the ice is broken up. Nor does it affect the keeping qualities of the ice.

(2) If there are any impurities in the water they are frozen up in the ice and tend to show to some extent in the center of the block.

(3) The blocks sometimes freeze up at different speeds, and it therefore may happen that, through carelessness in watching, some agitators get frozen in prematurely, causing their breakage.

(4) The cans, from having constant handling, sometimes leak and so cause a charge for repairs.

(5) Every time a block of ice is lifted out of the brine tank the can has to be lifted and handled with it, and there is a greater weight to handle over what there would

be if the ice only had to be dealt with. This and the extra handling of the empty cans may cause this plan to require a slight amount of extra labor.

(6) By carelessness water may be spilled or leaked into the brine, weakening it.

To reduce or obviate objections Nos. 1 and 2 a plan has been devised of placing a wood frame in the middle of the mould and letting the agitator work inside it—a block being frozen up at each end. This acts so far satisfactorily, but causes new difficulties. The wood freezes to the ice and has to be drawn out of the mold with it and removed by chisels and replaced in the mold; and a certain amount of dirty water has to be pumped out of each mold before removal of the ice, thus causing more hand-labor. In consequence, also, of the blocks freezing up at unusual speeds, some often come out of uneven shape, with a large hole in the center and of much less than the full weight.

To reduce objection No. 5, which is a very important one, various ingenious and complicated arrangements for handling a number of molds together with the assistance of steam-power have been devised. These have been more or less successful, but are evidently only imperfect attempts to overcome difficulties which do not exist in other plans of making ice.

ICE-MACHINE WITH BOXES ON THE WALL SYSTEM.

On this plan an ice-plant has two or more boxes. Thus a 2 or 4 ton plant has two boxes; a 6-ton, two or three boxes; a 9-ton, three boxes; a 15-ton, four or five boxes; and a 24-ton, eight to ten boxes.

The Wall box consists of a wood or wrought-iron water-tank. If made of iron, it is lagged with wood filled in with sawdust. In this tank a number of vertical galvanized cast-iron hollow walls or partitions are fixed by means of bolts to hollow cast-iron ends. Through these walls a circulation of brine cooled by the refrigerating machine is pumped by the brine-pump through the cold-brine pipe. The tank is filled with water, which, being cooled by the brine, freezes on to the hollow walls. The brine, warmed by passing through the walls and freezing the water, goes away to the cold brine tank, from which the brine-pump draws it and forces it through the cooler of the machine, where, being cooled, it again passes to the Wall box and so completes its circuit, the circulation being continuous until the ice has finished freezing. To keep the water in motion agitators reciprocate between the walls as shown, these being driven by means of shafting by the steam-engine, which also drives the ammonia, brine, and water pumps. The hollow walls reach nearly to the bottom of the tank, being kept a few inches above it, and in the space left all impurities voided by the water in freezing settle.

The brine-pipes to the wall boxes are provided with cocks so arranged that when freezing is finished (which is accomplished when the ice has grown to within about ¼-inch clear of the agitator) the brine can be shut off from the box (and turned on to others). The cold brine is then drained out of the walls into the cold-brine tank. There is a small warm-brine tank in which a reserve of brine, heated by means of a coil of steam-pipes by the exhaust steam of the engine or other means, is kept ready. This brine is forced by means of the small warm-brine pipes through the hollow walls of the wall-box, so melting the ice off, and leaving it ready for removal. The agitators are then lifted out. The ice-blocks so made are usually 14 feet long, 3 feet deep, and 6 to 10 inches thick. By means of a saw they are in the box cut into conveniently-sized blocks, say 3 feet 6 inches, by 3 feet, by 6 inches to 10 inches thick, and floating in the surplus water, are lifted out by the overhead traveler straight from the wall-box, and dropped into the cart standing ready to receive them, or dragged away to the store. The surplus water in the box is then filled up to the original level, the agitators are replaced, the warm-brine is shut off and drained out, the cold-brine turned on, and freezing commences. About once a week the water is all run out and the dirt at bottom of the wall-box washed out. Ice made on this plan is far superior to the best natural ice, being of much greater purity, and of the most attractive bril-

REFRIGERATORS IN FOREIGN COUNTRIES. 191

liant crystal clear appearance; and it can not be equalled by any other system of manufacture. Where purity and appearance are of great importance, as for restaurants, clubs, hospital, etc., this ice is always preferred to any other and fetches a higher price. The only objection to it is that it can not be obtained in blocks of uniform size and weight, without cutting up to shape, entailing waste and labor.

The advantages of this plan are:—

(1) Superior purity and appearance of the ice made.

(2) Scarcely any liability to breakage of agitators.

(3) No cans to handle or repair. The walls being fixed and of strong galvanized cast-iron are practically indestructible.

(4) Only the actual ice itself has to be handled, so much less weight has to be moved in comparison with the can system.

(5) When an ice box is finished it can be shut off by simply turning the cocks, and left till it is convenient to remove the ice. Thus all the boxes can be set so as to be completed during the day, and no night-shift of laborers is required.

(6) The water can not spill or leak into the brine and so weaken it.

The objections to this plan are:—

(1) The ice can not be produced in blocks of a given size and weight without waste and labor.

(2) If a box requires repairs it has to be shut off and the capacity of the machine is temporarily reduced in proportion. Repairs, however, are scarcely ever required; the shutting off is accomplished by simply turning cocks; and in a large machine the temporary proportionate reduction of capacity through a box being shut off for repairs is only from 10 to 20 per cent.

To remedy the objection No. 1, and to enable thicker ice to be made in a given time, Pontifex & Wood, limited, have designed their patent cell-box, which is next described.

ICE-MACHINE WITH PATENT CELL ICE-BOXES.

On this plan an ice plant has (as on the wall system) two or more boxes. Thus a 2 or 4-ton plant has 2 boxes, a 6-ton two or three boxes, a 9-ton three boxes, a 15-ton three or four boxes, and a 24-ton six to eight boxes.

The illustration opposite shows an ice plant to make 15 tons of ice per twenty-four hours, and provided with four-cell ice boxes. Opposite page twenty-two will also be found an illustration in detail to a larger scale of the patent cell ice-box. The cell ice-box consists of a wood or wrought-iron water tank. If made of iron it is lagged with wood filled in with sawdust. This tank is provided with (1) a galvanized wrought-iron hollow or double bottom; (2) two galvanized cast-iron hollow cross walls, or partitions; and (3) a number of short galvanized cast-iron longitudinal hollow walls fixed at right angles to the cross walls. Between the end of the tank and the ends of the longitudinal walls, open spaces are left. Each of these longitudinal walls is 3 feet 6 inches by 3 feet 6 inches, and they are fixed at a distance apart equal to the thickness of the blocks of ice it is desired to make, usually 9, 10, or 12 inches. Between each two of these longitudinal walls the ice forms, and therefore the blocks made are either: Three feet 6 inches by 3 feet 6 inches by 9 inches thick, weighing about 4¼ hundred weight each, or 3 feet 6 inches by 3 feet 6 inches by 10 inches thick, weighing about 5 hundred weight each, or 3 feet 6 inches by 3 feet 6 inches by 12 inches thick, weighing about 6 hundred weight each.

Blocks have also been made 3 feet 6 inches by 3 feet 6 inches by 15 inches thick, weighing 7¼ hundredweight each, and even of 3 feet 6 inches by 3 feet 6 inches by 1 foot 9 inches thick, weighing 10¼ hundredweight each; but these extremely thick blocks are not recommended commercially as they take such a long time to freeze up. Through the double bottom, cross-walls, and longitudinal walls, a circulation of brine cooled by the refrigerating machine is pumped by the brine pump H through the cold brine pipe I. The tank is filled with water, which being cooled by the brine freezes on to the double-bottom, cross and longitudinal walls. The brine, warmed by passing through the bottom and walls and freezing the water, goes away to the cold brine tank from which the brine pump H draws it and forces it through the cooler D of the machine, where being cooled it again passes to the cell box and so completes its circuit, the circulation being continuous until the ice is finished freezing. The two layers of ice gradually growing thicker between each two longitudinal walls at last meet and freeze together, when the block is finished. To keep the water in motion agitators reciprocate in the open spaces as shown, these being driven by means of shafting by the steam-engine, which also drives the ammonia, brine, and water pumps. The agitators in moving give an impulse to the water, causing it to rush in a wave between the longitudinal walls, and washing out all the impurities voided by the water in freezing, which settle at the bottom of the open spaces.

The brine-pipes to the cell boxes are provided with cocks so arranged that when freezing is finished the brine can be shut off from the box and turned on to others. The cold brine is then drained out of the double bottom and walls into the cold brine tank. There is a small warm brine tank in which a reserve of brine, heated by means of a steam coil of pipes by the exhaust steam of the engine or other means, is kept ready. This brine is forced by means of the small warm brine pump through the hollow double bottom and walls of the cell-box, so melting the ice-blocks off and leaving them ready for removal. The agitators are than lifted out. The ice-blocks are gently started away from the cross-walls to enable the ice-grips to grasp each end, and are lifted straight out by the overhead traveler P and dropped into the cart standing ready to receive them, or dragged way to the store. The surplus water in the box is then filled up to the original level, the agitators are replaced, the warm brine is shut off and drained out, and cold brine turned on, and freezing recommences. About once a week the water is all run out and the dirt at bottom of the cell-box washed out.

The ice turned out on this plan of cell-boxes is far superior to the best natural ice, being of far greater purity, clearness, and brilliancy, and produced in blocks of the most convenient form for commercial purposes.

The advantages of this plan are—

(1) The blocks are produced of a uniform size and weight, convenient to load and pack; and no weighing is necessary.

(2) The ice is of superior purity and appearance, and of great thickness.

(3) No liability to breakage of agitators.

(4) No cans to handle or repair. The walls are fixed and the general arrangement is of very great strength and practically indestructible.

(5) Only the actual ice itself has to be handled, so less weight has to be in comparison to the can system.

(6) No cutting up waste or weighing of ice, as in the Wall system.

(7) When an ice-box is finished it can be shut off by simply turning the cocks, and left till it is convenient to remove the ice. Thus all the boxes can be set so as to be completed during the day, and no night shift of laborers is required.

(8) The water can not spill or leak into the brine and so weaken it.

The only objection, if it can be called an objection, to the cell-box system, is that if a box requires repair it has to be shut off, and the capacity of the machine is temporarily reduced in proportion. Repairs, however, are scarcely ever required; the shutting off is accomplished by simply turning cocks; and in a large machine the temporary proportionate reduction of capacity through a box being shut off for repairs is only from 10 to 20 per cent.

COST OF WORKING AND PRODUCING THE ICE.

The cost of working varies considerably in different sized plants, working under different conditions; but Pontifex & Wood, limited, are prepared to guarantee, when required, that 15 and 24 ton plants shall be capable of producing in this country the best clear ice at a cost not exceeding 5s. per ton; the cost being for labor, coals, oil, chemicals, and water for making the ice.

The following are approximate estimates of the cost of working:

G or 24-ton ice-plant.

Per week of six days:	£	s.
Coal, 12 tons, at 10s. per ton	6	0
Ammonia, to replace any leakage, say	0	6
Oil, say	0	4
Water to make ice of, adding 50 per cent. for waste, 50,000 gallons, at 6d. per 1,000	1	5
Wages, day engineer	1	15
Wages, day, four laborers to remove ice, at 20s.	4	0
Wages, night stoker	1	5
	14	15
6 by 24 = 144 tons of ice made = 2s. $\frac{1}{4}$d. per ton of ice; if coal costs 20s. per ton add	6	0
= 2s. 10$\frac{1}{4}$d. per ton of ice	20	15

F or 15-ton ice-plant.

Per week of six days:	£	s.
Coal, 9 tons, at 10s. per ton	4	10
Ammonia, to replace any leakage, say	0	6
Oil, say	0	4
Water to make ice of, adding 50 per cent. for waste, 36,000 gallons at 6d. per 1,000	0	18
Wages, day engineer	1	15
Wages, day, three laborers to remove ice, at 20s.	3	0
Wages, night stoker	1	5
	11	18
6×15 = 90-tons of ice made = 2s. 7$\frac{3}{4}$d. per ton of ice. If coals cost 20s. per ton, add	4	10
= 3s. 7$\frac{3}{4}$d. per ton of ice	16	8

C or 4-ton ice-plant.

Per week of six days:	£	s.
Coal, 3 tons, at 10s. per ton	1	10
Ammonia, to replace any leakage, say	0	3
Oil, say	0	2
Water to make ice of, adding 50 per cent. for waste, 10,000 gallons at 6d. per 1,000	0	5
Wages, day engineer	1	15
Wages, day laborer to remove ice	1	0
Wages, night stoker	1	5
	6	0
6×4 = 24 tons of ice made = 5s. per ton of ice. If coals cost 10s. per ton, add	1	10
= 6s. 3d. per ton of ice	7	10

With the above figures, and a knowledge of the local cost of coals and labor, each intending purchaser will be able to calculate for himself the approximate cost of producing ice in his neighborhood. To the above figures depreciation and interest on capital, usually each calculated at 5 per cent. per annum, have to be added. It will be observed that the cost of producing small quantities of ice is, as might be expected, relatively very much higher than of producing large quantities.

In hot climates, as India, etc., the machines usually fall off in their production of ice from 10 to 30 per cent., while the cost of working remains the same or becomes higher, but no fixed rules can be laid down for this.

PROVISION COOLING STORES.

Pontifex & Wood desire to draw attention to the gain to be made by securing an additional source of income to an ice plant by providing in conjunction therewith cold stores for the use of butchers, poulterers, fish mongers and others. These stores can be very simply cooled by a small proportion of the power of the ice-machine, and worked by the same staff.

PONTIFEX REFRIGERATING MACHINES FOR ARTIFICIAL BUTTER MANUFACTORIES.

In this manufacture the various ingredients, after being melted and mixed together at about blood heat in churns, are mixed with and run out into ice-cold water contained in open troughs; the sudden application of the intense cold crystallizing and granulating the artificial butter, which is skimmed off; and the water at the same time washing out the butter milk, which would taint the butter by its rapid decomposition. Originally and still to a large extent ice is used for the production of the ice-cold water, ice being placed in tanks filled with water, and melting, the former imparts its cold to the latter. The objections to this plan are the great cost of the ice and of handling it, the impossibility of getting as low a temperature as desirable (because the best result obtainable by this process is the mean of the two temperatures of the ice and water); the impossibility of obtaining an exact regular temperature continuously, and the fact that the ice being always more or less dirty renders the water so, and so soils the artificial butter and spoils its appearance.

The Pontifex machine overcomes these difficulties. Its cost of working is so small that an amount of cold equal to that produced by the melting of a ton of ice is obtained at a working cost of less than 1s.; from the moment it starts to work a continuous stream of ice-cold water of a steady even temperature as low as $32\frac{1}{2}°$ Fahr. (or $\frac{1}{4}°$ Centigrade), if desired, is available; and the water coming in contact with nothing but the copper or brass tubes of the brine refrigerator leaves the machine as clean as it enters.

The machine itself has been previously described. A circulation of brine is pumped by the brine pump through the coils of pipes in the cooler and the ammonia gas cools this brine down to about $20°$ Fahr. In the churn room over the churns, or in any other convenient position, the ice water tank is fixed. Over this tank is fixed a patent copper or brass pipe brine refrigerator, consisting of horizontal rows of copper or brass pipes through which the circulation of cold brine is run, while over them the water to be cooled coming from the water company's mains at $55°$ to $65°$ Fahr. or any other temperature, is allowed to trickle, and in so doing it is cooled down to $32\frac{1}{2}°$ or $33°$ Fahr. by the brine inside the pipes, and after cooling runs into the ice water tank M, from which it is drawn as required for the use of the churns. The brine refrigerator is shown to a larger scale on the opposite page.

Some artificial butter makers are now using water cooled down only to $39°$ or $40°$ Fahr. In these cases the brine refrigerator is not required, the water to be cooled being simply run through the pipes in the cooler as in breweries.

The following is a table of the approximate quantities of water cooled by the Pontifix machine.

REFRIGERATORS IN FOREIGN COUNTRIES.

[In gallons per hour.]

Size of machines.	B.	C.	D.	D 1.	E.	E 1.	F.	G.
Ice equivalent in tons melted per 24 hours	3	8	14	17	20	28	35	50
Fahrenheit.								
From 73 to 33	100	270	500	620	730	980	1,240	1,800
" 68 to 33	115	310	570	700	815	1,115	1,410	2,050
" 63 to 33	135	360	660	825	975	1,300	1,650	2,400
" 58 to 33	160	430	790	990	1,170	1,565	1,980	2,880
" 53 to 33	100	540	990	1,140	1,460	1,950	2,475	3,600
" 48 to 33	270	720	1,320	1,650	1,950	2,610	3,300	4,800
" 70 to 40	150	400	730	920	1,080	1,450	1,830	2,660
" 65 to 40	180	480	880	1,100	1,300	1,740	2,200	3,200
" 60 to 40	225	600	1,100	1,375	1,625	2,175	2,750	4,000
" 55 to 40	300	800	1,465	1,830	2,165	2,900	3,660	5,330
" 50 to 40	450	1,200	2,200	2,750	3,250	4,350	5,500	8,000

The following is an almost similar table reduced to the metric system.

[In liters per hour.]

Size of machines.	B.	C.	D.	D 1.	E.	E 1.	F.	G.
Centigrade.								
From 24 to 1	445	1,186	2,173	2,692	3,211	4,259	5,434	7,905
" 21 to 1	511	1,363	2,500	3,097	3,693	4,899	6,249	9,090
" 18 to 1	602	1,603	2,941	3,643	4,345	5,763	7,352	10,694
" 15 to 1	730	1,948	3,571	4,424	5,276	6,998	8,928	12,986
" 12 to 1	929	2,479	4,541	5,630	6,715	8,907	11,363	16,528
" 9 to 1	1,278	3,409	6,250	7,742	9,233	12,247	15,624	22,727
" 22 to 5	668	1,782	3,268	4,048	4,822	6,404	8,169	11,883
" 19 to 5	811	2,164	3,968	4,915	5,862	7,775	9,920	14,429
" 16 to 5	1,033	2,754	5,050	6,256	7,461	9,896	12,626	18,364
" 12 to 5	1,628	4,328	7,936	9,831	11,724	15,551	19,841	28,859
" 11 to 5	2,894	5,050	9,259	11,469	13,678	18,143	23,147	33,366

PONTIFEX MACHINES FOR PARAFFIN OIL WORKS.

The Pontifex machine is specially advantageous for this purpose, not only on account of the great economy of the process, but particularly because the very low temperatures which can be maintained by it enable refiners to extract in the presses a far larger quantity of the valuable paraffin than can be obtained in any other way, and the quality of the oil separated is at the same time much improved.

Until recently ether machines have been largely used for this purpose, but the great difficulty with which by their use sufficiently low temperatures are obtained, and their very great reduction of sufficiency at these low temperatures, has caused them to be discarded in almost every case in favor of the Pontifex machine.

The illustration on the opposite page shows the most usual application of the Pontifex machine for paraffin oil cooling. The machine itself has been previously described. A circulation of brine is pumped by the brine pump through the coils of pipes in the cooler, and the ammonia gas cools this brine down to about zero, to 5° below zero Fahrenheit, or lower if desired. In an adjoining room are placed the cooling drums. Each drum consists of an open shallow trough in which revolves a hollow cast-iron or copper cylinder or drum. The oil to be cooled is placed in the trough. The surface of the drum in its revolution dips into this oil and becomes coated with a thin film of it, and is cooled by the circulation of cold brine from the machine, which is run through the drum by means of trunions with stuffing boxes at the ends. As the drum continues its revolution, the cooled oil is reduced to the temperature of 10° or 12° Fahrenheit, or to any other desired, and, in a pasty condition, is removed by a scraper, pressed against the side of the drum. The oil is then drawn away by plunger pumps and forced through filter presses which separate the paraffin wax crystals or scales from the oil.

In a new and improved apparatus the oil to be cooled is placed in large tanks provided with a number of vertical iron hollow walls or divisions. Through these hollow walls the circulation of brine is pumped, cooling down the oil in the spaces or chambers between them. After cooling, the oil is drawn away from the chambers by pumps and filtered as before. This plan is considered superior for several reasons, but chiefly because the oil having a much longer time to cool, the paraffin crystals or scales are formed very much larger, thus enabling the oil to be filtered more readily, and producing a larger quantity and better quality of wax and a better quality of oil.

PONTIFEX MACHINES FOR CHEMICAL WORKS.

Pontifex machines have been supplied to several chemical works, where they have been used chiefly for the reduction of mother liquors to low temperatures to increase the speed of crystallization, and the quantity of crystals produced. Also for the freezing of various chemicals and other purposes. The cold produced by the machine is usually imparted to a brine circulation which is used as a medium for reducing the temperature of the article to be cooled.

PONTIFEX MACHINES FOR BACON-CURING WORKS.

The Pontifex machines have been largely erected in bacon-curing factories, and their use in such is considered one of their most successful applications.

Originally the pigs after being killed were cooled simply by exposure to the atmospheric air, and afterwards cured in underground cellars at the temperature of the earth or 52° to 55° Fahr. These temperatures not being sufficiently low allowed of rapid decomposition and consequent taint in the bacon. To reduce this as far as possible, the bacon was charged with an excessive and objectionable amount of salt to preserve it. The public taste having latterly always moved in the direction of more and more mildly cured bacon, necessitated the artificial reduction of the temperature of the chill rooms and curing cellars. This has been usually accomplished by making the cellars with iron ceilings, above which were stored vast quantities—amounting in some cases to even thousands of tons of ice. This system was found very effective and is still largely in use; but it has many objections, of which the chief are (1) the large first cost of and amount of space occupied by the ice chambers, iron ceilings and their supports; (2) the great and continually recurring cost of the ice itself; (3) the cost and inconvenience of handling the ice; (4) the great risks ran and losses incurred when by any chance in the hot weather the supplies run short, and (5) the fact that the moisture rising in the air condenses against the underside of the iron ceiling and drips down on the bacon in process of curing.

The Pontifex system removes all these objections, and its application is so simple, powerful, and economical, and has proved in every respect so perfectly successful, that its universal adoption by the bacon trade in the United Kingdom is only a question of a very little time.

The illustration herewith shows the manner in which the Pontifex machine is applied in bacon factories. A circulation of brine (a solution of chloride of calcium in water) is pumped by the brine pump through the coils of pipes in the cooler and the ammonia gas cools this brine down to somewhere near its own temperature—say about 10° to 20° Fahr. or 22° to 12° of frost, or very much lower if desired. From this cooler cold brine flow and return mains are run through the factory to the chambers to be cooled. In the chill rooms and curing cellars rows of cast-iron flanged pipes are fixed overhead over the whole area, hanging from the ceiling; and through these pipes branch circulations of the cold brine are carried from the brine flow and return mains. This cold brine cools down the pipes to below freezing point, and the surfaces of the pipes cool the air in the rooms down to 40° Fahr., or any desired temperature. By means of cocks provided on the various branch mains, the speed of flow of brine through the various circulations, and consequently the temperature of the rooms can be regulated and reduced or increased at pleasure. In ordinary working the machine is run in the day-time; and when it is stopped at night and on Sunday, and the curing cellars, etc., are closed up, the large amount of cold stored up in the brine in the pipes is generally found sufficient to keep the rooms down to the desired temperature until next morning. In very hot weather and in very large bacon factories the machine is generally run at night as well as day.

The chill or cooling rooms and the curing cellars are fitted up in the same manner; the only difference being that in the chill or cooling rooms, where the work to be done in cooling down the hot meat is greater in proportion to their size but intermittent, a proportionately larger number of brine pipes are placed, and the brine is turned on or off as the rooms are full or empty; while in the curing cellars, where the work to be done in proportion to their size is less but regular, a proportionately less number of brine pipes are placed, and the brine is always kept in circulation while the machine is running, maintaining a steady and perfectly even temperature.

The machine is fixed by preference on the ground floor near the the factory steam-boiler, and placed under the charge of the regular stoker or engine driver, so that excepting where there is more than one machine no special man is required to work it. No special steam-boiler is required, so little steam being wanted that it generally only means the stoker putting on the boiler fire an extra two or three shovelfuls of coal per hour.

The approximate cost of running the machines will be found to be usually actually less than ice if the latter could be bought at 1s. per ton. Thus an E machine doing the same amount of work as the melting of 10 tons of ice per twelve hours, costs 7s. per twelve hours to run; and a D machine doing the same amount of work as the melting of 7 tons of ice per twelve hours, costs 6s. per twelve hours to run; and these costs are only reached when coal costs as much as 20s. per ton.

No insulation or other preparation of the cooling or chill rooms or curing cellars is necessary; the chambers being taken just as they are and the brine pipes fitted up in sections without stopping the ordinary work.

In some factories the machines have been applied to cooling the curing cellars alone, leaving the chill or cooling rooms to be cooled by cold-air machines.

PONTIFEX MACHINES FOR COOLING STORES, AND FOR PRESERVING MEAT, FISH, FRUIT, ETC.

This has become a very important trade, and the Pontifex machine is particularly suited for the purpose.

A chamber of any required size can be kept at a uniform temperature of say 30° to 40° Fahr. (which is found to be the best temperature for preserving food), at a very small cost.

The great amount of labor and the considerable expense which the use of ice entails is thus avoided, as is the injury done to the keeping properties of food when it comes in contact with either ice or moist atmosphere.

By the Pontifex process a perfectly dry atmosphere can be obtained with the greatest facility, or, on the other hand, when fish, for instance, is to be stored which is injured by too dry an atmosphere the natural moisture can be retained by a simple modification of the arrangements.

The chambers can, if desired, be kept at a temperature as low as 30° or 40° below freezing, but for most descriptions of food it is found injurious to expose it to a temperature low enough to freeze, and thus burst the vesicles of which flesh, etc., is constructed.

Until lately cold-air machines have been used almost exclusively for the purpose of freezing and keeping meat frozen, but in consequence of the enormous cost of producing the cold, which requires quite fifteen to twenty times as much steam power and coals as the Pontifex machine to produce the same result, with a proportionately large extra charge for labor working the machines, oil, etc., the Pontifex machines are now superseding the cold-air machines, on land where they are appliable. The Pontifex machines can not be used on shipboard, as they would not work properly if fixed on an unstable foundation.

The machine itself and its general arrangements are similar to those already described for bacon-curing works, with this alteration, that where exceedingly low temperatures are required as in the cases of stores for actually freezing meat and keeping it frozen, it is usually found desirable to fit up small wrought instead of large cast iron brine mains, as with the former the cold of the brine is more readily conducted through the thin metal of the pipes into the rooms.

PONTIFEX MACHINES FOR DISTILLERS.

These machines will be found of great value in hot weather to distillers, by keeping the spirit in the store tanks cool, thus effecting a great saving by avoiding the very considerable loss which occurs by evaporation.

PONTIFEX MACHINES FOR YEAST MERCHANTS.

The importance of the process to this trade is very large; the injury done to yeast and the disease set up in it by temperatures even only moderately warm, is well known. In consequence of this fact, the price in the market of German yeast rises fully 50 per cent. in warm weather.

PONTIFEX MACHINES FOR CHOCOLATE MANUFACTURERS.

For this purpose great advantages will be found by the use of this machine.

The cooling-room can be kept at a low temperature, and much waste saved by the rapid solidification which it renders possible, and also by the great advantage that the chocolate comes readily and perfect in shape out of the molds, and much fewer moulds are required to do the same amount of work.

For other works, too numerous to detail, this machine will also be found to be invaluable, both in facilitating and quickening the process employed, and also in enabling them to be carried on at a reduced cost.

THE PONTIFEX NEW PATENT IMPROVED AMMONIA PUMP.

The only parts of the Pontifex machine which move and therefore wear are the ammonia pumps. With a view of making these even less liable to give trouble than heretofore, Pontifex & Wood, Limited, have invented a new and greatly improved arrangement of pump which has been found to give the greatest possible satisfaction.

The illustrations on the opposite page show the new patent ammonia pump. Instead of being made as heretofore of the plunger type, and single acting, the new pump is made of the piston type and double-acting. Consequently, one pump throws double the quantity, and in a continuous stream, and each machine can do its full work with one pump only going. In addition to this, the place of the old pattern plunger of large diameter is taken by the new pattern piston-rod of very small diameter (only $\frac{3}{4}$ inch in the smallest and $1\frac{1}{4}$ inches in the largest pumps for corresponding machines), and the piston-rod gland being so small is very easily packed and kept tight, and the loss of ammonia in the ordinary working is almost entirely prevented.

These new pumps are so designed as to fit in the places of the old pumps on existing machines, on which Pontifex & Wood, Limited, strongly advise their adoption. These pumps are now put to all new machines.

SPARE PARTS AND FITTINGS.

The only parts of the Pontifex machines which wear are the **ammonia pumps**, which as already explained are in duplicate.

NEWCASTLE-UPON-TYNE.

REPORT BY CONSUL PUGH.

There is not a single refrigerator in use in the city of Newcastle, or, so far as I have been able to learn, in this district, in the sense in which the term is used in the United States, and about which information is sought.

The hotels and clubs use a small ice-box, crude in construction and of inferior capacity, but aside from these the refrigerator is not in use in any form.

This being a cool climate, butchers, poultry, fish, and game dealers have relied wholly upon the natural temperature for the preservation of their stocks, aiding nature simply by throwing the entire fronts of their rooms open during the day, and at night closing by means of open iron grating, thus securing a free circulation of air to all parts of the rooms.

By this means their meats are kept in comparatively salable condition without the use of ice or refrigerator, except on occasional hot days in summer, when a small per cent. of the dealers procure a small quantity of ice and place it on the benches and tables among the meats. However, a number of butchers in response to my questions have informed me that during the many years they had followed the business they had never bought a pound of ice.

As to interrogatory No. 5, I find the ice used here is imported from ports on the east side of the North Sea, principally Norway, at a cost of about $4.20 per ton in cargo lots, but the retail rate to the consumer is about 48 cents per 100 pounds.

The butchers, poultry, fish, and game dealers, recognizing the inconvenience of the present system, as it necessitated their carrying small stocks and occasioned frequent losses, have pretty universally agreed to adopt the plan of and have taken stock in the Northern Counties, Ice Making and Cold Stores Company, a prospectus of which is inclosed.

The necessity of some such plan as this, and the difficulty of introducing the American refrigerator, can only be appreciated by a knowledge of the diminutive quarters occupied by these dealers, the average size of which would not exceed 18 to 20 feet square; and yet this small room must accommodate counters, benches, scales, cutting-blocks, cash desk, stock, etc., with some little space for salesmen and customers.

A glance at any one of these will at once disclose the absolute want of space for a refrigerator of any valuable capacity.

The cold stores and ice company above alluded to was formed and stock apportioned long before the dispatch reached me, but in discussing the subject of refrigerators the members and officers of this company admit the importance and advantages of their use, and I therefore made to them this suggestion:

That as dealers in the outskirts of this city, those in the numerous surrounding towns, and especially those persons engaged in the very large fish trade at the mouth of the Tyne, would not be able to utilize the cold stores and become patrons of the ice company, and as they desired to extend the sale of their ice, would it not therefore be a good investment for the company to purchase a number of refrigerators of such size as could be used by dealers not accessible to their stores, furnish them to such persons at a stipulated rental and provide them with ice, thus extending their ice trade and making a profit off both ice and refrigerator?

The company appear to think it a good plan, at least in extending their ice trade and educating these dealers to the use of ice, and have asked me for estimates covering size, capacity, for both ice and meats, construction and costs, with a view to acting upon my suggestion.

I therefore suggest and recommend that our manufacturers forward to me their circulars and price-lists covering these points, to be placed before this company, or any persons whom I may be able to interest in the matter.

HORACE O. PUGH,
Consul.

UNITED STATES CONSULATE,
   Newcastle-upon-Tyne, November 25, 1889.

PLYMOUTH.

REPORT BY CONSUL FOX.

Refrigerators are not much used in this district except by confectioners, hotel proprietors and purveyors, only few private families using them.

The ordinary chest or box refrigerator is mostly used.

Refrigerators are made in many sizes commencing at 22 inches wide, 20 deep, 29 high, and continuing as large as 50 by 34 inches. Ice safes and refrigerators are also made as large as 75 inches high, 39 wide, 27 deep.

Most of the ice used in this district is obtained from Norway and is retailed at about $4.86 to $14.48 per ton of 2,240 pounds. There is also a local ice company whose prices are about the same as above stated.

To introduce American refrigerators I can only suggest the establishment of an agency here for their sale.

THOMAS W. FOX,
Consul.

UNITED STATES CONSULATE,
   Plymouth, January 2, 1890.

SHEFFIELD.

REPORT BY CONSUL FOLSOM.

The use of refrigerators in this consular district is exceedingly limited, as there is but little ice used. Dealers in ice here are the fishmongers and a few dealers in poultry, and hotel keepers employ small ones of a cheap class. I do not think the butchers use either ice or refrigerators and they are certainly unknown in private houses. Even in the summer iced drinks are considered a luxury, and in most places here a novelty.

The only peculiar requirement would be the keeping of a small block of ice for the longest possible time.

The most of the refrigerators in use are manufactured in London and Birmingham; a few, however, are manufactured by the Haslam Foundry Company, at Derby.

The few in use are small in size, not larger than those ordinarily found in private houses in the United States, and the prices of the same are not readily obtainab'e here.

Little or no ice is secured, and none to my knowledge is manufactured artificially. It is procured from Norway and Canada, and is sold, at retail, at about $1 per hundredweight of 112 pounds.

No doubt the use of refrigerators would be beneficial to the consumers of food, but the price of ice renders their use a luxury, and it is doubtful whether any successful introduction of the article could be made here except among a limited and wealthy class.

There is comparatively little hot or sultry weather experienced here, even in mid-summer, and but few precautions are taken for the preservation of foods and liquids. The former are bought in small quantities and the latter are kept in cellars where they retain a moderate degree of coldness. The inhabitants are so conservative in their views, and so disinclined to make radical changes in anything, that I doubt if even so useful, and to us so necessary, an article as the refrigerator could be successfully introduced.

It is possible, however, that something might be done in the way of introducing refrigerators of American manufacture through large commission houses—such, for instance, as that of W. B. Fordham & Sons, limited, 36 to 40 York Road, King's Cross, London.

BENJAMIN FOLSOM,
Consul.

UNITED STATES CONSULATE,
 Sheffield, January 15, 1890.

SOUTHAMPTON.

REPORT BY CONSUL BRADLEY.

Refrigerators are extensively used in this consular district.

There are no peculiar features in the construction necessary to the requirements of this climate. Those in general use are manufactured in London.

The principle of construction does not differ materially from those made for the temperate regions of the United States, but are more unwieldy, and not so light and convenient, and as a general thing do not present a neat appearance for family use. The cheapest refrigerator costs $15 and is used for cooling wines and waters only. The best and largest refrigerator for family use costs $125.

There are intermediate sizes and prices, and all are designed to preserve meats, fish, and butter free from taint of foreign flavor.

The chief supply of ice is brought from Norway, and the price per 100 pounds is usually 60 cents. Ice is manufactured at Portsmouth, but in small quantities.

We have frequent communications with reference to the most successful method of introducing wares, and we usually reply that "by commission" is the best manner.

Owing to the proximity of this district to London, it is supplied by agents there, and not direct from the manufacturers, thereby increasing the price to consumers.

Presuming that an article of commerce will sell more quickly by being cheapened, I would say that manufacturers should reach a desired market direct if possible.

Our opinion, therefore, is that advertising matter should be furnished to the principal consular offices with power to designate a per centum off that will bring the article to a basis of desirability.

No doubt an agency might be established in each consular district in this manner.

I would suggest that if a suitable place were secured for the exposition of the articles of manufacture most likely to sell, in each consular district, it would be the most successful method of introducing articles of American manufacture, but the plan is not feasible because of the restriction placed upon consuls by the consular regulations.

Otherwise consular officers could give the matter most profitable attention.

I am of the opinion that American refrigerators would come into general use by reason of their cheapness and lightness.

JASPER P. BRADLEY,
Consul.

UNITED STATES CONSULATE,
  Southampton, February 11, 1890.

IRELAND.

CORK.

REPORT OF CONSUL PIATT

Refrigerators are chiefly used in the dwellings of the wealthier classes of the people in this district, also in hotels, clubs, infirmaries, hospitals, etc., but only to a very limited extent. They are for the most part made at Birmingham, Sheffield, and other hardware manufacturing towns in England. They vary in size, the smaller ones being about 24 by 40 inches, having principally metal frames with zinc siding and roof perforated. The roof is oval in shape, forming a cone, at top of which is placed a wooden ball as ornament. These small refrigerators are suspended from a hook or spike under a shed or in some unexposed part of the house-yard at rear of kitchen. The price is from $2 to $2.50. The next size, similarly constructed, cost from $3.50 to $4.50. Larger ones, provided with shelves running through them, cost from $5 to $7.50, and rest on raised blocks or platforms.

The ice used in this district, where none is produced, is exclusively imported from Norway. There are but two firms or merchants in Cork who import whole cargoes of ice—one being a large bacon-curing establishment, which import it for their own use; the other imports cargoes for retail demand. About ten cargoes, averaging 500 tons each, are imported annually. The invoice price to the merchant is about $10 per ton, and it is sold retail at about 80 cents per 100 pounds. The price varies according to the season, it being sometimes in summer about $22 and in winter $14.60 per ton. Ice is secured or preserved for larger or wholesale uses in cellars fitted up specially for the purpose, large enough to contain several hundred tons. In households it is generally kept in wooden tubs, small barrels, or buckets covered over with sacks or cloth. Ice boxes or chests are not in use.

In households where refrigerators are not in use a surplus of food or liquids seldom accumulates, and ice is rarely used, except for medical purposes, as in cases of fever, etc.

For household purposes generally there does not appear to be any great need for refrigerators in this district, the supply of food and liquids being procured invariably tri-weekly. Again, the heat in summer seldom goes higher than 65°.

It is possible that refrigerators on an improved plan manufactured in America and put in the market at a cheaper price would find a sale— not directly, however, but through the English hardware centers. The demand here would not be sufficient for a direct trade with American manufacturers.

JOHN J. PIATT,
Consul.

UNITED STATES CONSULATE,
Cork, July 7, 1890.

DUBLIN.

REPORT BY CONSUL REID, OF DUBLIN.

Refrigerators are used in this consular district but to a very limited extent, and only in public and semi-public places. There are no peculiar features observed in the construction of those used here, except as noted below. As a rule, they are manufactured in the United States. The sizes and formation are not peculiar, while the prices are about the same as in the United States, with something added to cover the cost of transportation.

Ice in use in this district is brought from Norway and stored in icehouses, from which such demand as there is is supplied. Occasional consumers pay nearly two cents per pound therefor. The price charged to season customers is about three quarters of a cent per pound.

In further explanation of the foregoing answers, I have to say that the use of refrigerators in Ireland, even by the wealthy classes, is almost unknown outside of Dublin, Belfast, and Cork, except in hotels, in a few instances; and even in the larger cities the demand for them is very limited. They are in use only in hotels, cafés, etc.; very few private houses are provided with them. The reason for this is, first, that the extremes of temperature are very seldom, if ever, reached here. The mean annual temperature of the country is from 48° to 50°. The extreme of summer temperature is usually from 80° to 85°, but only a few days of each season are as warm as these figures indicate. In the winter, mercury only occasionally touches the freezing point. Secondly, because of the climatic conditions above mentioned, there is no ice produced in the country and but very little used—none at all in private houses. In fact, the need or want of it is but little felt. The breweries use machinery to establish a low degree of temperature for storage purposes.

Many of the refrigerators in use, being for special places and purposes, are made to order, and are stationary. Such limited general demands as exist in this line are supplied by refrigerators of American manufacture. I am so informed by the representatives of two firms in Dublin controlling whatever of trade there is in this direction. The particular kinds most in use here are the Alaska, manufactured by the Alaska Refrigerator Company, and the Belding, manufactured by the Belding Refrigerator Company. I am informed that the competition for the trade offered by British manufacturers is scarcely worth mentioning. The American manufacturers produce a much better article at a less price than British competitors offer.

As the best way of extending the refrigerator trade in this part of Ireland, I would recommend to parties or firms thus interested to correspond with Thomas McKenzie & Son, 212 and 213 Great Brunswick street, and John C. Parks, 110 and 111 Coombe, Dublin.

ALEX J. REID,
Consul.

U. S. CONSULATE,
DUBLIN, *January* 7, 1890.

SCOTLAND.

DUNFERMLINE.

REPORT BY COMMERCIAL AGENT REID.

Refrigerators, as understood in the United States, are unknown in this consular district.

Ice, in very limited quantities, is purchased in Edinburgh for the use of makers of ice-cream, and a still more limited extent by butchers, for a very short season in summer, for the preservation of meats.

The amount of consumption being well known, the killing of animals is regulated accordingly, and the cellars are always cool enough to render ice almost unnecessary. Price of ice per 100 pounds, 37 cents. Summer heat rarely exceeds 74° to 78°.

JAMES D. REID,
Commercial Agent.

UNITED STATES COMMERCIAL AGENCY,
Dunfermline, February 4, 1890.

GLASGOW.

REPORT BY CONSUL BROWN.

In answer to the first interrogatory as to the use of refrigerators in this consular district, will say that they are used but to a very limited extent as compared with their use in the United States.

There are no peculiar features required in the construction of refrigerators for use in this district, unless it be that refrigerators with less heat-resisting power would answer here, where it is called excessively warm when the thermometer registers 70° to 80°. I may add, the latter point is rarely reached.

Some of the refrigerators in use here are manufactured in London, but, as far as I can learn, the larger and better ones are of American manufacture. I should add that there are no small refrigerators or next to none in use here. I have visited a number of small or medium sized meat and fishmonger shops, and in no case found a refrigerator. They have a device of their own in most cases, and quite crude and unscientific. Refrigerators for family use are practically unknown.

The few that are in use, for the most part, are built within the rooms occupied by them. Of the smaller sizes, such as would be kept in stock, I have been unable to find any, though I have made inquiry of several alleged dealers. The trade is so small that quotations of prices are impossible.

Ice is secured in this district mainly from Norway, though some is secured from lakes near the city (thin and of consequent poor quality), and a small amount manufactured. Ice from the Baltic is worth, delivered here, $6.32 per ton, and is retailed at 48 cents per 100 pounds. I have talked with many persons, and all unite in saying that a more general use of refrigerators is most desirable, but in this connection it must be borne in mind that the climate here is far from what Americans would call hot, and refrigerators are not absolutely and indispensably necessary.

It is believed, however, that if the people came to understand the luxury, not to say the essential need, of refrigerators that a demand for them would spring up at once.

It is the unanimous judgment of those with whom I have conversed upon the subject that a refrigerator which would consume a minimum quantity of ice and which could be placed upon the market at a reasonable price would surely find sale. As to the best method of introduction, I am not so sure. Persons making the attempt should bear in mind what I have said of the climate, price, and quality, and remember that the Scotch are a conservative people, and that any new thing, however meritorious, would need "pushing."

A live representative, with refrigerators to confirm his statements in actual use, would, I believe, in time, be successful in building up a trade which would yield ample returns.

L. W. BROWN,
Consul.

UNITED STATES CONSULATE,
Glasgow, January 21, 1890.

LEITH.

REPORT BY CONSUL BRUCE.

Refrigerators are not extensively used in this consular district. Only here and there a brewery, a butcher's establishment, a hotel, or a private house form exceptions to the general rule. The weather is too cool to make them necessary in domestic economy. Younger & Co., of Edinburgh, large ale brewers, have an extensive pipe cooler (see Inclosure A), the cooling of the ale being accomplished not by ice but by water of natural temperature running against the ale pipes in opposite direction.

The ice in the ordinary domestic refrigerator is placed in the bottom of the chest, and the box is fitted with sliding zinc shelves.

The refrigerators used here are manufactured for the most part in London, although joiners or carpenters in Edinburgh often make them, as they may be required.

The domestic refrigerator (see Inclosure B) in use here, and known in the trade as refrigerator or portable ice house, is a square box from 22 to 50 inches in height, length, and width, resembling a wooden cube, on feet that raise it a few inches from the floor. The price ranges from $15 to $50.

REFRIGERATORS IN FOREIGN COUNTRIES. 207

Ice is brought to Edinburgh and the west of Scotland from Norway, and is worth at the unlading of ship about 40 cents per 100 pounds, and ranges from 50 cents to 60 cents when retailed during the season from June to August. There is one ice manufactory in Edinburgh, but I have been advised that the business is not profitable to the proprietors. In a word, the climate here is so cool and equable, even in the three summer months, that there is not the need or demand for ice or refrigerators as in warmer climates. It is only now and then that one comes upon ice-water on draught, and it is not common upon the table as with our people in the United States.

I also inclose herein a catalogue (illustrated) of "ice making and refrigerating machinery," recently published (marked Inclosure C), which will be of service in showing the kind of apparatus used in Great Britain.

WALLACE BRUCE,
Consul.

UNITED STATES CONSULATE,
Edinburgh, February 28, 1890.

Wort refrigerator, manufactured by Stewardson & Hodgson, 356 *Leith Walk, Edinburgh.*

[Inclosure A in Consul Bruce's report.]

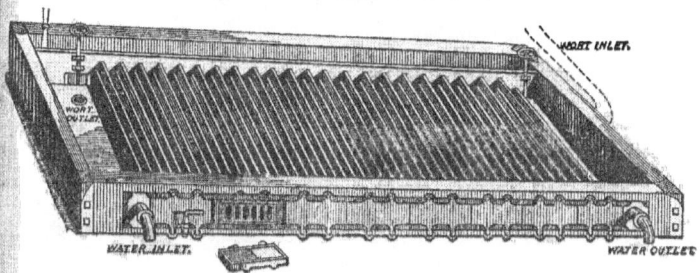

PRICES.

[Delivered f. o. b. or rail in Edinburgh.]

To cool 5 barrels per hour	£40	To cool 30 barrels per hour	£150
To cool 10 barrels per hour	70	To cool 35 barrels per hour	180
To cool 15 barrels per hour	90	To cool 40 barrels per hour	200
To cool 20 barrels per hour	110	To cool 50 barrels per hour	240
To cool 25 barrels per hour	130	To cool 60 barrels per hour	280

208   REFRIGERATORS IN FOREIGN COUNTRIES.

Refrigerator or portable ice house.

[Inclosure B in Consul Bruce's report.]

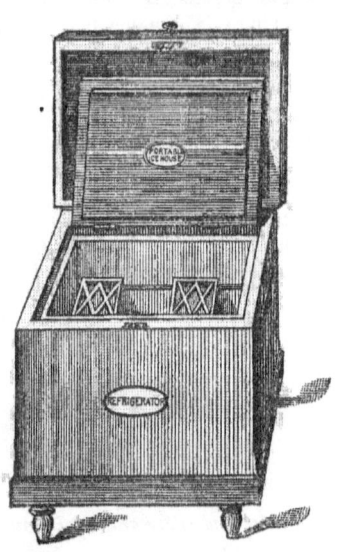

SIZES AND PRICES.

[Fitted with sliding zinc shelves, painted, grained, and varnished.]

This is the refrigerator said to be mostly in use in Leith and Edinburgh.

INDEX.

CONTINENT OF AFRICA.

EGYPT.

	Page.
Egypt (Vice-Consul-General Grant)	5
Styles, prices, ice, 5—Milk and butter preservation, 6.	
Madeira (Consul Jones)	6
Snow and hail, American refrigerators, 6.	
Morocco (Vice-Consul Stalker)	6
Refrigerators, ice, 6.	
Reunion (Commercial Agent Rayeur)	7
Refrigerators, ice and snow, 7.	
Senegal (Consul Strickland)	7
Refrigerators, ice manufactured and imported, 7.	
Zanzibar (Consul Pratt)	8
Refrigerators, manufactured ice, 8.	

SOUTH AFRICA.

Cape Town (Consul Hollis)	8
Refrigerators, artificial ice, 8.	

CONTINENT OF AMERICA.

BRITISH NORTH AMERICA.

Amherstburg (Consul Turner)	9
Refrigerators, ice, 9.	
British Columbia (Vice-Consul Martin of Victoria)	9
Refrigerators, ice, 9.	
Chatham (Commercial Agent Eddy)	10
Refrigerators, ice, 10.	
Coaticook (Consul Roberts)	10
Refrigerators, ice, 10.	
Fort Erie (Consul Whelan)	11
Refrigerators, sizes, ice, 11.	
Gaspé Basin (Consul Dickson)	12
Refrigerators, snow and ice, 12.	
London (Commercial Agent Leonard)	12
Refrigerators, ice, 12.	
Kingston (Consul Twitchell)	13
Refrigerators, 13.	
Manitoba (Consul Taylor)	13
Refrigerators, 13—Duty, ice, 14.	
Montreal (Consul-General Knapp)	14
Refrigerators, manufacturers, 14—Ice, 15.	
Nova Scotia (Consul-General Frye)	15
Refrigerators, ice, 15.	

	Page.
Ottawa (Consul-General Lay)	16
Refrigerators, styles, 16—Sizes, ice, 17.	
Port Hope (Commercial Agent Shaffer)	17
Refrigerators, sizes, 17—Ice, 18.	
Port Rowan (Commercial Agent Schooley)	18
Refrigerators, sizes, ice, and ice-chests, 18.	
Port Stanley and St. Thomas (Consul Quiggle)	19
Refrigerators, prices, ice, 19.	
St. Hyacinthe (Commercial Agent Moore)	19
Refrigerators, 19—Prices and sizes, ice, 20.	
St. John's, Quebec (Consul Fisk)	20
Refrigerators, 20—Prices, ice, 21.	
St. Stephen, N. B. (Consul Goodnow)	21
Refrigerators, ice, 21.	
Sherbrooke (Consul White)	21
Refrigerators, 21—Ice, 22.	
Three Rivers (Consul Smith)	22
Refrigerators, 22.	

MEXICO.

Guaymas (Consul Willard)	23
Refrigerators, artificial ice, 23.	
La Paz (Consul Viosca)	23
Refrigerators, ice, 24.	
Paso del Norte (Consul Sampson)	24
Refrigerators, ice, 24.	
Tuxpan (Consul Drayton)	24
Refrigerators, ice, 24.	

CENTRAL AMERICA.

COSTA RICA.

Costa Rica (Consul Mackey)	25
Refrigerators, ice, 25.	

NICARAGUA.

Bluefield (Consular Agent Simmons)	25
Refrigerators, 25—Ice, 26.	
Managua (Consul Wills)	26
Refrigerators, ice, 26.	

SOUTH AMERICA.

ARGENTINE REPUBLIC.

Argentine Republic (Consul Baker)	27
Refrigerators, 27—Ice, 28.	

BOLIVIA.

La Paz (Consul-General Anderson)	28
Refrigerators, 28—Ice, 29.	

BRAZIL.

Rio de Janeiro (Consul-General Dockery)	29
Refrigerators, ice, 30.	
Bahia (Consul Burke)	30
Refrigerators, 30—Ice, 31.	
Pernambuco (Consul Borstel)	32
Refrigerators, artificial ice, 32.	

INDEX. III

BRITISH GUIANA.

	Page.
Demerara (Consul Walthall)	33
Refrigerators, ice, 33.	

CHILI.

Iquique (Consul Merriam)	33
Refrigerators, manufactured ice, 33.	
Talcahuano (Consul Van Ingen)	34
Refrigerators, ice, 34.	

DUTCH GUIANA.

Paramaribo (Consul Brown)	34
Refrigerators, ice, 34.	

ECUADOR.

Guayaquil (Consul-General Sorsby)	35
Refrigerators, manufactured ice, 35.	

COLOMBIA.

Barranquilla (Vice-Consul Whelpley)	35
Refrigerators, ice, duties, 36.	
Colon (Consul Vifquain)	37
Refrigerators, ice, 37.	
Panama (Consul-General Adamson)	38
Refrigerators, ice, 38.	

VENEZUELA.

La Guayra (Consul Bird)	38
Refrigerators, duties, 38—Ice, 39.	

BRITISH WEST INDIES.

Bermuda (Consul Beckwith)	40
Refrigerators, ice, 40.	
Jamaica (Consul Allen)	40
Refrigerators, ice, 40.	
Antigua (Consul Jackson)	41
Refrigerators, ice, 41.	
Bahamas (Consul McLain)	41
Refrigerators, ice, 41.	
Tobago (Consular Agent Keens)	42
Refrigerators, ice, 42.	
Trinidad (Consul Sawyer)	43
Refrigerators, ice, 43.	

FRENCH WEST INDIES.

Guadeloupe (Consul Bartlett)	44
Refrigerators, ice, prices, 44.	
Martinique (Consul Garesché)	45
Refrigerators, artificial ice, 45.	

HAYTI.

Port au Prince (Minister Douglas)	46
Refrigerators, ice, 46.	

SAN DOMINGO.

Puerto Plata (Consul Simpson)	46
Refrigerators, ice, 46.	

SPANISH WEST INDIES.

CUBA.

	Page.
Havana (Consul-General Williams)	47
Refrigerators, ice, 47.	
Matanzas (Consul Pierce)	48
Refrigerators, ice, 48.	
Sagua La Grande (Commercial Agent Mullen)	48
Refrigerators, ice, 48.	
Santiago de Cuba (Consul Reimer)	49
Refrigerators, ice, 49.	

CONTINENT OF ASIA.

BRITISH ASIA.

Bombay (Vice-Consul Bode)	50
Refrigerators, artificial ice, 50.	
Calcutta (Consul-General Bonham)	50
Refrigerators, 50—artificial ice, 51.	
Straits Settlements (Vice-Consul Lyall)	52
Refrigerators, 52—Ice, 53.	
Hong-Kong (Consul Simons)	55
Refrigerators, ice, 55.	

CHINA.

Chin Kiang (Consul Jones)	54
Refrigerators, ice, 54.	
Shanghai (Consul-General Leonard)	56
Refrigerators 56—Ice 57.	
Tien Tsin (Consul Bowman)	57
Refrigerators, ice, 57.	

JAPAN.

Osaka and Hiogo (Consul Smithers)	58
Refrigerators, ice, 58.	
Nagasaki (Consul Birch)	58
Refrigerators, ice, 58.	

PHILIPPINE ISLANDS.

Manila (Consul Webb)	59
Refrigerators, artifical ice, 59.	

SIAM.

Bangkok (Consul-General Child)	61
Refrigerators, artificial ice, 62.	

TURKEY IN ASIA.

ASIA MINOR.

Smyrna (Consul Emmett)	62
Refrigerators, artificial ice, 62.	
Jerusalem (Consul Gillman)	63
Refrigerators, ice, 63.	

SYRIA.

Beirut (Consul Bissinger)	63
Refrigerators, artificial ice, 63.	

INDEX. v

AUSTRALASIA.

NEW SOUTH WALES.
	Page.
Sydney (Consul Griffin)	65

Food preservation, 65—Refrigerators, 67—Cooling chambers, 69—Chilled-meat export,70—Killing and chilling depots, 77—Refrigerating cars, 78.

New Castle (Commercial Agent Dawson) 80
  Refrigerators, ice, 80.

NEW ZEALAND.

Auckland (Consul Connolly) 81
  Refrigerators, 81—Ice, 82—Description Nelson Bros. freezing works, 83.
West Australia (Consular Agent Sandover) 86
  Refrigerators, ice, 86.

POLYNESIA.

Fiji (Commercial Agent St. John).. 87
  Refrigerators, ice, 87.
Hawaii (Consular Agent Furneaux).. 88
  Refrigerators, artificial ice, 88.

CONTINENT OF EUROPE.

AUSTRIA.

Reichenberg (Commercial Agent Hawes) 89
  Refrigerators, 89.
Trieste (Consul Hartigan).. 89
  Refrigerators, ice, 89.

BELGIUM.

Antwerp (Consul Steuart)... 91
  Refrigerators, 91—Ice, 92.
Brussels (Consul Roosevelt).. 92
  Refrigerators, 92—Ice supply, description of Schmidt patent, 93.
Liege (Consul Preston)... 97
  Refrigerators, ice, 97.

DENMARK.

Copenhagen (Consul Ryder).. 98
  Refrigerators, 98—Ice, 99.

FRANCE.

Marseilles (Consul Trail).. 100
  Refrigerators, ice, 100.
Limoges (Commercial Agent Griffin) 101
  Refrigerators, 101—Ice, 102.
Bordeaux (Consul Knowles).. 102
  Refrigerators, 102—Ice, 103.
Lyons (Consul Fairfield)... 103
  Refrigerators, 103—Ice, 104.
Nice (Consul Bradley).. 105
  Refrigerators, ice, 105.
Normandy (Consul Williams) 105
  Refrigerators, 105—Ice, 106.
Paris (Consul-General Rathbone).. 107
  Refrigerators, 107—Illustrations, 108—Ice, 115.
St. Etienne (Commercial Agent Malmros)....................................... 116
  Refrigerators, 116—Ice, 117.

GERMANY.

	Page.
Aix la Chapelle (Consul Parsons)	118
Refrigerators, price-list and descriptions, 118—Ice, 120.	
Annaberg (Consul Hubbard)	120
Refrigerators, 120—Ice, 121.	
Berlin (Consul-General Edwards)	122
Refrigerators, 122—Ice, 122.	
Chemnitz (Consul Merritt)	122
Refrigerators, 122—Ice, 123.	
Cologne (Consul Wamer)	124
Refrigerators, ice, 124.	
Crefeld (Consul Blake)	124
Refrigerators, 124—Ice, 125.	
Dresden (Consul Palmer)	126
Refrigerators, ice, 126.	
Düsseldorf (Consul Partello)	127
Refrigerators, ice, 127.	
Frankfort-on-the-Main (Consul-General Mason)	128
Refrigerators, 128—Ice, 129.	
Hamburg (Consul Johnson)	130
Refrigerators, ice, 130.	
Mayence (Commercial Agent Smith)	131
Refrigerators, 131.	
Munich (Consul Mealey)	138
Refrigerators, ice, 138.	
Stettin (Consul Fay)	139
Refrigerators, ice, 139.	

HOLLAND.

Amsterdam (Consul Eckstein)	140
Refrigerators, ice, 140.	

ITALY.

Catania (Consul Lamantia)	142
Refrigerators, ice, 142.	
Florence (Consul Diller)	142
Refrigerators, 142—Ice, 143—Duties, 143.	
Genoa (Consul Fletcher)	143
Refrigerators, 143.	
Palermo (Consul Carroll)	147
Refrigerators, ice, 147.	
Naples (Consul Camphausen)	148
Refrigerators, ice, 149.	
Venice (Consul Johnson)	149
Refrigerators, 149—Ice, 150.	

RUSSIA.

St. Petersburg (Consul-General Crawford)	151
Refrigerators, ice, 151.	
Finland (Vice-Consul Donner)	151
Refrigerators, 151.	
Poland (Consul Rawicz)	152
Refrigerators, ice, 152.	

INDEX.

SPAIN.

	Page.
Barcelona (Consul Scheuch)..	153
Refrigerators, ice, 153.	
Carthagena (Consul Molina)..	153
Refrigerators, ice, 153.	
Grao of Valencia (Consular Agent Mertens)	154
Refrigerators, ice, 154.	
Cadiz (Consul Turner)...	154
Ice, 154.	
Jeres de la Frontera (Consular Agent Hall).................................	155
Refrigerators, 155—Ice, 156.	
Seville (Consular Agent Caldwell)	156
Refrigerators, ice, 156.	
Port St. Mary's (Consular Agent Daniels)....................................	156
Refrigerators, ice, 156.	
Malaga (Consul Marston)	156
Refrigerators, ice, 156.	
Gibraltar (Consul Sprague)	158
Refrigerators, ice, 158.	

SWEDEN.

Gothenberg (Consul Man)..	159
Refrigerators, ice, 159.	
Stockholm (Consul Elfwing)...	160
Refrigerators, ice, 160.	

SWITZERLAND.

Horgen (Consul Adams)...	161
Refrigerators, 161—Ice, 162.	
Zurich (Consul Catlin)..	162
Refrigerators, 162—Ice 165.	

TURKEY.

Constantinople (Consul-General Sweeney)	167
Refrigerators, ice, 167.	

UNITED KINGDOM.

ENGLAND.

Birmingham (Consul Jarrett)...	168
Refrigerators, ice, 168.	
Bradford (Consul Tibbits)..	169
Refrigerators, ice, 169.	
Bristol (Consul Delille)..	170
Refrigerators, 170—Ice, 171.	
Falmouth (Consul Fox)...	171
Refrigerators, 171.	
Leeds (Consul Wigfall)..	171
Refrigerators, 171—Ice, 173.	
Liverpool (Consul Sherman)...	174
Refrigerators, ice, 174.	
London (Consul-General New)..	175
Refrigerators, 175—Ice, 176—Pontifex ice-making and refrigerating machines, 176.	

New Castle-upon-Tyne (Consul Pugh)... 199
 Refrigerators, 199—ice, 200.
Plymouth (Consul Fox).. 200
 Refrigerators, ice, 200.
Sheffield (Consul Folsom) 201
 Refrigerators, ice, 201.
Southampton (Consul Bradley)... 202
 Refrigerators, ice, 202

IRELAND.

Cork (Consul Piatt).. 203
 Refrigerators, ice, 203.
Dublin (Consul Reid)... 204
 Refrigerators, ice, 204.

SCOTLAND.

Dunfermline (Commercial Agent Reid) 205
 Refrigerators, ice, 205.
Glasgow (Consul Brown)... 205
 Refrigerators, ice, 205.
Leith (Consul Bruce)... 206
 Refrigerators, 206—Ice 207.